Theater in a Crowded Fire

The publisher gratefully acknowledges the generous support of the General Endowment Fund of the University of California Press Foundation.

Theater in a Crowded Fire

Ritual and Spirituality at Burning Man

Lee Gilmore

UNIVERSITY OF CALIFORNIA PRESS
Berkeley · *Los Angeles* · *London*

University of California Press, one of the most distinguished university presses in the United States, enriches
lives around the world by advancing scholarship in the
humanities, social sciences, and natural sciences. Its
activities are supported by the UC Press Foundation and
by philanthropic contributions from individuals and institutions. For more information, visit www.ucpress.edu.

University of California Press
Berkeley and Los Angeles, California

University of California Press, Ltd.
London, England

For credits, please see page 223.

Library of Congress Cataloging-in-Publication Data

Gilmore, Lee, 1969–.
    Theater in a crowded fire : ritual and spirituality at
Burning Man / Lee Gilmore.
        p.   cm.
    Includes bibliographical references and index.
    ISBN 978-0-520-25315-5 (cloth : alk. paper)
    ISBN 978-0-520-26088-7 (pbk. : alk. paper)
        1. Burning Man (Festival).   2. Ritual—Nevada—
Black Rock Desert.   3. Black Rock Desert (Nev.)—
Religious life and customs.   4. Festivals—United
States.   5. United States—Religion—1945–.   I. Title.
    NX510.N48G55   2010
    394.2509793'54—dc22

                                        2009052480

Manufactured in the United States of America

19   18   17   16   15   14   13   12   11
10   9   8   7   6   5   4   3   2

This book is printed on Cascades Enviro 100, a 100%
post consumer waste, recycled, de-inked fiber. FSC
recycled certified and processed chlorine free. It is acid
free, Ecologo certified, and manufactured by BioGas
energy.

For Spencer Daniel Ardery Meiners

Contents

Illustrations

Tables

Acknowledgments

As solitary a process as writing often is, this book could not have been created without an extensive community to support it. First and foremost, I wish to thank the global community of Burning Man participants, without whom this project would quite obviously not have been possible. I am especially grateful to each of the hundreds of Burners who participated in my research by giving the gift of their time in interviews, conversations, or filling out the on-line survey I conducted in July 2004.

A number of Burning Man staff members were very helpful in facilitating data collection, fact checking, and obtaining permission to produce the DVD that accompanies this text, especially Andie (Action-grl) Grace and Jess (The Nurse) Bobier. Special thanks are also due to (Maid) Marian Goodell, who—unbeknownst to either of us at the time—helped to inspire much of the work that follows in these pages when she invited me to join the fledgling Burning Man Media Team in 1998, thus deepening my involvement in and commitment to this community. Finally, I am indebted to Burning Man's founder and ongoing executive director, Larry Harvey, for his time, invaluable insights, and inspiration.

As will become apparent in the pages that follow, I am embedded in a rich and colorful community of Burners with whom I have camped at the event over the years. Thus I should like to thank all the members of the "BLD Village" for providing a welcome place to call home in Black Rock City, especially Patrice (Chef Juke) Mackey. As core organizers and founders of the BLD for many years, Eric (Frog) Pouyoul and Rachel Ruster are to be commended for their patience and service to the greater community. A special debt of gratitude is also due to Craig (Newt) Lauxman for taking me to my first Burning Man in 1996. James Marshall provided an invaluable service in helping me to configure the more difficult technical components of my on-line survey. Lisa Hoffman generously granted permission to reproduce her original artwork (chart of Black Rock City). Other nods of appreciation are due to Jeff Anderson, Yoni Ayeni, Amacker Bullwinkle, Bridget Connelly, Felix Baum, Jennifer Baum, Jeanie Bier, Kathleen Craig, Margot Duane, Will Francis, Mike Fusello, Katrina Glerum, Dennis Hescox, Jennifer Hult, Jessica Spurling, John Spurling, Candace Locklear, Blair Miller, Yu-Shen Ng, Argyre Patras, Kate Shaw, Shin, Hillary Sommers, Tim Spencer, Kayte Stasny Kelly, Dawn Stott, Dan Terdiman, Jan Voss, Michael Urashka, Alx Utterman, and Michael Wolf. I am also grateful to friends and colleagues who provided helpful feedback on portions this manuscript, including Jonathan Korman, Niki Whiting, and Ben Zeller.

Critical intellectual and financial support was provided by the Media, Religion, and Culture Fellowship program of the University of Colorado School of Journalism. I am especially grateful to Stewart Hoover, Lynn Schofield Clark, and Diane Alters for instituting and administering this program, and to Ronald L. Grimes, who participated in one of the seminar discussions held in conjunction with this program, for his singularly insightful and helpful grilling. The Graduate Theological Union (GTU) also provided generous financial support through its Newhall Fellowship Program, as did the Association for the Sociology of Religion, which granted a Fichter Research Award in partial support of fieldwork expenses.

Within my camp at Burning Man, I have been joined by a number of other academics throughout the years who, in becoming part of my ethnographic landscape, came to indelibly shape many of the directions this work would take through sharing their insights and analyses of the event over many a dusty cup of coffee. First and foremost among these compatriots has been Mark Van Proyen, of the San Francisco Art Institute, with whom I was privileged to coedit a collection of essays titled *After-Burn: Reflections on Burning Man*. Mark has been a great colleague, friend, and mentor dating to my first years on the playa, and much of the ultimate success of this project is due to his early faith in my work. Patrick Gavin Duffy also deserves a nod for organizing the first panel of academics to present a session on Burning Man at the conference "Community and the Environment," held at the University of Nevada, Reno, in 1997, in which I was privileged to participate. D. S. Black was likewise an early intellectual colleague who helped to inspire me to write about this event. I am very fortunate to have been joined by other colleagues who became campmates over the years in Black Rock City, in particular, Rob Kozinets (York University), John Sherry (University of Notre Dame), Graham St John (University of Queensland), Sarah Pike (California State University, Chico), Adrian Ivakhiv (University of Vermont), and Grant Potts (Austin Community College).

Pike also served as the outside reader for my Ph.D. dissertation, which brings me naturally to extending my deep gratitude to each of my committee members and mentors whose support and critical insights became so central to this work. My adviser, Ibrahim Farajaje, stood steadfastly by my side throughout my years at the GTU and was an inspirational model of creativity, difference, and innovation; without his support this project almost certainly would not have come to be. From the first day I walked into his office, he shared his unbridled enthusiasm for my work, and the knowledge of his abiding faith in my scholarly abilities kept me going at many a frustrating moment. Clare Fischer's close mentoring and support over the years was likewise indispensable to my success; her consistently careful reading of my work and critical feedback were invaluable. Jerome Baggett was also an important critical reader and enthusiastic champion of this work. Finally, Sarah Pike has provided immeasurable professional support and encouragement far beyond her role as outside reader for my dissertation.

Some of the material included in this book has been previously published elsewhere, as listed in the credits. Specifically, I wish to thank the University of New Mexico Press, the University of Arizona Press, Rutgers University Press, Brill Academic Press, Greenwood/Praeger, and Berghahn for their support of my work and for graciously granting permission to reproduce some of my earlier work for this book.

The DVD that accompanies this book has been a collaborative project between my husband, Ron Meiners, my mother, Elizabeth Gilmore, and me. Ron in particular played a foundational role in creating this portion of the project by setting out with his video camera to document his perspective on Burning Man—including interviewing a number of our friends and campmates—from the moment he first set foot on the playa in 1998. Without this footage, the production of the DVD would have been impossible. My mother generously spent countless hours editing the footage into its final form, and thus played an indispensable role. I also wish to thank University of California Press, especially Reed Malcolm for his enthusiastic support and encouragement of all facets of this project, and Juliana Froggatt for her thorough and adept assistance in shepherding this book into publication.

Last, but most certainly never least, I wish to thank my husband, Ron, for providing unwavering support, inspiration, and love throughout the long years of doctoral study and beyond. As a Burner in his own right, he and I have shared countless conversations about Burning Man. His perspectives and analyses are inextricably infused and woven into the pages that follow. I am deeply and enduringly grateful for his love and companionship.

Introduction

Every summer during the week leading up to Labor Day weekend, tens of thousands of people from around the globe descend on the Black Rock Desert, a desolate and otherwise obscure corner of northwestern Nevada whose principal feature is an ancient and absolutely barren plain of crackled clay known as the playa. Their destination is a colorful and eclectic arts celebration known as Burning Man. For a brief time Black Rock City—or BRC, as this settlement is sometimes called—becomes the fifth largest metropolis in the state of Nevada as participants—collectively referred to as "Burners"—design, construct, and dwell in thousands of makeshift shelters and tents. Laid out along a carefully surveyed system of streets forming an arch of concentric semicircles, BRC stretches over two miles from end to end, surrounding a large central open space within which an extraordinary assortment of interactive and often monumental art installations are created (see chart 1, pages 36–37). Many of those in attendance don fanciful costumes as they carouse in this carnivalesque setting, making merry and making themselves at home in the desert's harsh and alien environment.

At the center of it all stands a forty-foot sculpture called the Burning Man—a towering wooden latticework figure perched atop a fanciful platform, lit with multicolored shafts of neon, and filled with explosives designed to detonate in a carefully orchestrated sequence when the figure meets its fiery demise at the festival's climax. Ostensibly genderless and void of any specifically stated meaning, this effigy—affectionately called "the Man"—retains the same general humanoid shape and appearance from year to year and is ultimately offered up in blazing sacrifice with each annual iteration of the event (fig. 1; see also DVD, chaps. 1, 3, 4, and 7). Marking the festival's traditional climax, this dramatic rite—colloquially termed "the Burn"—is met by participants with considerable fervor and enthusiasm. Once the flames have transformed the Man into a mound of flaming coals, ecstatic celebration reverberates throughout the city until daylight returns. Finally, at week's end, all physical traces of this temporary community are completely eliminated, and the city fades back into the dust, as everyone packs up and returns to the mundane routines of everyday life, or what some Burners have termed the "default world." Yet for many participants, emotional and other intangible traces remain in memories and friendships formed, lingering like the alkali desert dust that still adheres to one's camping gear months after returning home.

Burning Man is many things, and most participants would probably agree with an oft-spoken dictum that it can be "whatever you want it to be." Indeed, independent and idiosyncratic points of view, alongside ongoing participant critiques about the nature of the event and its meaning, are cornerstones of this community's ethos. Yet among the many frameworks within which this event can be situated—arts celebration, social experiment, or orgiastic revelry—one of the experiences that it fulfills for many participants is *ritual*. In particular, Burning Man can be a venue for those who wish to express and ritualize individualized conceptions of spirituality but who resist the doctrines and institutions of religion. On both large and small scales, Burning Man participants may partake of a variety of unconventional and inventive rites—from the central shared rite of the Burn to intentional gatherings among smaller groups and individual private gestures to the embodied experience of the entire event as a transformative journey or pilgrimage. I am far from alone in noticing a general social trend as many individuals seek after spiritual experiences while conceptually positioning these quests outside the rubrics of what they understand as religion.[1] In this regard, I argue that Burning Man is an important site on the vanguard of this contemporary movement in which creative expressions of spirituality and alternative conceptualizations of religions are favored, thereby destabilizing and reinventing normative cultural assumptions about what constitutes "religion."

I use the terms *spirituality* and *religion* with considerable caution—and others such as *alternative* and *ritual* can be similarly problematic—recognizing the difficulties and ambiguities inherent in any attempt to unequivocally define them. They are the sort of terms whose meanings

FIGURE 1. The Burning Man, 1996. Photo by Lee Gilmore.

seem perfectly obvious, until one tries to unpack their countless associations or definitively fix their meanings. As perhaps befits our infamously individualistic society, interpretations of spirituality and religion tend to be highly individualized and context-specific. Even thornier is the notion of somehow separating "spirituality" from "religion," given the mutually self-referential and ultimately synonymous nature of the various ideas implied by these terms. Still, a reasonably sized segment of the U.S. population may describe themselves as "spiritual but not religious"; this number has been estimated to be as high as 19 percent, although other surveys place the number of "unaffiliated believers" closer to 5 percent.[2] Yet it remains difficult to ascertain precisely what is meant here, let alone determine a reliable head count given the inherently diverse nature of such outlooks.

There is difficulty too in labeling this social phenomenon a "movement," as that term can imply something far more unified than the loosely aggregate affinities into which the so-called pastiche or cafeteria spiritualities of "new age" seekers, "neo"-Pagan devotees, Buddhist dabblers, and yoga practitioners (along with myriad other communities and spiritual ideologies) are usually, and sometimes uncharitably, lumped. Such associations may be united only by their self-conscious locations outside traditional or mainstream religious institutions, and even this stipulation can be called into question, as some members of more mainstream traditions may also use the term *spiritual but not religious* in describing their perspectives.[3] If taken too literally, the many vagaries surrounding "alternative" spiritualities or "spirituality but not religion" render these distinctions ultimately meaningless. Yet these critical precautions aside, "spiritual but not religious" is a commonly used turn of phrase and one that many Burners themselves employ. For these individuals, this outlook implies a quest for spiritual experience and expression, and an often-ritualized connection with "something more," that takes place apart from most traditional religious institutions. Burning Man constitutes a place to encounter and ritualize this sensibility.

This ritualizing often involves creative appropriations of cultural and religious motifs from a vast global well of symbolic resources. Crosses, devils, buddhas, goddesses, labyrinths—the list is potentially endless— are here patched together in a heterodox hodgepodge, through which participants explore, comment on, play with, and parody religion and spirituality. (See DVD.) At Burning Man, the random flotsam of human history and global cultures washes up on the Black Rock playa for one week, then washes out as participants return to the default world, having shared in an experience that often leaves residual traces on participants' senses of self and notions of culture. This phenomenon could be said to exemplify what the anthropologist Claude Lévi-Strauss famously termed bricolage, a process by which we cobble together our belief systems about the world based on the sensory, cognitive, cultural, and historical ingredients available to us, or in Lévi-Strauss's terms, by "whatever is at hand."[4] It is also akin to what some scholars have characterized as syncretism, a term originally applied—often disparagingly—to the merging of two different religious traditions to create a third tradition, although at Burning Man the sources are as infinite as the bounds of human culture, history, and imagination, and the result is unmistakably indeterminate and dynamic. To borrow yet another term, this one from the electronic music and deejay cultures that intersect with the festival, Burning Man is a *mash-up*, an idiom that refers to the mixture of two or more popular songs from different genres to form a new polyphonic creation. In this implicit invitation to play with the stuff of diverse cultures, reshaping them to one's likings or whims, Burning Man serves to render the constructedness of cultures transparent, highlighting their native hybridity, adaptability, and plasticity. Through this process of creatively exploiting a vast array of cultural signs, Burners ritualistically and self-consciously de- and reconstruct ad hoc frameworks in which to create and perform self-reflexive spiritualities, which can become for many a profound life-changing experience.

It must be acknowledged that many participants and observers alike deny that Burning Man has any spiritual or other redeeming qualities whatsoever. Certainly there are thousands of participants—as I discuss at greater length in the pages that follow—who state emphatically that Burning Man does *not* entail any sense of individual or collective spirituality per se, although many of these individuals may still engage in a ritualized quest for self-discovery while electing not to cloak such experiences in mystical terms. Such competing perspectives are part and parcel of the very nature of the event. It is through an ongoing process of argument and dissent that participants themselves come to define, refine, and perform collective notions of what the event is all about. Furthermore, many would argue that Burning Man is merely a grand party—an excuse for debauchery and a license for transgressive behavior that is disconnected from any overt sense of spirituality, or any occurrence of significant change in one's life, community, or culture. Yet while the event is undeniably rife with opportunities for bacchanalian and hedonistic indulgence, this aspect of Burning Man need not preclude its spiritual, introspective, and transformative qualities. Indeed—America's Puritan heritage notwithstanding—religious traditions that do not include some opportunity for joyous, and occasionally excessive, ritualized celebration as part of the package deal are comparatively rare.

I should also state at this juncture that I have chosen to forgo a specific examination of the consumption of either licit or illicit consciousness-altering substances at Burning Man. Although such activities are for some an undeniable aspect of the festival—and at times the subject of gratuitous media attention—my observation has been that drug use is by no means a universal practice in this context. I therefore concluded early in the research process that although there may indeed be some connection between the use of substances that have been called "entheogenic"—that is, engendering an awareness of God or the divine—and participants' reports of transformative or spiritual experiences in this context, a focus on these questions would shift attention away from the inquiries into ritual and cultural performance with which I am primarily interested here and that I find ultimately more compelling.[5]

ONE PARTICIPANT'S ARRIVAL STORY

I entered into Burning Man as a participant first and as a participant observer second, and this insider position has had inevitable and interesting consequences for shaping the perspectives that are indelibly stamped on this text. Before I attended the event in 1996, I had heard about it from various friends and acquaintances but had been of the opinion that it would not be the sort of thing I would enjoy. I felt that I would generally prefer to appreciate the desert environment on its own terms, if at all, rather than overrun by crowds and revelry. However, when a couple of good friends announced that they were planning to go, I figured if they could handle it, so could I.

On arriving at Black Rock City, I discovered a hot, dusty, and somewhat dangerous place populated by several thousand hearty souls. My friend and I had driven through the night from San Francisco and pulled off the two-lane highway onto the Black Rock playa at dawn. We were greeted by the ticket taker, stationed with one or two lonely compatriots in a trailer just off the pavement. She told us that a fatal motorcycle accident had happened a few nights before and warned us to drive very carefully. Black Rock City itself was still several miles off, and she pointed us in a straight line farther east, instructing us to watch the odometer and then turn sharply north after a number of miles, proceeding with caution a few more miles toward the Burning Man encampment. My companion, already a veteran Burner, followed these somewhat vague directions with little trouble. My imagination raced as we traversed the vacant expanse of the playa—kicking up clouds of dust in our wake—and I was swept away by the feeling of heading into the unknown. Finally, as we drove along the edge of the encampment in search of our party, I could see that many tents and other forms of shelter were already haphazardly set up within a generally circular space. Along the sides of a wedge-shaped open space within this circle—then called "no man's land"—was a sprinkling of art installations: a small Stonehenge-like monument named *Mudhenge,* a cacophonous assemblage of piano parts called the *Pianobell,* the still-under-construction mock–strip mall *HelCo,* and Pepe Ozan's imposing monument the *City of Dis.* (See DVD, chap. 6.) At the center of "no man's land" stood the Burning Man—the same forty-foot-high skeletal mannequin that continues to be built and burned each year—propped up on a short stack of hay bales, awaiting its fate.

Many things about the event are rather different now. For one, it is much closer to the road and four or five times as large in both population and physical size (in 1996 the number of participants was about 8,000, as opposed to almost 50,000 a decade later). Arriving at night, one is immediately confronted with a glittering vista of colorful lights and throbbing sounds as Black Rock City pulsates and tantalizes in the darkness. Where once participants set off alone or in small caravans into the vast desolation of the playa, now they typically sit in multiple lanes of traffic temporarily laid out just off the pavement before proceeding through one of several ticket-taking stations. But all this had not yet taken shape when I rolled onto the playa that first morning and found myself unexpectedly thrown in with a group of organizers and other already longtime attendees who were the denizens of Safari Camp, my first home base. This provided me immediately with a glimpse into the event's inner workings, civic issues, and assorted politics and gossip, all of which I found quite fascinating.

It was also a much wilder event in those days. Population growth and attendant safety concerns would lead to regulations prohibiting both firearms and unfettered driving the next year. But these regulations were not yet in place, and one night I found myself tagging along with my campmates as they loaded pickup trucks with tanks of propane, a small catapult launch, and a number of guns and drove a few miles from camp for their annual "wild propane hunt"—skeet shooting one-gallon tanks of propane. I was absolutely terrified. I was put off by the guns, afraid of stray bullets, and fearful of the exploding fireballs above my head. Although I was somewhat reassured by the generally responsible demeanor of those around me and what appeared to be their genuine safety concerns (it should be noted that they also collected all the spent casings, leaving no trace of our doings), I still stayed far from the action.

Yet my experience of the totality of the event that year pushed my boundaries, as I have come to believe it was in some sense designed to do. I began to ponder my feelings and question many of my assumptions about what constitutes community, creativity, and self-expression. A couple of nights later, after the Burn, I found myself back on the distant reaches of the playa with some of the same characters, and this time I was offered the chance to join in. Someone handed me a rifle, gave me some quick pointers, and invited me to "take out" a small can of propane sitting on the ground maybe twenty feet away—an easy shot, perhaps, but the resulting fireball was no less cathartic. I had never before held a gun, and this experience caused me to challenge my preconceived limitations and enabled me to face one of my fears head-on.

After the event was over and I had returned gratefully to the comforts of my comparatively dust-free home, some impulse in me longed to be back on the playa. I subscribed to the Burning Man e-mail discussion list in an attempt to keep some connection to the event alive and present even in my dreary office cubicle. As a result, I was immediately plugged in to the San Francisco Burning Man scene in a way that I don't think would have happened otherwise. Because most list members were in the Bay Area, parties and other opportunities to meet were frequent. Despite the adventures they had provided, I hadn't really connected with most of my fellow Safari Camp mates, but through the list I met numerous people with whom I did feel an affinity, many of whom I still count as good friends.

My association with the Burning Man community became fairly extensive over the following year, so there was no doubt that I would attend in 1997. A large core group from the e-mail list, including me, banded together into what was to become the event's first "village," a large grouping of smaller camps.[6] Many individuals from this group became involved in helping to organize the festival, and I began to volunteer by writing for the *Black Rock Gazette*, the event's internally published newspaper. The next year this morphed into a role with the newly formed Media Team, which would be responsible for managing the increasing number of professional reporters who wanted to cover the event, responding to their queries throughout the year and staffing an on-site media hub during the event, as the organization developed increasingly savvy public relations strategies.

Also in 1996 and 1997, I was working on my master's degree and immediately saw the ethnographic potential of the festival. I was especially intrigued by the emphasis on being a participant, not a spectator, which offered some obvious parallels to the notion of reflexive participant observation, as well as by its ritual elements and transformative possibilities, which serve as central concerns in the present study. After the 2000 event, I withdrew from most active participation with the Media Team, in large part because by then I'd decided to focus on Burning Man as a dissertation topic and needed more time to experience and examine other aspects of the event.[7] Yet my years on the Media Team also served as an invaluable aspect of my early participant observation by giving me close access to core event organizers and providing me with a unique understanding of the media's relationship to the event (see chap. 5).

I share these stories in order to illustrate the extent to which I am thoroughly, deeply, and personally embedded in the Burning Man culture and community. A clear advantage of this immersive methodology is the wealth of data that my participation has afforded; I know my subject intimately. One could be legitimately concerned that my "native" status has resulted in an overfamiliarity with my subject and that I might be too close to the material to be able to analyze it empirically and rigorously. However, once I began undertaking formal research in 2001, my extensive acquaintance with the event came to be a benefit in terms of gaining a somewhat more distanced perspective. My basic understanding of the nature of Burning Man had become solid enough that I found I could reflect on the participants' narratives and performances in a more nuanced manner. In part, this can be attributed to the fact that I was no longer surprised by much of anything that goes on there. While the event's numerous works of art and silly costumes may still be impressive, even awe-inspiring, they are nevertheless just more instances of a long succession of expressions. But furthermore, it had become more apparent that most participants, including me, were on some level merely playing out a well-defined set of themes and narratives.

I continue to thoroughly enjoy occasional sojourns to the playa—especially the simple joy of camping out for a week with a tight-knit and ever-shifting group of friends. However, the experience typically no longer touches me as deeply as it once did. I am not alone in this; many longtime Burners have begun to experience burnout, resulting in extensive and ongoing internal critiques of the event. After several years

I concluded that those aspects of the event that had prompted my experiences of life transformation and personal epiphany no longer had the same effect. It seemed that because I had been to the event so many times it had nothing new to teach me. Or so I believed.

Given the harsh desert setting, severe dehydration is a constant concern, and all participants must take care to drink a minimum of one gallon of water every day. The regular intake of protein, salt, and electrolytes is also a very good idea. Yet despite my many years of experience and my conscientious efforts to attend to these necessities, the desert finally caught up with me toward the end of my final year of dissertation research (2004). On Saturday afternoon—the next to last day of the event—I began to feel light-headed and nauseated, which I knew were signs of dehydration, so I headed back to camp and spent the rest of the day sitting in the shade and drinking water. Although this course of action had always done the trick in the past, this time my symptoms were not improving and in fact began to get worse just before sunset. I knew I needed to go to the medical tent, where I was promptly fitted with an IV and administered two liters of saline. Since Saturday night is when the Man is burned, I missed the climactic spectacle that year.

While by all rights I should have been deeply disappointed, the experience was an odd personal highlight for me that year. My husband stayed by my side throughout the evening, and several dear friends stopped by to check on me on their way out to watch the Burn. It was comforting to know that I had good people watching my back. Furthermore, it was a new experience and a new perspective on the event. In nine years on the playa I had never had occasion to observe the inside of the medical tent. Despite my wooziness, my researcher's eyes came alive with delight to see a series of wall hangings adorning the interior of the tent: an image of the Virgin Mary, another of the Buddha, and a third of Elvis (on black velvet, of course). Data! The inclusion of these icons in this setting demonstrated the medical team's awareness not only that such spiritually resonant images might be comforting to those facing physical and emotional trials but also that this was a doctrinally diverse community. But beyond simply providing still more samples to catalog in my already bloated field notes, the experience provided a new opportunity for self-reflection and observation of my own behavior and reactions to an (albeit relatively minor) medical emergency. As I had in my first year on the playa, I was able to set aside my fears and remain rational and present. Thinking back on the experience during the long drive home, I realized that Burning Man might have still other new experiences for me and that I could rise to the challenge.

In reviewing my experiences at the festival, it is clear that many of the questions explored here—transformation, spirituality, and ritual—were already becoming apparent from my very first day on the playa and that I too participate in the cultural themes and streams that emerge through the event. Furthermore, my extended community of friends and campmates and other Burners with whom I am personally acquainted constitute a network within which I occupy a particular stance as both participant and observer, thereby implicitly and explicitly defining the perspectives through which I've come to view the Burning Man phenomenon. This is bound to be the case in nearly any ethnographic endeavor, as one inevitably establishes better rapport with some individuals than others. Yet while this is undeniably *my* story of Burning Man, it is by no means mine alone. The voices of the many Burners who shared their thoughts and experiences with me in countless hours of conversation, as well as in field interviews and via the Internet, are woven into this narrative and deeply shape my understandings of the event.

One anonymous voice unknowingly gave me the gift of the title of this book. In 2002 I was told of a man overheard in the midst of the ecstatic and chaotic moment following the flaming collapse of the Man shouting, "Theater! Theater!" My sources puzzled over this for a moment: was this simply an obscure commentary on the spectacle of it all? Then they realized that he was, in fact, shouting "Theater!" in a rather "crowded fire." I immediately seized on this phrase as an apt title.[8]

Burning Man is an interactive stage on which to perform, interrogate, and negotiate the meanings of religion, spirituality, ritual, identity, and culture, alongside a multitude of concurrent themes and possibilities. On a fundamental level, I see this project as my own performative and participatory contribution to the event—my gift and enactment of time, love, and intellectual commitment. Certainly, I receive things in this exchange—as do all Burners—which in my case includes a degree of professional status and a small amount of financial compensation that doesn't begin to cover the personal investment I made in attending the event for more than a decade. But by far the most important gifts I have received are my raw experiences on the playa in hundreds of moments and my memories of love, friendship, community, and the simply surreal that have shaped my life and perspectives in innumerable ways.

METHODOLOGY

My research on the Burning Man festival relied primarily on the ethnographic methods of participant observation, which can be understood as means by which to *reflexively* engage in lived cultural contexts, embedding cultural observations and analyses in ongoing examinations of one's self and relationships in both field and text. This requires a rigorous and strategic balance between points of focus, remaining attentive to diverse perspectives and ever-shifting relationships between participatory observers and observed co-participants. It is only in the past few decades that anthropology has begun to embrace this dimension of the study of cultures, but reflexive ethnographic strategies are increasingly understood and accepted as critical methods.[9] With these concepts in mind, I have attempted to remain attentive to my location as both participant and observer within and throughout this project. Given the Burning Man community's emphasis on being a participant rather than a spectator, this has been an especially challenging and rewarding endeavor. I have undeniably been changed by my encounters at Burning Man, and this is no doubt reflected in my search to understand how and why the experience of Burning Man is so often said to be transformative, a primary theme that runs through this text.

Beyond the realms of personal experience, my fieldwork included dozens of formal semistructured interviews and hundreds of informal conversations about participants' perceptions of and experiences at the festival. I also distributed a survey via the numerous, global on-line communities associated with Burning Man, with the intent to garner a broader set of data on participants' experiences of the event than would have been possible had I limited my research to the festival site alone. The survey generated over three hundred responses, and I followed up one-on-one with a handful of respondents. Because my interests lay primarily in individual and collective experiences, my intent in the interviews and surveys was qualitative rather than quantitative, although I did discern and tabulate some common themes. I also recorded basic demographic data on respondents for the purposes of context and compared these data to quantitative survey data compiled by the Burning Man organization.[10] Finally, media reports on the event constitute another major source of data, and I have amassed an extensive personal library of these.

As to questions of methodology, this work engages with a range of disciplines, including anthropology, sociology, media studies, and especially ritual studies. Ritual studies is itself an interdisciplinary field that draws on the anthropology and sociology of religion, the history of religions, liturgics, and performance studies, among other areas, in order to observe and analyze ritual in diverse cultural contexts. An influential theorist for ritual studies—whose ideas have proven especially fruitful for understanding Burning Man—is the anthropologist Victor Turner.[11] Turner's work on ritual process significantly expanded the concept of rites of passage and their tripartite structure as developed by an earlier anthropologist, Arnold van Gennep.[12] This framework describes rites of passage as entailing *separation* from the mundane world into a sacred *liminal* realm understood as transitional, marginal, and set apart from ordinary society. Finally, in *aggregation* the initiate returns to the ordinary world having gained a new status or new experiential knowledge. Turner broadened and amplified the liminal phase, characterizing it as prompting social experiences marked by feelings of communal unity, egalitarianism, and connectedness that he called *communitas,* experiences that he saw as disrupting the structure of normative hierarchical relationships and social institutions. Turner later developed the term *liminoid* to refer to liminal-like phenomena in industrial societies—such as pilgrimages, carnivals, and theater—reserving liminality itself specifically for the transitional phase in "traditional" or "indigenous" cultural rites.[13]

The concepts of liminality and communitas in particular resonate with and illuminate many of the ritual and experiential aspects of Burning Man and have influenced my thinking on this event.[14] This festival can be seen as a quintessentially postindustrial liminoid event, as participants themselves tend to view it as a transgressive, marginal, and otherworldly space for "countercultural" resistance. In this context, the transformations experienced by Burners do not typically transpire in terms of overt or externally defined changes in status or identity but rather involve connecting with others in community. Through a process of reflexively playing with various elements of culture—as well as through the viscerally challenging physical experience afforded by the playa—the event provides opportunities for participants to peel away layers of default cultural messages and constructions of identity. In so doing, they may discover a core sense of self that is deemed somehow more authentic and construct new or renewed identities based on the performative cultural ethos of the festival.

Burning Man's ritual events also generate a sense of communitas, a key reason so many people attend—and do so repeatedly—although as the festival has matured many find that this communitas has become routinized. The event's rites sometimes trigger experiences of collective integration and individual epiphanies, but many participants deem such encounters no longer reliable (if they ever were). The festival fosters an "alternative" atmosphere intended to directly challenge whatever is deemed culturally normative. Yet at the same time, Burning Man must increasingly capitulate to the demands of the default world, putting it in tension with what Turner called "structure" and "anti-structure." Finally, Burners' narratives at times refer directly to Turner's ideas, indicating that these concepts have permeated popular culture and now recursively *reflect and shape* our cultural conceptions of what the categories "ritual," "religion," and "spirituality" should be, thus outlining the context in which this event has come, for some, to constitute an alternative to conventional religions. My intent here is to use these and other theories of ritual, religion, and culture as frameworks for thinking about the ritualized behaviors that proliferate at Burning Man, looking to what they say (or do not say) when put in conversation with this event.

OVERVIEW

This book aims in part to paint a comprehensive and definitive ethnographic portrait of the Burning Man festival. Each chapter explores a different aspect of or perspective on the event, entailing thick descriptions of the ritual, media, and cultural contexts in which the event thrives, alongside participants' narratives and negotiations of spirituality, transformation, and culture. I thereby seek to demonstrate that Burning Man not only is a space in which to ritualize alternative and individualized constructions of spirituality but also calls into question both academic and popular culture assumptions about what constitutes religion, ritual, and spirituality in the first place.

Chapter 1 presents a history and overview of the festival, looking briefly to its contextual antecedents and parallels as a cultural phenomenon, and also describes its basic constituent elements and ideologies. Chapter 2 addresses the evocations of spirituality and religion within Burning Man by examining participants' narratives and perspectives on these concepts, relating these to their larger contemporary sociocultural contexts. Chapter 3 looks to the event's rites and ritualistic contexts, some of the more prominent, as well as a few smaller-scale examples, and their significance for understanding Burning Man's ritual dynamics and reflexive engagements with ritual theory.

Chapter 4 considers the ways in which Burning Man serves as a transformative pilgrimage, understood here as a culturally diverse ritual journey that may serve multiple social purposes. In so doing, this chapter examines participants' narratives of identity and transformation as connected to their experiences at the event, illustrating the ways in which these reflect the overarching ethos of the Burning Man community. This chapter also situates the event in its contemporary economic and "touristic" social contexts, as well as in its spatial and ecological milieu. Chapter 5 interrogates Burning Man's complex relationship with the mass media as a critical space for cultural production and negotiation, looking at how this has shaped experiences and understandings of the event. In particular, specific tropes used in media depictions of Burning Man are uncovered—including "technopaganism," "neotribalism," or "modern primitivism"—indicating tensions and tendencies that often serve to describe and frame the event in the public domain. Chapter 5 also considers elements of ritual and media reflexivity that are present in my own project by way of the DVD that accompanies this text. Chapter 6 concludes the book with a summary of my basic arguments by looking outward to the ways in which the cultural, religious, and ritual discourses that are framed, constructed, and performed through Burning Man may have significance for informing and transforming a wider social context.

Burning Man is perhaps most famous for its striking and provocative imagery, and this project includes a digital visual companion alongside the text. Our intent in producing the DVD has been to provide a vibrant complement to the text that extends its usability by enabling multiple modes of conversation and interaction between readers and the material. Like the text, the DVD, consisting of seven chapters, highlights narratives of transformation and spirituality alongside the festival's ritualistic and performative features, loosely corresponding with and reiterating key ideas in the text. Relevant segments and illustrations are noted throughout the book, tying together its descriptive analyses with the visual representations as much as is possible. It is hoped that these digital video elements will provide a particular vantage point on the ground—or in this case, on the playa—offering a richer depiction of the event than would be possible by the text alone. As with the text, the visual component does not purport to be an objective or comprehensive view of the events of Burning Man but rather is filtered through the lenses of those of us who worked closely to produce this portion of the project.[15]

In marshaling and weaving together these images, ideas, and narratives, this book and the DVD illustrate the ways in which Burning Man constitutes a theater for individual and collective spiritual expressions and experiences, as situated within broader narratives of cultural production. I locate Burning Man's intersection with ritual theories and religious discourses within overarching themes such as spirituality, pilgrimage, transformation, authenticity, otherness, liminality, and communitas as they are performed in this context—by which I mean the extent to which Burners' spoken accounts about and actions surrounding the event encounter, express, and live out these themes. The playful performance of religious and cultural motifs, symbols, and theories is abundantly observable in Burning Man's imaginative ritualistic and theatrical performances, as well as in many of the interactive art installations. By describing and locating some of these diverse spiritual and ritual motifs that proliferate at Burning Man, I intend to show how thoroughly they permeate our culture and are inscribed on individuals and communities while also highlighting their inherent heterogeneity and flexibility.

Thousands upon thousands of individuals have made a pilgrimage to the Burning Man festival. A majority make this journey more than once, despite the numerous challenges and hardships necessitated by the harsh desert environment, and many return with the feeling that their lives have been irrevocably changed. What compels people from all over the world to create an ephemeral city in the middle of nowhere? How is this remarkably enduring community forged from a temporary gathering of strangers? What are the historical and cultural contexts of this event, and what is its significance for our global society? Finally, what is it about this journey that engenders a sense of transformation for many participants, and how do they bring these experiences home? This book seeks to answer these and other questions by telling the story of Burning Man.

CHAPTER I

Into the Zone

By the time I first got to Burning Man in 1996—which turned out to be a pivotal year for the event—it had already changed dramatically from its humble beginnings a decade before. On summer solstice eve in 1986, a man named Larry Harvey and his friend Jerry James decided, for no premeditated reason, to host an impromptu gathering on San Francisco's Baker Beach, where they constructed a primitive wooden effigy and burned it. Having invited just a handful of friends to join them, they were delighted to discover that as they set flame to the eight-foot-high sculpture, the spectacle attracted onlookers from up and down the beach. As Harvey tells the often-repeated tale, someone began to strum a guitar, others began to dance and interact with the figure, and a spontaneous feeling of community and connectedness came upon those gathered— friends and strangers alike (see DVD, chap. 1). Flushed with the unanticipated success of the gathering, Harvey and James soon decided to hold it again the next year; with each subsequent iteration, both the crowd and the sculpture grew substantially.

Numerous legends have accumulated around the birth of the festival and—as is often the case with largely oral traditions—the elements of the narrative have shifted with each retelling, as some aspects have been emphasized and others lost in the dust. For his part, Harvey insists that he had no consciously preconceived ideas about the meaning of the Burning Man, let alone about starting a global movement. But this has not prevented observers and participants from ascribing a fanciful array of intentions and interpretations to the event's origins.

Over the many years that I have been studying the event I have noticed that most longtime Burners know the story of its origins and subsequent developments, but many recent attendees do not seem to have been introduced to this lore. Still others—both participants and interested observers—have heard half-truths, misrepresentations, and other distortions that have been propagated through popular culture and the media. It therefore seems helpful at the outset to lay the groundwork for the remainder of this work by putting the event in context. In so doing, I explain how Burning Man evolved into its present form and provide brief accounts of other festivals to which Burning Man can be compared, as well as an overview of the current state and organization of the event. This history also begins to illuminate some of the themes and issues that have most prominently shaped the event—spirituality, ritual, transformation, symbolic and artistic expression, countercultural resistance, and the challenges and opportunities of the desert setting—that are explored in the chapters that follow.

CREATING THE MAN

One of the most widely circulated legends surrounding the festival's inception contends that Larry Harvey was motivated by the demise of an important romantic relationship, a tale that has become a frequently repeated and occasionally distorted media myth: Larry was burning his ex-girlfriend; Larry was burning his ex-girlfriend's new boyfriend; Larry was burning his ex-girlfriend's lawyer; and so on. While Harvey characteristically shrugs off such notions, he admits that prior to the inception of what was to become Burning Man he had attended a number of "spontaneous art-party happenings" with his girlfriend.[1] At these happenings (staged by an artist named Mary Graubarger) attendees were invited to build small sculptures out of driftwood and scrap and burn them at Baker Beach on the summer solstice. Harvey has stated that the memory of these visits to the beach with his now-lost love were on his mind that first year, but he insists that this was not the cause or, more important, the *meaning* of the Man's creation and destruction. He instead credits his inspiration for the event simply to a spontaneous desire to have fun. This absence of conscious intention or specified significance became a cornerstone of Burning Man's guiding philosophy from the outset. As Harvey stated many years later, "The Burning Man's famous for our never having attributed meaning to him, and that's done on purpose. He is a blank. His face is literally a blank shoji-like screen, and the idea, of course, is that you have to project your own meaning onto him. You're responsible for the spectacle."[2] (See fig. 1.) With the Man remaining a blank canvas—an open signifier devoid of explicit or fixed meaning— the amorphous image continues to be available for multiple interpretations, as individuals are invited to transfer their own impressions and feelings onto it.

What started as a small gathering of friends in 1986 proceeded to grow phenomenally in size over the next few years, as word of the event spread through San Francisco's art and alternative culture scenes. By 1988 roughly 150 to 200 people joined in and the figure, now thirty feet high, was officially dubbed "the Burning Man." By 1990 there were approximately 800 in attendance when the local Park Police stepped in to prevent the combustion of the Man, by this time forty feet high. As the crowd grew restless and unruly, it became clear that the event was no longer sustainable as a free-for-all beach party. Undaunted, Harvey teamed up with a group called the San Francisco Cacophony Society—a loose-knit confederation of self-proclaimed "free spirits" and "pranksters" who orchestrated absurd public performance happenings and theatrical private parties. Members of the Cacophony Society had already been attending and helping to spread the word about Burning Man for a couple of years, and with the organizational support of these Cacophonists—in particular, John Law and Michael Michael—it was determined to take the Man out to Nevada's Black Rock Desert to meet its fiery destiny. James (who withdrew from the event after 1991) and other Cacophonists had gathered there a year before for a wind-sculpture exhibition.[3] For his part, Law had also been thinking about organizing an as yet unspecified Cacophony event in the Black Rock Desert. Thus various forces serendipitously converged, and a plan was hatched to orchestrate a collective pilgrimage to Nevada on the next Labor Day holiday, the first weekend of September.[4]

The stark setting of the Black Rock Desert has significantly influenced how the event has unfolded over the decade and a half since this fateful decision. Located approximately a hundred miles northeast of Reno, it is dominated by a four-hundred-square-mile prehistoric lakebed, or playa. Ringed by distant mountains, this expanse of hardpan alkali clay is completely flat, bone dry, utterly empty, and devoid of vegetation and animal life.[5] (See DVD, chap. 1.) The weather is extreme, as temperatures in late summer typically range from below 40 to well over 100 degrees Fahrenheit, and fierce dust storms with winds sometimes exceeding seventy-five miles per hour are not uncommon. The winds vigorously assault all in their path, easily taking down tents and shade structures that are not adequately secured with guy wires and rebar stakes, and even then they can wreak havoc on participants' temporary homes. Dehydration is also a constant threat, as the intensely arid environment inexorably wicks the moisture out of one's body, such that all participants need to be *constantly* drinking water. And then there is the dust. Though the surface of the playa is baked hard after the winter rains—which temporarily return this expanse, once home to prehistoric Lake Lahontan, to a shallow lakebed—the sudden influx of thousands of people breaks up the encrusted plain into a fine alkali powder that coats everything within moments. The high-powered winds capture this particulate matter, thereby fomenting dust storms that can create whiteout conditions and that have been known (albeit on rare occasions) to last for days.

This dramatic landscape can seem like the surface of an alien planet and presents numerous physical challenges. In its seemingly endless expanse and otherworldly terrain, the Black Rock playa evokes feelings of both fantastic and limitless possibility, and the austerity of the desert stirs up the themes of hardship, sacrifice, mystery, and boundlessness that are deeply ingrained in the Western cultural imagination. It is not without significance that deserts have a long history as loci of transformative possibilities—from Moses to Muhammed and from Christ to Carlos Castaneda—and Burning Man plays to these ideational sensibilities. Participants today often speak of being "on the playa" in a way that references this sense of environmental and cognitive otherness, helping to set the stage for transformative experiences.

Also significant has been the festival's relationship with the nearby towns of Gerlach and Empire and the surrounding counties of Washoe and Pershing. Perhaps one of the reasons Burning Man was able to thrive in this location during the early years is the fact that there was a certain sympathy (and a shared enthusiasm for recreational firearms) between the eccentric and reclusive residents of this remote high desert and the aging punks and pranksters of the Cacophony Society, both groups identifying themselves as cultural outsiders. Like every other aspect of this event, the relationship between Burners and locals became more complex as the years wore on, but by and large Burning Man continues to be tolerated by local residents, supported in no small part by local businessmen who profit directly from the annual influx of thousands of people in need of gasoline and other last-minute supplies, as well as by the organizers' conscientious efforts to participate in and give back to the local community.

Fewer than one hundred individuals made the trek out to Black Rock for Burning Man's first desert adventure in 1990, which was dubbed a

"Zone Trip," as Cacophonists called their practice of occasionally taking events on the road.[6] (See DVD, chap. 4.) These trips were conceived
as adventures of both the imagination and the body, as participants traveled to a conceptual otherworld of space and time. The Zone could just
as easily be an ordinary American suburb—approached with a nonordi-
nary gaze—as a remote desert, although the playa lends itself well to a
sense of the surreal and mysterious. The original announcement in the
Cacophony Society's monthly newsletter, *Rough Draft,* read:

> An established Cacophony tradition, the Zone Trip is an extended event
> that takes place outside of our local area of time and place. On this partic-
> ular expedition, we shall travel to a vast, desolate white expanse stretch-
> ing onward to the horizon in all directions. . . . A place where you could
> gain nothing or lose everything and no one would ever know. A place well
> beyond that which you think you understand. We will be accompanied by
> the Burning Man, a 40-foot-tall wooden icon which will travel with us
> into the Zone and there meet with destiny. This excursion is an opportu-
> nity to leave your old self and be reborn through the cleansing fires of the
> trackless, pure desert.[7]

This invitation to seek transformation in and through the heat and
emptiness of the desert, coupled with the sacrificial notes sounded by the
Man itself, already evoked the event's central, symbolically resonant elements. As one of the original travelers later described the experience:

> Did we know what we were doing? Probably not. Did we care? Yeah! We
> knew that whatever we were doing, it would be different. If only for that
> weekend, we were going to put some meaning into a special experience,
> recreating an ancient pagan ritual that was actually 1000s of years old. In
> Cacophony, we called these adventures a "Zone Trip." The Zone was
> some other dimensional place, it could be the past, the future, something
> weird, it didn't matter. We were going there, and we would challenge it
> and be better for it. . . . We all got out of our cars as one member drew a
> long line on the desert floor creating what we accepted as a "Zone gate-
> way." This was one of our Cacophony rituals, for the zone as we defined
> it took on many forms, it could be a weird house, a particularly strange
> neighborhood (like Covina, CA), or a desolate, deserted warehouse. To-
> day it was the base of a mountain range in Northern Nevada. We crossed
> the line and knew we were definitely not in Kansas anymore.[8]

As these intrepid adventurers literally stepped across a threshold
from one Zone into another, they performed a ritual passage into what
Turner and van Gennep termed a liminal realm—a conceptual zone "betwixt and between" the everyday and the extraordinary, the sacred and
the mundane, where transformation and the unexpected can occur.[9] Par-

ticipants would eventually turn to another Zone metaphor, specifically, the concept of the Temporary Autonomous Zone (or TAZ), proposed by the cultural critic Hakim Bey: "The TAZ is like an uprising which does not engage directly with the State, a guerilla operation which liberates an area (of land, of time, of imagination) and then dissolves itself to re-form elsewhere / elsewhen *before* the State can crush it. Because the State is concerned primarily with Simulation rather than substance, the TAZ can 'occupy' these areas clandestinely and carry on its festal purposes for quite a while in relative peace."[10] First published in the early 1990s, just as Burning Man was itself beginning to take off, this concept quickly caught on among Burners, despite Bey's original intention that "the TAZ be taken more as an *essay* ('attempt'), a suggestion, almost a poetic fantasy," rather than a specifically instituted (and institutionalized) reality such as Burning Man has become.[11] Yet this concept seemed to appropriately capture the "ontological anarchism" inherent in the Burning Man spirit, especially in its earlier, more anarchistic permutations, and continues to be an ideal among Burners and other countercultural denizens.[12]

A somewhat similar concept in this regard is that of the *heterotopia*—a term coined by the philosopher Michel Foucault to contrast with the literal "no place" of a utopia. Heterotopias are instead taken to be "places that do exist and that are formed in the very founding of society—which are something like counter-sites, a kind of effectively enacted utopia in which the real sites, all the other real sites that can be found within the culture, are simultaneously represented, contested, and inverted [and which is] capable of juxtaposing in a single real place several spaces, several sites that are in themselves incompatible."[13] As Burning Man grew into a site resounding with the strains of multiplicity, difference, paradox, and countercultural ideology, this would serve as an increasingly apt description.

The marriage of these elements—a voyage through the desert into an otherworldly and heterotopic zone to meet oneself in the guise of a burning effigy—readily forms a compelling symbolic stew that has remained central to the Burning Man mythos throughout its evolution, shaping its trajectory and persisting as a foundational narrative to this day. Despite its clear symbolic references to ancient transformative rites, the festival remains explicitly unaffiliated with any religious movement—Pagan or otherwise. Instead, both participants and organizers consistently reject any one fixed meaning for the event, locating it outside the realm of doctrine and dogma. But these refusals of canonical significance notwithstanding, neither the Burning Man festival nor the effigy for which it is named emerged out of a vacuum. The Man conveys allusions to a wide range of mythological and prehistoric rites of sacrifice and regeneration that can be traced to ancient sacrificial bonfires, carnivals, festivals, and other similar cultural acts.

BURNING THE MAN

Among the oldest popular legends are those concerning massive wood or wicker figures containing human or other living sacrifices that are said to have been erected and burned by the ancient Druids. Julius Caesar wrote of such practices nearly two thousand years ago in his tale of the conquest of Gaul, although corroborating archaeological or other evidence remains ambiguous at best.[14] Nevertheless, numerous bonfire-centric folk practices persisted in the British Isles through to medieval and contemporary times, and there remains a reasonably widespread belief that such events did in fact take place in ancient Europe. This notion was popularized in part by Victorian sources such as James Frazer's *The Golden Bough,* which proposed, among other things, that myths and rituals concerning a dying and reviving vegetation deity were a *universal* religious phenomenon, a claim that has long since been disproved.[15] Some believe that echoes of these bonfires can be found in popular events such as the English tradition of Guy Fawkes night, in which effigies of an Elizabethan-era Catholic rebel—the "Guy"—are set ablaze in bonfires throughout the Commonwealth in early November—although most scholars hold that the origins of this celebration are coincidental.[16]

In North American and European popular culture, the idea of ancient sacrificial bonfires flourishes in association with the 1973 horror movie *The Wicker Man,* which drew on Frazer's and others' ideas to imagine a quaint, remote, and fictional Scottish island where such practices are reborn with malicious intent and a hapless, puritanical police officer is caught up in the community's annual fertility sacrifice.[17] Beginning in 2002, a music event called the Wickerman Festival has taken place in Scotland each July, patterning itself in part in homage to the romantic neopagan ideas presented in the film.[18] Culminating in the burning of a thirty-foot-high "wickerman," this commercially sponsored independent music festival is in the tradition of several other summertime music fests in the United Kingdom, such as Glastonbury and the Stonehenge Free Festivals of the 1970s, that also lay some claim to England's pre-Christian "Pagan" heritage.[19]

Imagined Celtic wicker men are far from the only effigies that are central to carnivalesque events. For example, in northern India during September and October numerous regional pageants, celebrated in conjunction with the annual festival of Dussehra, reenact the epic *Ramayana* in which the divine Lord Rama rescues his wife, Sita, from the clutches of the demon Ravana. Highlighted by several daylong "Ram-lila"—or plays about Rama—these festivals typically culminate in spectacular conflagrations of Ravana effigies, often towering over one hundred feet high.[20] Another, much more recently devised example is the annual Zozobra festival in Santa Fe, New Mexico, in which a fifty-foot marionette called Zozobra—or "Old Man Gloom"—is burned in early September. Organized by the local Kiwanis Club, Zozobra is said to date to the 1712 introduction of the Spanish fiesta tradition in New Mexico. However, records indicate that the Santa Fe Fiesta as currently celebrated began in the early twentieth century, and the figure of Zozobra was the brainchild of the artist Will Shuster, who first devised the puppet in 1924.[21] Another contemporary event to which Burning Man has been compared—with even stronger ties to the "dominant" culture than Zozobra—is the Bohemian Club's annual revels at their Grove in the Northern California redwoods. The Bohemian Club, which began as a writers' guild in San Francisco in 1872, is today a private men's social club whose membership roster infamously includes the highest-ranking U.S. and international politicians and businessmen. The group's annual July encampment in the Bohemian Grove opens with a mock-Druid rite known as the "Cremation of Care," in which a humanoid effigy ("Care") is sacrificially burned by costumed "priests." The intention here is that these world leaders should let go of "dull care" for the duration of the two-week event.[22]

Contemporary events such as these, each in its own way, take some inspiration from romantic and exoticized ideals of a bygone era, and there are doubtless many more such festive events featuring sacrificial effigies and bonfires across cultures and histories, too numerous to cover thoroughly here. But the obvious parallels notwithstanding, Harvey and his fellow organizers have repeatedly emphasized that their Burning Man is not to be taken as an explicit re-creation of any particular mythological symbol or rite, and they have made several statements to this effect, including the following:

> Larry informs us that he had not seen this film [*The Wicker Man*] in 1986 when he first burned the Man. However, while listening to the sound track of a video made in 1988 at Baker Beach, he did hear a bystander shout,

"Wicker Man." Provoked by this, it occurred to him that "Lumber Man" would be a more appropriate, though not particularly inspiring, name. He decided to call the figure (which had been anonymous) "Burning Man," and so it has remained. Any connection of Burning Man to "Wicker Man" in fact or fiction—or, for that matter, to Guy Fawkes, giant figures burned in India, or any other folk source—is purely fortuitous.[23]

With or without a central flaming figure, there are countless other popular and alternative culture festivals, both contemporary and historical, to which the Burning Man event owes some debt for its existence. Burning Man takes its place in a lineage stretching back at least as far as the European medieval pilgrimage and carnival traditions and including the popular Christian camp revival meetings of the eighteenth- and nineteenth-century "Great Awakenings" in the United States, along with much more recent events like 1969's Woodstock concert. Traces of these diverse predecessors can be found throughout a contemporary network of alternative camp-out events that flourish across the United States and elsewhere. These include the relatively well known Rainbow Gatherings—free camping events held on public lands in the United States—that annually attract thousands of "hippies" and other countercultural types.[24] There is also a thriving network of contemporary Pagan and other alternative spirituality–oriented camp-outs and nature retreats such as the Pagan Spirit Gathering in the Midwest, Ancient Ways in Northern California, and Starwood in upstate New York, among many others.[25] In addition, numerous small-scale music-oriented and other camp-out events take place in the United States and internationally.[26]

Members of the international community of Burning Man participants have formed local networks in order to organize a number of Burning Man-esque events—ranging in form and scale from parties and art exhibits to multiday camp-outs—many of which are officially endorsed by the Burning Man organization. Among these events are Flipside in Texas (the first such spin-off), Playa del Fuego in Delaware, InterFuse in Missouri, Toast in Arizona, Element 11 in Utah, Apogaea in Colorado, Critical Massive in Washington State, and Soak in Oregon, to name just a few.[27] Most of these so-called regionals involve—like the Burning Man festival that inspired it—some kind of flaming effigy, though these are often constructed to be different from the Burning Man itself, such as the Texas Flipside community's "Stranger," which changes in appearance from year to year.

These various camp-out festivals are in many ways radically different from one another in their thematic or aesthetic orientations, as well as in their outlooks on commercial activity and expectations of participants, yet they also share similarities and cultural legacies. There are countless parallels, overlaps, and connections between these events, not only symbolically and thematically, but also in terms of constituency.

CACOPHONISTS AND CULTURE JAMMERS

Another cultural thread to which Burning Man owes its existence is a practice that has come to be called "culture jamming," referring in this context to various acts of public surrealism, reversal, and irreverence that aim to throw a conceptual monkey wrench into the cogs of normative social expectations and orders.[28] These acts are often intended to demonstrate the absurdity or injustice of globalized, corporate society, although some culture jammers may intend their pranks to be just good (if weird) fun, taking delight in confounding hapless citizens and bending the boundaries between everyday social expectations and surrealist sensibilities. Much of the inspiration for these varied movements can be traced to the dadaist works of Marcel Duchamp and others, the Situationist International movement theorized by Guy Debord, and Jean Baudrillard's conceptualizations of hyperreality and simulacra, as well as the "happenings" originated by the artist Allan Kaprow, Ken Kesey's band of Merry Pranksters, Abbie Hoffman and the Yippies, and the quasi-satirical Discordian religious movement, among many others.[29]

The Cacophony Society in particular is an important and influential exemplar of this larger phenomenon. Its roots can be found in a group called the Suicide Club, which started in 1977. The Suicide Club recommended that one should "get all worldly affairs in order, to enter into the world of Chaos, cacophony and dark saturnalia, to live each day as if it were the last."[30] The group lost momentum and disbanded in 1982, after performing such feats as repeatedly scaling both the Golden Gate and Bay Bridges, entering a Bank of America in downtown San Francisco dressed as clowns and Keystone Kops singing, "We're in the Money," and modifying commercial billboards to make ironic statements about cultural hypocrisy (leading to a related group that would come to be called the Billboard Liberation Front).[31] Former Suicide Club members, including John Law, regrouped in 1986 as the Cacophony Society. Michael Michael soon became involved and, with fellow Cacophonists, organized numerous similar public pranks and other edgy events during the late 1980s and the 1990s.[32]

One version of its mission statement, which, in keeping with the mercurial nature of the group, is always in flux, declared:

The Cacophony Society is a randomly gathered network of free spirits united in the pursuit of experiences beyond the pale of mainstream society through subversion, pranks, art, fringe explorations and meaningless madness. We are that fringe element which is always near the edge of reason. Our members include a wide variety of individuals all marching to the beat of a different din. We are the merry pranksters of a new decade. Our ranks include starving artists living on a diet of sacred cows, underemployed musicians listening to their own subliminal messages, postmodern explorers surveying urban environments, dada clowns working in the neural circuits, and live actors playing the theater of the street. We are nonpolitical, nonprophet and often nonsensical. . . . You may already be a member.[33]

Most Cacophony events have typically been geared to acts of public weirdness, although members have also orchestrated clandestine events such as "sewer tours," in which participants dressed in elegant formal attire and hip waders for (literal) underground cocktail parties. Perhaps most famous, or infamous, among all Cacophony and Cacophony-inspired events are those known as Santarchy or SantaCons, in which hundreds of people don cheap Santa Claus suits at Christmastime and irreverently roam the streets and shopping malls of various U.S. and international cities, including London, Tokyo, and Berlin.[34] From its inception on Baker Beach, Burning Man attracted participants from various segments of San Francisco's artsy alternative scene, including several denizens of the Cacophony Society who left an indelible fingerprint on the festival through their active involvement in and co-organization of the event throughout the early 1990s (although their specific presence as an organizing force ceased after 1996).

Each of these social movements has contributed to the context from which Burning Man emerged and in which it has flourished. Ancient burning icons, traditions of carnival, festival, and pilgrimage, and bands of Cacophonists—our Burning Man rides these cultural streams, often referencing and projecting romanticized concepts of premodernity into our so-called postmodern context. Burning Man organizers acknowledge these historical antecedents but disavow any direct causal relationship between their event and these various parallels. With no preconceived source or definitively ascribed interpretation underlying either the image of the Man or the annual rite of the Burn, its *meaning* is left open to individual interpretation and imagination.

BUILDING BLACK ROCK CITY

Once Burning Man took root in the Black Rock Desert, the event began to take on what would become its defining characteristics as a major international festival. For starters, it roughly doubled in size each year, so that by 1996 there were about 8,000 "citizens" of what by this time had come to be called Black Rock City.[35] In many ways 1996 would prove a watershed for Burning Man. Previously, the event was able to get by with minimal organization and oversight, and many saw it as an essentially anarchistic event where one of the only guiding rules was, "Don't interfere with anyone's immediate experience."[36] The festival's image as a feral and potentially dangerous happening was fueled not only by the ecstatic tenor of the Burn itself but also by highlights such as the Drive-by Shooting Range, located several miles from the main campsite and targeting stuffed animals.

Also contributing to this perception in 1996 was the event's first "annual theme"—The Inferno, loosely inspired by Dante's *Divine Comedy* and often referred to as "HelCo," after a prominent art installation that year. Intended as a spoof of corporate culture, this theme feigned a hostile takeover of Burning Man by HelCo, said to be fresh on the heels of its successful leveraged buyout of hell. It was an ironic comment on Burning Man's potential—and refusal—to sell out, even as the event underwent radical population growth and became increasingly structured.[37] The mock–strip mall of the *HelCo* art installation featured larger-than-life facades emblazoned with sarcastically modified corporate logos: CacaHell in place of Taco Bell, Submit in place of Subway, and Starfucks in place of Starbucks, along with other cleverly mutated brand images.[38] The Inferno also featured the *City of Dis*—named after one of Dante's levels of hell—which was an impressive forty-foot-high, three-towered sculpture with large gargoyle-like heads made of mud and wire mesh and designed by the artist Pepe Ozan (see DVD, chap. 6). In conjunction with this installation, Ozan and friends orchestrated an ambitious opera titled *The Arrival of Empress Zoe*, featuring nude and seminude performers depicting devils, demons, and insects and chanting the lyrics "devils' delight, fire tonight" while dancing around the hollow structure, which was filled with wood and set aflame.[39] Such satirical flirtations with religious (and irreligious) symbolism have become typical of Burning Man, here simultaneously acknowledging and lampooning the event's ostensibly "heretical" tendencies.

In addition to these outward affectations of defiance and danger, the first serious accidents occurred in 1996. A few nights before the official opening of the event, a man riding his motorcycle on the open playa—reportedly playing chicken while very drunk and with his headlight off—collided with another vehicle and was killed. Later, two other people were seriously injured when their tent was run over by a driver who was said to have consumed a large quantity and variety of illicit drugs. These tragic incidents—which remain among the most serious accidents related to Burning Man to date—spurred an awareness of the need to establish more effective safety regulations.

An additional ramification of the fact that until 1997 cars were allowed to come and go as they pleased was that gate crashers could not be easily prevented, as the "gate" was nothing more than a trailer off the side of the highway, staffed with one or two volunteers who provided directions to the event, which during these early years was located several miles into the interior of the playa. Presuming one could find Black Rock City in the featureless expanse of the playa without guidance, this meant that paying the then-$50 admission fee was deemed optional by some. In 1996 in particular, the gate was disregarded by a large influx of local Nevada youths on the final day and night of the Burn who drove onto the site with no supplies other than cheap beer, apparently intent on gawking at the freaks (and the sometimes scantily clothed or unclothed women). Although organizers encouraged locals to attend, they also needed them to be prepared for survival in the occasionally capricious environment of the Black Rock Desert and, furthermore, wanted them to participate and immerse themselves in the experience along with everyone else. It was from incidents like this that one of the event's guiding principles was born: "No Spectators."

As with the final Burn on Baker Beach in 1990, the difficulties of 1996 made it clear that the event could not sustainably continue as it had. From this point forward, the default world of government bureaucracy and business interests intervened more vigorously, requiring organizers to work much more closely and carefully with the local Nevada authorities, who up to this time had been relatively uninterested. These authorities primarily consist of the Bureau of Land Management (BLM)—the federal agency that oversees the Black Rock Desert—and Washoe and Pershing Counties, which straddle the playa. Burning Man's organizers correctly understood that they would have to impose certain limits and more explicit rules if the event was to continue. John Law, who had been a driving force behind Burning Man, did not want to see things move in the direction of greater regulation and control, so he withdrew from the organizing team and has not attended since.[40] Harvey and many others, however, wanted to see Burning Man continue to grow so that as many people as possible could have the opportunity to experience what was understood to be a remarkable and potentially life-changing event, and they proceeded to take the necessary steps to reorganize and restructure the festival as it exists today.

In order to institute a new organizational and fiscal umbrella for the event, Harvey formed the Black Rock City Limited Liability Corporation (BRC LLC) with Michael Michael and other longtime friends and co-organizers, Crimson Rose, Will Roger, Harley Dubois, as well as a relative newcomer, Marian Goodell, who became involved after the 1996 event. These individuals would fulfill important roles in event management. For example, as Director of Business and Communications, Goodell manages Burning Man's public interactions, including negotiations with local governments, the BLM, and the media, thereby serving a key role in shaping the public's perception of the event. Rose is Managing Art Director, which also entails oversight of pyrotechnics and fire performances during the event; and Michael (also known as Danger Ranger) could perhaps be best described as a futurist and visionary, fulfilling the enigmatic role of Ambassador and Director of Genetic Programming. As Director of Community Services, DuBois has perhaps the most noticeable impact on participants' experiences of the event itself as the City Manager of Black Rock City. Roger's active role in managing BRC's infrastructure was scaled back in 2003, although he still serves on the LLC board and as Director of Nevada Relations and Special Projects.[41]

In 1997 these organizers instituted a number of changes to address safety and other infrastructural concerns. Driving on the festival grounds by vehicles other than official or emergency transport was henceforth prohibited, although an important exception was made for "art cars," which were now prohibited from traveling at speeds over five miles per hour. Also known as "mutant vehicles," art cars are creatively and often elaborately modified autos that have been transformed into various sorts of mobile interactive sculptures (fig. 2; see also DVD, chaps. 1 and 2). A roaming community of art car aficionados had started attending Burning Man in the early 1990s and became a beloved feature of the event.[42]

In addition, the event site was relocated much closer to the highway so that the gate and festival boundaries could be more tightly controlled.[43] Now, rather than embark into the immense void of the playa—with fingers crossed that sufficient attention to the odometer would in fact bring

FIGURE 2. "Mahayana Bus" and "Silver Skull" art cars by unknown artists, 2003. Photo by Lee Gilmore.

one to the event site—one must typically wait in a long line of other vehicles before proceeding through an uncompromising ticket-taking station, where the surly, desert-hardened punks of the Gate and Perimeter staff brook neither fools nor stowaways. Where once the threshold into the Zone was physically and symbolically breached by stepping across a

simple line, this extended entrance is now marked with numerous and frequently humorous signs intended to help set the tone and evoke the annual
theme.[44] Following a rigorous check for tickets, adequate supplies, and
stowaways, arrivals proceed to a Greeters station, staffed by a much more
cheerful bunch of volunteers who warmly welcome "home" both new-
comers and old-timers. Their role is to orient people to community standards and expectations, as well as to help people figure out where to set up
camp or, for those whose friends are already on-site, how to locate pre-
arranged campsites.

The journey to Black Rock City requires considerable preparation. At
a minimum, everyone must supply their own food and water—at least
one and a half gallons per person per day—along with other survival
gear such as tents and general camping equipment. Most participants
also construct a temporary shelter or shade structure to shield themselves from the blistering sun, and these must be securely tied down and
capable of withstanding the occasional near–hurricane force winds.
Popular shelters include store-bought canopies and carports, homemade
lean-tos, covered geodesic domes, and other temporary buildings pieced
together out of PVC pipe and tarps or constructed of colorfully painted
plywood. (See DVD, chap. 1.) Some participants rent recreational vehicles for their journeys to and stays on the playa. Admission is itself a
nontrivial expense, as tickets in 2010 ranged from $210 to $300, depending on date of purchase, a cost that typically rises incrementally
each year.[45] In addition to these basics, many participants make enormous commitments of time, energy, and money—well above the cost of
admission and supplies—in order to create and transport the event's numerous elaborate art projects, theme camps, and costumes.[46]

After overcoming numerous external and internal political challenges
during the late 1990s, the Burning Man organization achieved relative
financial and social stability. The rate of Black Rock City's annual population growth is no longer exponential, having slowed to a more manageable rate.[47] In addition to the LLC board, the organization now employs
several full- and part-time salaried and contract office and event staff.
Participants occasionally refer to this body as "the BMorg," pronounced
"bee-morg," but sometimes shortened to "the Borg," a derogatory reference to a dystopian race of cyborgs from the *Star Trek* television shows.
The Borg moniker indicates the extent to which many Burners contest
and resist social structures deemed authoritative or hierarchical, but for
their part, Burning Man organizers and staff members dislike this term
and prefer that their collective endeavors be referred to as "the Project."

In addition to paid staff members—and perhaps more important— there are several thousand volunteers who help make the event happen every year, collaborating with paid staff leadership to provide the infrastructure and basic civic amenities for Black Rock City. This includes a volunteer peacekeeping force of specially trained Rangers, who act as intermediaries with various governmental and law enforcement agencies that maintain a presence at the event and whose roles also include conflict mediation, crowd control, and emergency response. There is also a couple-hundred-person-strong construction crew known as the DPW (Department of Public Works) who begin building the city's infrastructure more than a month in advance.[48] Although participants are encouraged to travel around Black Rock City's several-square-mile terrain on foot and bicycles, art cars are now "licensed" by the DMV (Department of Mutant Vehicles). Burning Man staff and volunteers also liaise with and contribute to professional emergency medical services, and a local agency, the Reno-based Regional Emergency Medical Services Authority (REMSA), is hired to staff the event. To facilitate communication, from 1994 to 2004 organizers published a daily newspaper, the *Black Rock Gazette*, which in 2005 was reduced to a single "gate edition" following a decision to reallocate resources. Other participants have independently produced their own daily publications during the event, most famously the long-standing and self-proclaimed alternative newspaper *Piss Clear*— named after a phrase used colloquially at the event in order to promote sufficient hydration—which published from 1995 to 2007.[49] Black Rock City is also home to dozens of low-frequency radio stations, including the official Burning Man Information Radio station. The Center Camp Café serves as a central gathering spot in the heat of the day and provides a venue for participants' spoken word and musical performances. (See DVD, chap. 1.) A final and indispensable civic requirement is met by several hundred chemical toilets, regularly serviced by the Reno-based provider Johnny on the Spot.

Many Burning Man participants organize themselves into groups that create "theme camps." (See DVD, chaps. 1 and 2.) These are usually presented as imaginative temporary locations dedicated to a particular motif or affinity, each functioning both as interactive entertainment venues for the city populace and as hubs for their own extended communities. Some groups also organize "villages," which are larger groupings of smaller theme camps that share some collective identity and organizational effort. A typical theme camp might be devoted to a particular preference in music, such as the Church of Funk or Spike's Vampire Bar, and many theme camps host nightly deejayed dance venues—typically involving some genre of electronic, or "techno," music—that are open to any and all interested revelers.[50] Others feature regularly scheduled performances or theatrical contests of some type, as is the case with the "Thunderdome"—faithfully adapted from a scene in the *Mad Max* movie of the same name and reproduced every year since 1998 by the Death Guild theme camp. Another popular contest called Dance Dance Immolation, based on a popular interactive video game, "Dance Dance Revolution," appeared at Burning Man in 2005–6. Where the original game's goal is to correctly keep up with a programmed sequence of dance steps, at Dance Dance Immolation participants (safely ensconced in fire-proximity suits) were blasted with flames whenever they made a mistake. Still others might proclaim themselves sanctuaries for particular erotic identities and practices, such as PolyParadise, the Temple of Atonement, JiffyLube, or Bianca's Smut Shack. In other cases, theme camps are based on idiosyncratic parodies of well-known popular figures or corporations, such as the Spock Mountain Research Labs or Motel 666. The Burning Man organization, for its part, now carefully oversees a theme camp proposal and mapping process; those groups that successfully indicate that their efforts will create an exceptional venue for interactivity and participation are given preferential placement along Black Rock City's main drag—usually called the Esplanade—which faces a large, central open area reserved for art installations, as well as other close-in locations that are mapped in advance.[51]

The city itself—now more than ten times larger than a decade ago—is ringed by a dozen or so precisely surveyed semicircular rows of campsites bisected by cross streets at regular intervals (chart 1). The latitudinal streets are typically named in accordance with the annual theme—for example, Authority, Creed, Dogma, Evidence, Faith, Gospel, Reality, Theory, and Vision in 2003 when the theme was Beyond Belief—while the longitudinal streets are designated by degrees of time ranging from 2:00 to 10:00.[52] Participants generally refer to the city's open area simply as the playa, although technically this term applies to the entire landscape on which Black Rock City resides. This uninhabited zone—an open-air playground of the imagination—is conceptually and physically distinguished from the city's residential area and is populated by dozens, if not hundreds, of participant-created and frequently interactive works of art, including the Burning Man itself standing at Black Rock City's geographic center.[53]

The layout of Black Rock City is designed to generate a particular sense of community, and Harvey has stated that he chose to leave the circle open because he wanted to invite a sense of boundlessness and wilderness into this civic space and also because he wanted the Man to reside at some distance from the main camp area.[54] When viewed from above, the semicircular layout is reminiscent of a labyrinth or mandala. The placement of the Man at the center of the city's concentric semicircles and radial spokes readily suggests a template that the historian of religion Mircea Eliade called the *axis mundi*—a symbolic manifestation of the sacred center of the cosmos and the location of *hierophany*, the eruption of the sacred into the profane world.[55] Here the Man forms the axis around which space and time are fixed—space, because the Man forms the locus around which streets are laid and in relation to which most of the other art is placed; and time, because the Burn is generally perceived as the festival's zenith.

Starting in 1996, Burning Man organizers devised a series of annual themes, beginning with The Inferno, as previously mentioned.[56] Although intended in a satirical and cacophonous spirit, the Inferno theme contributed to a somewhat dark atmosphere in 1996. Hence subsequent annual themes have attempted to inspire a more cheerful or contemplative mood: Fertility (1997), which vaguely nodded to notions of pagan goddess worship, love, and sexuality; Nebulous Entity (1998), hinting at beliefs in extraterrestrial intelligence; the Wheel of Time (1999), a loosely millennial theme in which the Black Rock City layout became patterned as a monumental clock face; the Body (2000), featuring artistic representations of body parts arranged as kundalini chakras along the city's central causeway;[57] the Seven Ages (2001), which celebrated the human life cycle from birth to death (see chart 1); and the Floating World (2002), which loosely alluded to the Japanese artistic tradition of *ukiyo-e* (images of the floating world), although the artwork inspired by the theme largely had nautical and watery motifs, transforming the desert into an oceanic spectacle of boats, fantastical marine life, and pirates.[58]

The 2003 theme, Beyond Belief, was intended as an exploration of the boundaries of the world's religions, rituals, and faiths, drawing the event closer than ever before into direct dialogue with notions of religion and spirituality. The Vault of Heaven (2004) paid homage to cosmic grandeur, alien worlds, and scientific discovery; and Psyche (2005) encouraged reflections on the mind, dreams, and the unconscious.[59] The Future—Hope and Fear (2006) set out to examine both utopian and

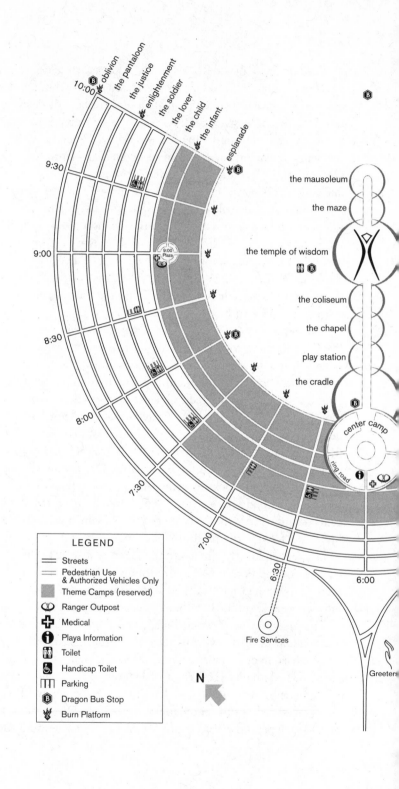

10:00

the pantaloon
oblivion
the justice
enlightenment
the soldier
the lover
the child
the infant.
esplanade

9:30

9:00
Plaza

9:00

8:30

8:00

7:30

7:00

6:30

6:00

the mausoleum

the maze

the temple of wisdom

the coliseum

the chapel

play station

the cradle

center camp

ring road

Fire Services

Greeters

N

LEGEND

Streets

Pedestrian Use
& Authorized Vehicles Only

Theme Camps (reserved)

Ranger Outpost

Medical

Playa Information

Toilet

Handicap Toilet

Parking

Dragon Bus Stop

Burn Platform

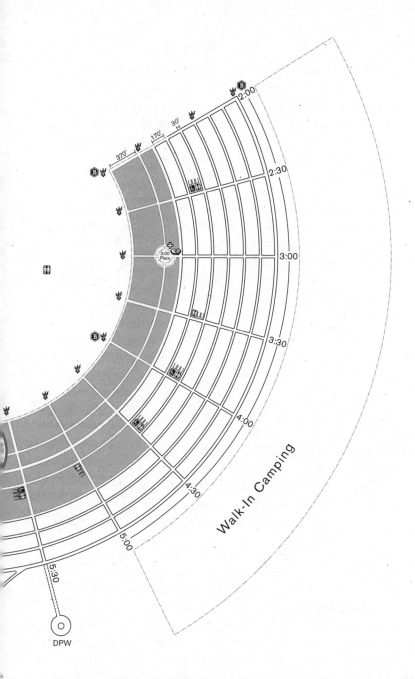

CHART 1. Black Rock City, 2001. Chart designed by Larry Harvey and Rod Garrett. Adapted by Bill Nelson from an illustration by Lisa Hoffman (www.burningman.com/whatisburningman/2001/photos/2001_map.gif). Copyright Black Rock City LLC. Used with permission.

dystopian notions of what may come; the Green Man (2007) invoked a popular pagan motif while also striving to improve the event's environmental profile; and the American Dream (2008) invited participants to imagine, reimagine, critique, and celebrate the mythos of this contested nation. Most recently, Evolution (2009) examined change, chaos, nature, and culture, while Metropolis (2010) set out to explore questions of urbanity and civilization.[60] These annual themes are advanced in order to furnish a conceptual common ground and provide a starting point for the event's creative expressions. The themes serve to spark the collective imagination and occasionally provide opportunities for both self- and cultural reflection. Yet, in keeping with Burners' typical resistance to authority and fixed meanings, many participants pay little heed to the themes, nor is all the art necessarily congruous with or inspired by them. It is much more important that artworks involve some form of interactivity, in keeping with the event's participatory philosophy.

NO SPECTATORS!

Over the years Burners have cultivated and nurtured an overarching ethos that reflects and reinforces the values and standards developed within the larger community of participants. These ideals were eventually explicitly formulated by the organizers into the "Ten Principles," which serve as guidelines for community behavior: radical inclusion, gifting, decommodification, radical self-reliance, radical self-expression, communal effort, civic responsibility, leave no trace, participation, and immediacy.[61] The organizers conscientiously promote these values through their Web site, newsletters, e-mails, and personal appearances, and they are embraced and championed by participants, who propagate them throughout the community. In advancing these principles, the organizers have not only framed and helped to define the nature of Burning Man but also selected for a set of participants who are, by temperament and social location, more likely to be drawn to an event of this sort in the first place.

A handful of established rules are spelled out in the *Survival Guide*, required reading for all participants; given the antiauthoritarian bent of most participants, these are sometimes referred to as "Participant Responsibilities" and "Community Standards" rather than "rules."[62] However, a few points are officially codified as the event's "Ten Fundamentals," prohibiting dogs, firearms, vending, driving non–art cars, leaving garbage behind, and camping outside the limits of Black Rock City and requiring that everyone purchase a ticket, follow basic sound and safety ordinances, and adhere to all applicable local and federal laws.[63] In this vein, the concepts of participation, radical self-expression, and radical self-reliance serve more as behavioral ideals than as strictly codified doctrines.

The need to preserve the natural desert environment led to one of the event's primary mandates: *leave no trace,* a catchphrase initially developed by the U.S. Forest Service, the National Park Service, and the BLM in order to encourage visitors to wilderness areas to protect the natural environment from potentially damaging human activities and waste. This requirement—both enforced by the BLM and largely embraced by the community—entails scrupulously cleansing the playa surface of all physical traces of the festival at its conclusion, down to the last pistachio shell, cigarette butt, or speck of glitter, and requires participants to pack out all their own garbage. This means that as the playa is returned to its natural condition, Black Rock City disappears like Brigadoon at the festival's conclusion and must be rebuilt from scratch each year. Because Burners generally support environmental responsibility, and share a deep appreciation for the rugged beauty of the desert, they have by and large earnestly adopted this model, packing out all their own refuse and methodically combing over their campsites to remove as much minute litter as possible. The community has even coined its own unique moniker for random debris: MOOP, which stands for "matter out of place." This principle was extended in 2007 when organizers sought to reduce the event's carbon footprint by arranging for solar- and biodiesel-powered generators to supply all their infrastructural power needs, in keeping with that year's Green Man theme.

However, the implementation of this edict is not always perfect, and some participants inevitably leave behind messes, both large and small. Another problem has been that garbage bags are sometimes found strewn along the side of the highway between Black Rock City and Reno, due to failure to securely fasten them to roof racks or trailers or to willful littering. Either way, it's a problem that has brought the event to the attention of the local communities in a distinctly negative fashion, and as a result the organizers have made concerted efforts to educate participants about this problem, which seems to have reduced its incidence. Also, the organization uses its e-mail newsletter to publicly shame groups that leave behind large amounts of garbage by announcing the name of the camp, if known, or the location of the problem camp within the Black Rock City grid, as the dominant attitude among most Burners is that such behaviors are unacceptable.[64] After the festival is over, many volunteers remain behind for weeks to finish the clean-up, as the BLM randomly checks parcels of the event site in order to verify that only a very small amount of MOOP has been left on the playa, a stipulation on which the annual permit depends.

The principles of *decommodification* and *gifting* mean that both corporate and independent artisan vending is strictly prohibited at Burning Man, as are advertisements. The no-vending policy distinguishes Burning Man from both commercial events like the neo-Woodstock concerts or the Coachella Music Festival, as well as from other so-called counterculture festivals such as the Rainbow Gathering and most contemporary Pagan festivals, at which many attendees fund their travels by selling food or arts and crafts.[65] As an alternative, organizers promote the event as a *gift economy* in which participants are encouraged to freely share their resources and creativity while also practicing *radical self-reliance* in keeping with the requirement to supply all one's own food, shelter, water, and any other items needed for survival. By and large, Burners have come to heartily embrace this edict, and indeed the promise of a space temporarily removed from the consumer culture that dominates in the default world is for some a main attraction of the event.

The innumerable creative acts that drive the heart and soul of Burning Man are also seen as contributions to the gift economy. In this regard, Harvey has been especially inspired by the poet and literary critic Lewis Hyde's meditation on gift economies as an "erotic" commerce, based on relationship, attraction, and union, that binds communities together by creating ties between individuals, where art itself becomes a form of gift giving.[66] This ideal situates Burning Man within a larger cultural critique of corporate consumption and commodification and also blends seamlessly with the other key principles, as individuals are encouraged and inspired to share of themselves as a way to participate in the larger community.

The Burning Man organization consistently refuses all offers of corporate sponsorship and is vigilant about maintaining an event free from outside corporate advertising, product placement, and vending of any sort. This means that the event is funded almost exclusively by ticket sales, although the organization also produces a limited supply of products such as T-shirts and calendars, which are available for purchase only via the burningman.com Web site. However, the income generated by these sources constitutes a minuscule portion of Burning Man's annual budget, which was nearly $8.4 million as of 2006.[67] These funds are used to rebuild the considerable infrastructure of Black Rock City each year, pay the hefty BLM fee, cover insurance and miscellaneous administrative costs, and sponsor select art projects, such that the organization basically breaks even every year. Participants tend to be vocal critics of any perceived breach of the gift economy principle, and some have charged that—given the high ticket prices and increasingly complex bureaucracy—the Borg itself has become overly corporate or commercialized, despite its rhetoric. In response, the organizers carefully distinguish their own revenue-generating activities as "commerce," not "commodification":

> We have drawn a dividing line around our desert event in order to separate direct, immediate experience from the commercial world of manufactured desire. It's not that we are against commerce, but we are against commerce without community, consumption without purpose and profit without value. The small amount of schwag we offer to the public is created by and for participants. Its aim is to communicate the experience of Burning Man and your involvement in our culture. We do not advertise outside of our community. We challenge other commerce to provide an equal value.[68]

Once past the gate, money can be exchanged in only two places within the Black Rock City limits: the Center Camp Café and an ice concession devised as a theme camp called CampArctica. The Café, which sells only beverages such as coffee and chai, has been a feature of Black Rock City since 1993, with its proceeds mostly serving to fund its own existence. (See DVD, chap. 1.) Given the length of time during which participants must maintain perishable food supplies in the desert heat, the pragmatism of an ice concession seems indisputable, and some portion of the profits of this enterprise are traditionally donated to the local communities of Gerlach and Empire. However, some participants still find the Café controversial, feeling that it represents a commodified space, providing a service that participants would do better to fulfill in their own self-reliant (and gifting) ways. Indeed, many longer-term and other attendees never go into the Café, a fact also borne out by the fact that most of interviews I conducted there were with first-time (and sometimes solo) attendees who may not have had anywhere else to find shade and shelter in the heat and dust of the day.

In addition to declining all offers of corporate sponsorship or product placement, the organization vigorously defends the Burning Man "brand"—with its indisputable hipster cachet—from being used by any outside party or to promote anything other than the event.[69] Most participants would perceive blatant commercialization of the event—such

as corporate logos on tickets, the sale of branded beverages or food, or
any statement like "Burning Man is brought to you by [fill in the name
of any commercial entity here]"—as a betrayal of the event's core values.
In resisting corporate branding, many participants go so far as to carefully mask or creatively alter all logos on the rented trucks and other gear
they bring with them, so that Black Rock City can remain a kind of puri-
fied space, ideologically (if not practically) removed from the tainted
forces of the market.

The consumer researchers Robert Kozinets and John Sherry examined
the ways in which Burning Man simultaneously resists and participates in
traditional market economies. Noting that participants must engage in
commerce with some corporate interests in order to obtain supplies for
the event—a conclusion reached in part by the extent to which the task of
traveling to and adequately supplying themselves for Burning Man resulted in the rapid depletion of their research budgets—they also observed that participants distance themselves from corporate consumption
once they have arrived at Black Rock City. Kozinets concluded:

> Rather than providing a resolution to the many extant social tensions in
> contemporary life—such as those surrounding the beneficial and oppres-
> sive elements of markets—it offers a conceptual space set apart within
> which to temporarily consider, to play with and within those contradic-
> tions. It falls short of some ideal and uncontaminated state, but it may be
> all the consumer emancipation most consumers want or need.[70]

Yet, even if only a fleeting ideal, it is one that participants sometimes embrace and promote even more enthusiastically (almost fanatically) than
the organizers.

Finally, perhaps the most popular principle at Burning Man is the injunction to participate, with the corollary that there should be, as stated
above, no spectators. (See DVD, chap. 1.) The concept of participation
undergirds the entire event, which, simply put, means that everyone is
expected to actively engage in Burning Man and make a positive contribution to the collective experience, in whatever unique way individuals
so choose. As the organizers state, "The people who attend Burning
Man are no mere 'attendees,' but rather participants in every sense of the
word: they create the city, the interaction, the art, the performance and
ultimately the 'experience.' . . . We often like to say there are no spectators at Burning Man. It doesn't mean there isn't a lot to look at—it
means that even the process of viewing is active."[71] The twin concepts of
radical self-expression and radical self-reliance are closely allied with

the ethos of participation. The term *radical self-reliance* underscores the edict that participants are expected to supply their own material needs at the event and also reflects the values of responsibility, autonomy, and freedom that are extolled at Burning Man. However, this injunction is not intended to breed isolation or greed but rather is framed such that individuals are encouraged to turn their self-reliance outward, starting with the self and reaching out to the greater community. The term *radical self-expression* is likewise intended to encourage creative and reflexive exchanges between individuals and the larger community. As Harvey has stated, "We [ask] that participants commune with themselves, that they regard their own reality, that essential inner portion of experience that makes them feel real, as if it were a vision. . . . No one can say what that vision might be. We just ask people to invent some way of sharing it with others."[72]

In this regard, there is no official mandate as to *how*, specifically, one should participate in or express oneself through the event. (See DVD, chap. 1.) For some people, this may mean volunteering in some capacity for the Burning Man organization, which has developed a number of volunteer teams that are responsible for managing diverse aspects of the event. There are those who assist in administrative capacities year-round— for example, the Media Team or the Web Team—as well as those whose efforts take place on-site at the event, including the Greeters, the Rangers, and the DPW. Others produce the event's numerous and often ambitious artworks or organize elaborate theme camps, and still others play and interact with those objects and camps while decked out in eclectic and whimsical costumes, thus contributing to the performative and ritualistic ambience that saturates the festival. Furthermore, the various elements of this ethos—especially participation, radical self-expression, and radical self-reliance—have come to be among the key elements of the event that participants most frequently cite as having inspired a sense of life transformation or critical change in perspective, as I explore further in chapter 4.

CONCLUSION

Ritual, religion, and spirituality have always been thematic undercurrents at the Burning Man festival. Soon after Larry Harvey and his compatriots first erected an artistically primitive effigy on the beach, Harvey discovered that he had tapped into something powerful, something that had the ability to touch people in compelling and potentially transformative ways, even if only by providing a momentary joy or a fleeting sense of connectedness to others in the age-old fascination with fire. Although there was ostensibly no conscious intention behind that act, religious or otherwise, the simple performance and the spontaneous community that formed around it tapped into a primal attraction to fire and referenced ancient "pagan" sacrificial rites and totems, triggering a mood that was at once contemplative and celebratory. A few years later, when Harvey and his culture jamming friends in the Cacophony Society first set foot on the playa, intent on burning the Man, they consciously evoked the liminal metaphors readily suggested by the desert's other-worldly terrain in stepping across a threshold into the Zone. In this simultaneously imaginal and physical space, they could be "reborn through the cleansing fires of the trackless, pure desert," framing the experience as a rite of passage.[73]

This once-simple event grew into an increasingly complex and well-organized festival as participants have created a mini-metropolis on the surface of a barren and unforgiving desert floor. Thousands now perform this annual pilgrimage to the Black Rock Desert, taking part in a long legacy of carnivalesque celebrations and retreats into the wilderness in search of a temporary heterotopia or an alternative to the mundane routines of the default world, and perhaps a sense of connection to something larger than oneself. Today's Burners bring with them an extraordinary proliferation of artwork, much of which references global religious symbolism in both overt and subtle ways. (See DVD.) In tandem with this, many participants use Burning Man as a space in which to create quirky, unorthodox, and hybrid forms of ritual expression through which participants cobble together independent symbol and meaning systems. Many also report that the shared, immediate experience of the event contains deeply transformative and spiritual dimensions, although they typically refuse to associate Burning Man with any explicit metaphysical, theological, or religious doctrine.

CHAPTER 2

"Spiritual, but Not Religious"?

Burning Man emerged at the crossroads of the twentieth and twenty-first centuries and is an expression of the trends, circumstances, and desires arising at this juncture in contemporary American cultures. Its existence derives in part from a variety of cultural movements that include but are certainly not limited to eighteenth- and nineteenth-century camp revivals, contemporary outdoor festivals, so-called New Age and other alternative spiritual movements, countercultural and utopian movements of the 1960s (and before), rebellious punk movements of the 1970s and 1980s, and the electronic music and dance scenes of the 1990s (and beyond). Going farther back, it is linked to a long tradition of pilgrimage, carnival, and festive collective ritualizing that reaches into the antecedents of Western and global cultures.

Many of these movements can be traced in turn to various pursuits for something deemed more "real" or more "true" that resides outside the bounds of the ordinary social world, or in Burners' terms, the default world. Such movements have a long legacy in numerous religious reform impulses across cultures and histories, wherever the dominant or normative religious institutions have come to be seen as somehow corrupt or otherwise lacking in "authentic" spirituality. In recent decades, one guise such critiques have taken is desires for a spirituality that is positioned as conceptually distinct from religion, and the Burning Man festival is one place in which this broad contemporary trend prevails as an influential narrative. This chapter looks to the ways in which participants describe their understandings of religion and spirituality, placing these themes in dialogue with the findings of select relevant social theories. (See DVD, chaps. 4 and 5.)

IS BURNING MAN A RELIGIOUS MOVEMENT?

It is difficult to discuss Burning Man as a venue of ritual and spirituality as for the most part neither participants, nor organizers, nor observers see it as constituting a religion. For many, Burning Man is simply seen as a fantastic party and as an arena for creative and rebellious behavior, with no more lofty aspiration than to be a celebration of outsider art.[1] Burners employ a multitude of diverse and sometimes contradictory frameworks to describe their perspectives on the event, and if there is a dominant principle that most could agree with, it may be that Burning Man "can be whatever you want it to be." Yet the abundance of experiences that some participants claim as spiritual—alongside numerous and culturally eclectic expressions of religious themes and symbols that are readily observable within the event's rituals, artwork, and costuming—begs the question as to why Burning Man is *not* considered a religion.

One important reason is that most participants tend to come to this endeavor with an idea of religion that carries a lot of negative baggage—laden with notions of institutionalization, oppression, stultification, and irrationality—that they seek, in part through this festival, to be free of. For their part, organizers also make conscious efforts to conceptually demarcate these realms; for example, they declare in their mission statement, "We believe that the experience of Burning Man can produce positive spiritual change in the world."[2] (See Appendix 3.) Yet, at the same time, they consistently disclaim the notion that Burning Man is intended to be understood as representing any specifically "religious" ideology or doctrine, as in this statement:

> We have never attached any kind of supernatural dogma to [Burning Man's] practices. Undoubtedly, the act of pilgrimage to a remote location and the ritual sacrifice of a ceremonial figure has real religious resonance for many people, and any spiritual faith, however arrived at, is certainly worthy of respect. Valid comparisons have also been drawn between events at Burning Man and religious ceremonies in the ancient world—in particular, the observances of the Mystery Religions of the Hellenic and Roman eras. [See DVD, chap. 3.] The ritual aspects of Burning Man, however, have wholly evolved in the context of artistic endeavor, and their significance, as with any work of art, is explicitly left open to interpretation.[3]

This paradoxical framework, positing a distinction between the spiritual and the religious, is not an isolated phenomenon; the concept of a spirituality absented from religion has increasing currency for a constituency that has little faith in mainstream or traditional religious options as means by which to determine personal and cosmological meanings. Instead, many people are engaged in new religious movements, individualized and hybridized spiritual paths, and alternative systems of faith and practice through which to connect with both personal and communal senses of spirituality.

Such maneuvers to differentiate the concepts of spirituality and religion aside, any attempt to unequivocally or universally define these terms is nearly insurmountable as they emerge from and exist in specific historical and cultural contexts and represent concepts that may or may not be more or less applicable in other settings.[4] It is furthermore unwise to attempt to bifurcate these into somehow *essentially* separate categories, as the two terms are endlessly recursive and often synonymous. Ultimately, both terms grasp at ineffable human experiences, beliefs, and desires and therefore are perhaps best understood as culturally constructed signifiers that attempt to contain these illusive qualities. I do not wish to belabor these points, or to dwell exhaustively on defining these terms—let alone the troublesome phrase "spiritual, but not religious." What is most significant here is not what should or should not be construed as either religion or spirituality in any essence but rather how Burners describe and frame their own experiences and orientations to the underlying concepts these terms reference, and why.[5]

FRAMING NARRATIVES

Through my decade of immersion in and observation of the Burning Man community, I developed a strong sense of the event's general cultural ethos—especially given my interests with regard to religion—and quickly perceived that, by and large, the event attracted people who were deeply ambivalent about so-called organized religion. With few exceptions, the majority of my friends, acquaintances, and campmates at Burning Man eschew involvement in traditional religious institutions, and many see themselves as completely secular, perceiving both religion and spirituality as irrational and repressive realms. There is some general sympathy for alternative spiritualities and practices such as contemporary Paganism, along with other, more generic new age spiritualities and mysticisms, but very few people whom I encountered actively embrace or adopt specific practices or identities.[6] Instead, the preference tends to be to pick and choose elements of faith and practice that individuals deem most suitable or appropriate for them in a given situation.

Instructive and ultimately supported though these observations have been, I want to include a broader perspective than that offered by my immediate and extended community. This has been achieved in part through field interviews, as I sought out participants more or less randomly in the Center Camp Café and also visited specific theme camps throughout Black Rock City whose descriptions indicated a religious or ritual focus and where I thought I would find individuals who would have unique or interesting perspectives on my questions. In most of these conversations, I heard similar narratives of desires or quests for spirituality paired with a rejection of organized religion, along with various experiences of personal transformation and ritual catharsis in the desert's crucible. Still, I wanted to reach out to a broader range of perspectives than would have been possible by relying solely on one-on-one contacts and so turned next to the Internet, where the international community of Burners has developed an extensive network of e-mail lists and Web sites.[7]

Among the key questions I put to participants was, "In general, do you consider yourself a religious or spiritual person? Please say more about what that means to you, why you do or do not. What has been your religious / spiritual background?"[8] Combining the results of this survey with those gleaned in field interviews, I discovered that although the responses reflected diverse perspectives, several common themes emerged. These typically reflected eight basic tendencies, which I grouped into three broad categories, as follows:[9]

EIGHT BASIC TENDENCIES

"Alternative" (58 percent)

GROUP 1. Those who clearly stated—in more or less as many words— that they considered themselves "spiritual, but not religious" (31 percent).

GROUP 2. Those who indicated that they thought of themselves as in some way "spiritual" but who did not explicitly indicate that they either rejected or embraced any particular religious tradition, or "religion" in general (11 percent).

GROUP 3. Those who described themselves as "spiritual" while also identifying an interest in multiple religious traditions (and no explicit affiliation with any one tradition) (10 percent).

GROUP 4. Those who named a current affiliation with one particular nonhistorically Western or Abrahamic religious tradition, such as Buddhism or contemporary Paganism (6 percent);

"Mainstream" (6 percent)

GROUP 5. Those who indicated a current affiliation with Judaism or Christianity, or particular denominations thereof (6 percent).

"Secular" (28 percent)

GROUP 6. Those who stated clearly that they were specifically atheist or who saw themselves as decidedly neither "spiritual" nor "religious" (15 percent).

GROUP 7. Those who identified themselves as largely ambivalent or agnostic (9 percent).

GROUP 8. A subset of atheists and agnostics who said they experienced some larger meaning, purpose, or connection to a greater (and ultimately mysterious) cosmos but who understood this connection in scientific rather than spiritual terms (4 percent).

I wish to be clear that these general groupings—as well as the broad descriptors *alternative, secular,* and *mainstream*—are not intended to constitute a comprehensive or global typology. Instead, this thematic organization of narratives serves to reveal pertinent dimensions about Burners' perceptions and feelings on questions of religion, spirituality, and the Burning Man festival itself.[10]

"Alternative"

Given my suppositions going into the survey, I was not surprised to find that those whose replies indicated some alternative perspective on spirituality and religion in their lives constituted a majority of respondents. *Alternative* is, of course, a somewhat problematic term, as it would seem to be defined solely in opposition to an equally illusive and variable "mainstream." However, for the purposes of facility and utility, I take this term here to indicate non-Jewish and non-Christian or otherwise outside normative American religious categories, at least as they have traditionally been understood. Of the four thematic tendencies included under this rubric, the framework most commonly referenced—totaling nearly one-third of all respondents—was "spiritual but not religious." These participants tended to cite a number of common qualities that they associated with both celebrated notions of spirituality and rejected concepts of religion, deemphasizing doctrine in favor of diverse and distinctive points of view. For example, one San Francisco resident in his early thirties gave this evocative statement on what he considered the defining qualities of spirituality:

> Spirituality is a flow, emotions not logic, analog not digital, music not words. Senses (music, sexuality/sensuality), feelings outside of physical senses, subtlety and heightened perception. . . . It's a way of interpreting the universe as we experience it, a manner of interacting and reacting. It's being connected with the universe rather than separated. Spirituality is connectedness, including connecting with people. It's about riding the experience as if you're surfing, not about dominating or controlling it.[11]

These general sentiments—invoking and underscoring an individualistic view while simultaneously reflecting a search for connection and community—were echoed in many other responses. Participants also spoke of constructing an ad hoc and personal spirituality out of an assortment of available resources, as with this young woman from the Lake Tahoe region of California:

> I consider myself a spiritual person. I wouldn't consider myself religious. . . . I don't call myself anything. I kind of extract what I need from everything I come in contact with, with no judgment. I believe that we all have our journeys and our beliefs, and I think love is the essence of all the religions I've read about and looked into and talked about.[12]

For most of the people grouped here, rejection of religion stemmed from associations with inflexibility, closed-mindedness, and hierarchical authority, all qualities viewed as inherently opposed to their lauded notions of spirituality. For example, a woman in her early sixties who lived in the mountains above Santa Cruz, California, said:

> I consider myself a spiritual person but not a religious person. Religious, to me, implies [being] stuck in some hierarchical group with a set belief system. Spiritual, to me, means being open to all life and all people and feeling part of nature and all creation. It has nothing at all to do with particular beliefs.[13]

For others, rejection of religious institutions stemmed more specifically from their own negative experiences or impressions, resulting in a deep distrust of those institutions, as explained by this Idahoan in his early thirties:

> I came to believe that religious doctrine is more about power and politics than about spirituality, and also to believe that religion has lost all concept of the beauty and power of metaphor, instead demanding that we take Scripture at its literal face value (which I think is a shame, and that the metaphor is ultimately so much more powerful and can be digested at such a more personal level).[14]

A second and related theme discernible in a number of responses—constituting roughly 11 percent—was the understanding of being spiritual, or otherwise engaged in a quest for "spirituality." But these respondents made no specific statements either rejecting or accepting the term *religion* per se. While I was therefore hesitant to include them with the previous set, the concepts of spirituality they voiced were generally similar. For example, a San Franciscan in her mid-thirties stated:

> I consider myself a spiritual person, which to me is about expanding myself, opening my heart to compassion for everyone. It is also about questioning my assumptions and lifelong-held perceptions of people and the world. Spirituality is about me being guided by the divine universe and acting from that expanded self place rather than small self place.[15]

A third contingent—totaling approximately 10 percent—similarly described themselves as spiritual while also not categorically rejecting religion. However, these voices were somewhat distinct from the previous two groups in indicating an interest in *multiple* religious traditions while not naming any one specific, current affiliation. These included such statements as this one from a nineteen-year-old woman in Vancouver:

> I consider myself pretty spiritual, for the most part. . . . I was into Wiccanism for a while, but I've recently discovered what I believe is a mix of Wiccanism, Buddhism, and Hinduism all together. I suppose if I had to label that, it would make me a Unitarian, yes? I choose not to label it. It's just what I believe. I think that spirituality is a very personal thing. It is for me, anyway.[16]

Finally, there was a fourth identifiable trend among respondents—comprising about 6 percent: these individuals identified themselves as adherents of specific religious traditions that are not conventional or typical in the West, most frequently Buddhism or a particular branch of contemporary Paganism. For example, one respondent in his mid-fifties stated,

"I am a Druid and very active in the Pagan community."[17] A few individuals in this group indicated that they maintained a Buddhist practice, such as this fifty-six-year-old woman from the California Sierra foothills: "I have had a Zen Buddhist practice since 1991. I sit daily and attend sesshin regularly."[18] Still others offered unique responses, such as a twenty-six-year-old woman from Seattle who stated, "I have been a Kabbalist for years. The Kabbalah is more pragmatic than most 'mysticisms.' I feel I have spirit, but I am not 'new age.' "[19]

Participants in this fourth group tended not to employ either the term *spiritual* or *religious* in their responses—instead naming specific traditions—and in this way they might be seen as having more in common with those in the so-called mainstream group than with the spiritual but not religious narratives offered by most of the others, who seemed to best fit under the "alternative" heading.[20] Yet while the numbers of explicitly religiously affiliated respondents—either "alternative" or "mainstream"—were a distinct minority, their perspectives help to flesh out a fuller understanding of the wide variety of religious discourses expressed through Burning Man.

"Mainstream"

Challenging what many people might assume, I encountered a number of participants who identified with religious traditions that could be considered mainstream or normative; approximately 6 percent of respondents named a specifically Christian or Jewish religious affiliation.[21] As previously noted, all the broad descriptors applied here have certain problems, and "mainstream" may be the most troublesome of the lot. For example, is Judaism, whose adherents remain a distinct minority in the United States, properly to be understood as "mainstream"? Further, many of the self-identified Christians I encountered through Burning Man might be seen as atypical of what is most commonly assumed to be the "center" of their traditions. Ultimately, however, given the dominant position that Western monotheisms hold in U.S. society, I opted to use the term *mainstream* in recognition of this privilege.

These voices also reflected complex and challenging understandings of self in relation to religion, as some indicated that they pushed the boundaries of what might be considered typical of their tradition by including the teachings of other religious traditions in their practices. For example, one individual I encountered who could be seen as somewhat unorthodox in his orthodoxy was a cofounder of a theme camp called the

BRCJCC (a.k.a. Black Rock City Jewish Community Center), which—among other activities—hosted Shabbat services and Kabbalah lessons. He would not let me tape record our conversation because it happened to be a Saturday morning when I stopped by his camp, and he felt that recording would violate religious proscriptions against working on the Sabbath. However, he also told me that I could walk along and chat with him while he headed over to another theme camp, the HeeBeeGeeBee Healers, that was hosting a Buddhist Vipassana meditation session he wanted to attend. As we discussed his perspective on Burning Man, he told me that he had needed to carefully consider his understanding of what the Burning Man "idol" meant, so as not to engage in any way in the worship of "false gods."[22]

This was somewhat reminiscent of an earlier conversation I'd had with a sixteen-year-old from North Carolina who indicated that she had felt the need to negotiate some of the specific teachings of her church with some of the more hedonistic or potentially "idolatrous" aspects of participation in Burning Man: "I'm an Orthodox Lutheran. Which is one of the reasons that I haven't participated in anything ritualistic [here] that would be against my beliefs."[23]

Other individuals in this general group indicated that their experience of Burning Man, in particular, its desert setting, had enhanced or reinvigorated their faith in some way. For example, a woman in her mid-thirties from New York City stated, "I grew up very Christian in the South and in fact struggled with wanting to let that go until I came to Burning Man. Finding god in the desert just in the spirit of the event and the attitude of my fellow Burners helped me set aside my fears and religious hang-ups."[24] Another individual—a lifelong Quaker in his late thirties from Oakland, California—also cited an encounter with the physical environment in describing how Burning Man had changed his life; he quoted the Old Testament: " 'I will entice you into the desert and there I will speak to you in the depths of your heart.' Hosea 2:14. It happened to me. I won't presume to speak for the meaning for anyone else."[25] In instances such as these, it can be seen that while some Burners who have conventional religious affiliations may feel a need to negotiate a potential conflict between their faith and their experience of the festival, its transformative reach does not necessarily preclude "mainstream" religious affiliators and can in some cases even enhance them.

This was also the case for Randy Bohlender, a young evangelical pastor who made repeated trips to Burning Man from the Midwest with members of his flock starting in 2000, in order to witness his faith and distribute thousands of bottles of water as a way to "show God's love."[26] After conversing with several participants, he discovered that many of his own preconceptions about what lay at the heart of Burning Man had been challenged; he was profoundly struck by the ways in which the event fulfilled people's desire to connect with one another in community. He returned to find that Burning Man had changed his "personal definition of weird" and had deepened his own relationship to God. In an essay that he initially posted on his church's Web site, he stated:

> I no longer find it weird when people express themselves in ways I never thought of. . . . I think God likes our rough, creative ideas better than professional presentation. I have a gut feeling he delights in our most creative attempt to get his attention, because it shows our heart. With this in mind, I find it weird that the church world appears to have been made from a cookie cutter. While worshipping a God that values creativity, the church has managed to squash it at every turn. . . . Particularly in America, we have homogenized worship to the point where our distinctive [gifts], given to us by God to be celebrated, have dissolved into an evangelical unitarianism. . . . I do find it weird that the church strives to convenience people when people really thrive on challenge. Getting to Burning Man is a challenge, but it's a challenge people rise to. The church in America has done everything they can to remove all challenge from attending, in hopes that if it's convenient, people will stumble into a walk with God. . . . Let me make it simple for you. Following God, pursuing him, is not as easy as getting to Burning Man.[27]

Bohlender returned in 2002 and 2004 with increasingly large groups in order to continue his mission to educate other participants about what he understood as Christ's message in a way that was sensitive to the cultural contexts of Burning Man. Although he never wavered from his faith in what he termed "the exclusivity of the Gospel," he also remained open to the creative and transformative possibilities of the event.[28] After his second trip to Burning Man, he wrote:

> I go to Burning Man because the playa puts me in my place. I spend entirely too much time in boxes. I have a ranch style, suburban box, where I keep my family and most of my stuff. I have a small, German-made box with wheels where I keep most of my CDs and spend a lot of time on the phone. I have another box where I keep coworkers. In those boxes, I am someone. I have the power to change the climate. I can manipulate the auditory environment. I crown myself king of my boxes, and when my boxes wear out, I will get new ones. The playa is the ultimate out-of-the-box experience. In our boxes, we are in total control. On the playa, we are at the mercy of God (some would say the universe, but remember . . . I've got a paradigm). It's on the playa that I realize my finiteness.[29]

Bohlender's story is a striking example of the religious heterogeneity that can be discovered among Burning Man participants. The spiritual diversity of this alternatively oriented event nevertheless has room for evangelicals and the mainline religious beneath its wide tent. These individuals may hold highly individualistic orientations to their faith, but—as it does for those of more "alternative" or "secular" orientations—the experience of Burning Man can offer encounters with spirituality or transformation for them as well.

"Secular"

The group collectively labeled "Secular" rejected both the concept of religion and the concept of spirituality. This theme constituted the second most prevalent outlook reported by participants, totaling 28 percent. Of these, 15 percent stated that they were either explicitly atheist or otherwise nonreligious and nonspiritual. Some individuals in this group simply said "No" to the question of whether they were religious or spiritual.[30] But most others elaborated their perspectives with statements reflecting a general disbelief in supernatural forces. For example:

> Not religious. Atheist. By this I mean that I don't believe in spiritual forces, beings, or apparitions that independently exist outside of human imagination. I don't generally refer to myself as spiritual as the word is so often associated with belief in supernatural forces. I value compassion, honesty, love, truth, beauty, and knowledge.[31]

Those of atheistic dispositions often spoke of their reasons for rejecting religion in terms similar to those who saw themselves as spiritual, viewing "religion" as something irredeemably corrupt, oppressive, and hypocritical. But for these individuals, all matters of faith and spirituality were suspect and rejected. For example, one participant in his mid-thirties from San Francisco stated, "I think that religion is stupid and spirituality is a crutch that the human mind requires to make sense of the world. My background is that I was raised Catholic and did a brief stint with Wicca before deciding it was all bunk."[32]

Another 9 percent of respondents in this group identified their perspectives as largely agnostic or ambivalent, as typified by the following statement from a forty-year-old man in Portland, Oregon: "I'm an agnostic. In general, I believe human events and activities tend to have whatever meaning you bring to them, and that our human minds are far too limited to comprehend the divine, if the divine indeed exists at all."[33]

Many of the other statements included here indicated some degree of ambivalence or uncertainty rather than explicit agnosticism or atheism. For example, a thirty-three-year-old woman in the south Bay Area said, "I have no religious or spiritual background. I don't really consider myself a religious or spiritual person. I do believe that there is a greater being or beings. I am still in the inquiry as to who or what that may be and how my life is influenced by that being."[34]

Such responses demonstrate a perhaps predictable rejection of religion that is similar to many of the "alternative" voices noted above, based on their perception of numerous institutional problems or personal negative experiences that led them to a generalized mistrust of organized religion. Many also spoke of the impossibility of empirically assessing the existence of an essential spiritual or sacred realm. However, a handful of respondents—4 percent—similarly indicated that they could be best understood as primarily atheist or agnostic but also that they experienced some connection to a greater reality understood from a scientific or secular perspective. A biochemist and computer programmer in his mid-forties living in Emeryville, California, stated this sentiment most evocatively:

> The universe is such an amazing place, why would anyone want to muck it up with religion? . . . I suspect what others may get from spirituality, I get from standing somewhere, looking at a beautiful Douglas fir, and thinking down, down, down through the various scales from the overall tree and it's structures and systems . . . back up to the macro level and photosynthesis, forest as community, the biota that exists within the tree[,] . . . which leads you to the formation of planets, solar systems, [and] stellar formation . . . followed by the structure of galaxies, local clusters, and the strings and voids that make up large-scale stellar structures in the universe. . . . Is that sequence of thoughts "spiritual"? I suspect that others might describe it that way. I'm certain that any number of followers of a lot of religions have marveled at those same ideas and sang hosannas to the "glory of God." I simply don't understand why people feel compelled to believe that anyone is driving.[35]

Although most respondents did not specifically mention such understandings of cosmic or scientific mystery, I suspect that many other Burners with a secular orientation might embrace something like this experience of connectedness to creation. My suspicion is based on numerous conversations with self-described atheists who have also thought deeply on these topics and expressed similar sentiments.

In all the narratives shared by these participants, it becomes apparent that, even as Burners' viewpoints on spirituality and religion are multiple and individualistic, certain common threads can be discerned. Most simply, "religion" in this context tends to mean *organized* or *institutional* religion and is also usually associated with doctrinal beliefs or ideologies, as well as particular ritual and symbol systems. "Spirituality," on the other hand, is conceived as better found outside the realm of institutional religious structures and doctrines and evokes a broadly and variously conceived sense of connection with something more that is beyond the individual and the ordinary. Spirituality as performed in this context is fundamentally *experiential* (based on the primacy of personal experience and personal authority), *reflexive* (inspiring reflections on self, self/other, and self/culture), and *heterodoxic* (constituted by multiply layered, fluid, and noncentralized constructions of meaning). This may include a sense of connecting with a diversely understood sacred realm, a sense of connection with others in community, a quest for some meaning or purpose in life, an expanded and deepened experience of self in particular communities and cultural contexts, and experiences of transformation, transcendence, or mysticism. Finally, for most—but, of course, by no means all—Burning Man participants, this quest takes place largely outside the context of traditional religious institutions.

ASSESSING BURNING MAN

If Burners' perspectives on questions of religion and spirituality in their own lives are heterogeneous and independent, their views on whether or not Burning Man should be understood as a religious or spiritual event are likewise multifaceted and defy easy categorization. In this regard, a second question I posed to participants was, "Do you think Burning Man is a religious or spiritual event? Why or why not?" Common threads were also discernible here, although I found that in this case it was more accurate and instructive to track the overall frequency of given themes—counting the total number of individuals who sounded general notes rather than attempting to subdivide these into distinct categories—as over half (53 percent) gave voice to more than one perspective. The most prevalent sentiments can be summarized within five broad areas:

THEME 1. Those who affirmed that their own experience of Burning Man was, in various ways, "spiritual" (46 percent).

THEME 2. Those who made some reference to Burning Man as spiritual but not religious (11 percent).

THEME 3. Those who firmly rejected any notion of Burning Man as either spiritual or religious (15 percent).

THEME 4. Those who noted Burning Man's ritualistic features and other traits that parallel traditional religious institutions and structures (39 percent).

THEME 5. Those who stated that Burning Man could be whatever participants wanted it to be (42 percent).

When correlated with responses from the previous section, not surprisingly, individuals who described themselves as spiritual or religious (Groups 1–5) were also more likely to characterize Burning Man as spiritual or religious, whereas those whose perspectives tended toward the secular (Groups 6–8) were less likely to ascribe such qualities to the event. In most other regards, however, participants' voices on these general concepts and subjects remained diverse and personal (table 1).

While not constituting a clear majority opinion, the most frequently voiced theme—46 percent of respondents—affirmed that this festival contained some spiritual aspect. In describing what about this festival led them to such understandings, many referred to a sense of connection to others or to community. For example, a woman in her mid-thirties from Eugene, Oregon, stated, "It is deeply spiritual for me because of the connectedness that Burners feel towards one another. It's an exercise in love and loving everybody I come into contact with for an entire week. The spiritual strengthening that results from this is something that resonates with me forever after."[36] Others spoke of spirituality as in some way inherent in the event and as stemming from something beyond ordinary reality. A participant in her mid-forties from Sacramento stated, "Burning Man calls to the part of us that is really spiritual, that understands our connection with the Universe. Accordingly, it doesn't need to have dogma; the Subconscious doesn't need rules, it needs Experience. At Burning Man one can Experience."[37] And as a thirty-one-year-old woman from Oakland put it, "There is a very real connection people are feeling out there to the divine, to ancestors and the dead, and especially to the divine within each participant."[38]

Others spoke of encountering a means of self-expression, self-exploration, or self-renewal through this event, as a woman in her mid-thirties from San Francisco attested: "There are aspects of it which seem spiritual to me. . . . It really opens me up emotionally and creatively. It is

TABLE 1

Participants' Perspectives on Religion and Spirituality

	All Respondents (%)	Group 1 (%)	Group 2 (%)	Group 3 (%)	Group 4 (%)	Group 5 (%)	Group 6 (%)	Group 7 (%)	Group 8 (%)
Theme 1	—	31	11	10	6	6	15	9	4
Theme 2	46	48	68	69	59	61	24	40	42
Theme 3	11	10	3	13	12	11	14	20	8
Theme 4	15	13	16	6	0	22	24	7	17
Theme 5	39	36	59	28	47	56	28	37	42
	42	51	25	44	41	22	32	50	50

a safe place to be the person I am—whoever it is that I am is OK."[39] A woman, also in her mid-thirties, from Alberta, Canada, stated, "Burning Man brings out the spiritual in people who didn't even know they were. Burning Man helps you to see that life is more than who you are, more than what your job is, where you live, what you own. Burning Man is you and the world that you live in."[40]

It is significant that most of these replies did not employ the terms *religion* or *religious,* and those that did tended once again to turn to the concept of spirituality but not religion. Roughly 11 percent explicitly mentioned an understanding of spirituality as distinct from religion. Most of these responses were from individuals who felt that the event itself was in some way spiritual. For example, a thirty-seven-year-old woman from the north Bay Area stated, "Religious? No. Spiritual? Probably, if only because it elevates that thing we most regularly call the 'spirit.' It raises my spirits and my awareness of the world around me. It quiets my internal dialogue, and simultaneously makes it scream with the affirmation, *I am alive!*"[41] And a fifty-year-old man from Reno, Nevada, stated, "I think it is highly spiritual, and nonreligious. Religions are merely cults. Burning Man is not a cult, because it doesn't require Faith or promise salvation or control people."[42]

In keeping with this general resistance to institutionalized religion, as well as with the significant number of individuals who professed largely secular orientations, 15 percent of respondents stated that the Burning Man event lacked any inherent spirituality—a perspective that tended to be more prevalent among those who identified themselves as atheist or agnostic (see table 1). A few of these replies were as simple as "No";[43] others reflected a certain cynicism, as exemplified by this response from a thirty-nine-year-old Bay Area man: "No, it is not! It is someone's way to make a shitload of money."[44] Others based this assessment on their own ideas about spirituality and religion, as with this thirty-nine-year-old man from Austin, Texas: "There is no god/goddess. I've never understood why folk find Burning Man somewhat religious, but I've never felt it to be."[45]

However, in keeping with the fact that a majority of responses to this question referenced more than one common theme, about one-fifth of those who rejected the notion that Burning Man was either spiritual or religious also indicated that they understood that the event could ultimately be whatever participants wanted it to be. For example, a forty-four-year-old man from New Jersey stated, "Burning Man is not religious.

Spiritual? What does that mean? Many people I've met have tried to construe it as one, but Mr. Harvey has been very careful to avoid reducing the event to anything that can be easily defined. Burning Man is what the participants make of it."[46] In addition, nearly one-third of those who did not see Burning Man as either religious or spiritual noted a ritualistic resonance in the event, such as a man in his late twenties from Portland, Oregon, who stated, "Personally, I don't think that Burning Man is religious or spiritual in the traditional definitions of the terms. However, I can see how it might be considered religious or spiritual, referencing a more tribal, reptilian form of ritual that is lacking in regular society today."[47]

Indeed, 39 percent of all respondents noted various ritualistic aspects—or other structural elements commonly perceived as characteristics of religions—as in some way intrinsic to the event, most of whom also concurred that these conditions lent the event a spiritual quality or flavor. For example, a woman in her late twenties from Los Angeles stated:

> Absolutely, I am deeply fascinated with Burning Man as it manifests every belief pattern at once, reflecting the oneness of such diverse spiritual experiences. As soon as I saw the Man in the center of the city my first year, I knew that Black Rock City was a place of *deep ritual,* a sense of connectedness rarely achieved in modern communities.[48]

Other responses did not explicitly implicate ritual as an element of Burning Man's spiritual qualities but did allude to other aspects of religious faith, such as a twenty-nine-year-old woman from San Francisco who stated, "I think it can be, since it has been for me. Since it encourages community, which was always my favorite part of my religious experience, and presents many opportunities for personal mystic / divine / love experiences which I see as a major component of my spirituality."[49] Finally, it should also be noted that a few respondents perceived the event's ritualistic and religious parallels with disdain, as did this thirty-nine-year-old man from San Francisco:

> Religion is a recent disease at Burning Man. For me, Burning Man has always been a great escape from the painful pseudoreligious stupidity I have to listen to and live with in the real world. . . . It was not a spiritual event for many years, but as more people come, everything gets easier, safer, and more like a rave in downtown [San Francisco]. People stop discovering what it is about and just lean on the old tired mindless religious ideas, because it is so much easier than discovering something new.[50]

Yet even while he rejected and expressed his distaste for the embrace of spirituality within Burning Man, this man nevertheless acknowledged the extent to which this theme has become prevalent at the event.

As already touched on above, a final common theme—which emerged in 42 percent of participants' responses to this question—came from those who described Burning Man as capable of being whatever individuals, or communities, choose or seek to make it. One response that typified this perspective came from a forty-four-year-old man from Seattle who stated simply, "It has an amazing power to be whatever the hell you want it to be."[51] Another participant, a Canadian in his late twenties, said:

> Burning Man is what you make of it. That's all it is. It's the removal of expectations, and the reminder that expectations leads to disappointments. One year it's too hot, one year it's too cold, one year it's too rave-y, one year it's too sexual. One year it may be spiritual, but Burning Man is the quintessential embodiment of the idea that you shouldn't label something.[52]

Whether participants relate to Burning Man as a spiritual experience—or in some other way observe (or resist) its religious parallels—it is clear from these narratives that Burning Man can, indeed, be whatever participants want it to be, as it both absorbs and reflects an enormous variety of ideals and expectations. Though I did not find that a clear majority of respondents directly subscribed to this theme, it can still be seen as a dominant position among many Burners, as reflected in the fundamental semantic flexibility ascribed to this event and in the diversity of attitudes about Burning Man's spiritual or religious qualities.

The interpretive openness evidenced in participants' widespread rejection of religion as a meaning-making frame—and in turn the collective dismissal of any pretense of orthodoxy in defining the event itself—is a central and critical aspect of this festival. As all the above narratives illustrate, most Burners describe both Burning Man and their own perspectives on spirituality in ways that largely resist or ultimately reject normative ideas about religion, and most understand it as an arena that by design invites multiple constructions and layers of meaning. Instead Burners seek—in part through this festival—to realize and ritualize their desires for connectedness, community, and meaning by constructing individualistic narratives that privilege experiences and expressions of spirituality over traditional religious institutions and doctrines.

ASSESSING THE LANDSCAPE

Burning Man's rituals and spiritual quests have not, of course, emerged from a vacuum but rather must be viewed in light of the social contexts out of which they have developed—in particular, the ever-shifting American religious landscape. Over the past several decades many social theorists, beginning with such founding figures as Max Weber, have claimed that religion—as an authoritative social and ideological force—was on the wane in the Western world as a result of the increasing secularization of social structures and a concomitant increase in the authority of scientific knowledge over the authority of religious claims to "truth."[53] This trend eventually came to be understood not as the total disappearance of religion from society but rather as the disestablishment of religion from the public sphere, which was thought in turn to result in an increased privatization and individualization of the religious sphere. Whatever the tenor of these now-controversial theories, it has become increasingly apparent that religious and spiritual discourses have certainly not disappeared from the public sphere in the United States. Indeed, overall religion and spirituality remain strong forces in individual and communal lives.

For example, a 2006 Gallup Poll found that 84 percent of Americans said that religion is a very or fairly important aspect of their lives, and 63 percent said they were members of a church or synagogue.[54] Furthermore, most polls taken in the past few decades have consistently found that 85 to 95 percent of Americans say they believe in God or some higher power, although precisely what is meant by this statement no doubt varies widely.[55] While these polls seem to show that a majority of the U.S. population remains affiliated with more or less traditional religions, extrapolating from Gallup's figures, there remain 37 percent who are not members of a church or synagogue and 21 percent who would say that religion is important to their lives but who remain institutionally unaffiliated. Contrary to a popular notion that the United States has always been a Christian nation, religious and spiritual practices have historically been far more diverse than is generally acknowledged; scholars have found that so-called alternative spiritualities have been part of the American landscape since its beginnings.[56] In this regard, the persistence of alternative spiritualities and the apparent manifestation of spiritual expressions in ostensibly secular venues such as Burning Man is ultimately nothing new.

In the 1980s and 1990s sociologists increasingly began to characterize apparent trends toward nontraditional and noninstitutional religion in terms of *individualization* and *seeking*. An influential study by Robert

Bellah and colleagues concluded that U.S. society is increasingly characterized by a spiritual individualism that threatens to weaken the social
fabric of healthy communities rooted in traditional, church-based understandings of faith, morality, and community responsibility.[57] Others,
such as Robert Wuthnow, concluded that as individuals feel less compelled to cleave to particular religious territories, there is a corresponding lack of boundaries around religious identities. He worried that this
new spiritual freedom was ultimately rootless and lacking any foundation in historical, cultural, and community-based traditions.[58] Wade Clark
Roof, in his examination of "seekers" in the so-called American spiritual
marketplace, found individuals across the social spectrum striving to engage in reflexive, personal experiences of spirituality, in which they create their own spiritual identities, practices, and beliefs, connecting this
process to Lévi-Strauss's concept of bricolage. In so doing, they become
more aware that their perspectives are but one among a plurality of possibilities instead of relying on inherited faith and church teachings as the
sole authorities on the divine.[59]

Roof's and Bellah's studies in particular were pointed primarily at the
so-called Baby Boom generation, typically defined as those born between
1946 and 1964. Burning Man, however, attracts participants from many
different age groups, with the largest bloc belonging to what came to be
known as Generation X, or GenX—that is, those born between 1965
and 1984. For example, respondents to my 2004 survey ranged in age
from 17 to 66, with a median age of 37.5 (table 2). A 62 percent majority reported that they were 20 to 39 years old (born between 1965 and
1984), while 35 percent reported that they were 40 to 59 years old (born
between 1946 and 1964).[60] (See Appendix 1.)

As can be readily observed within the multigenerational Burning Man
community, Generation X and Baby Boomers—in the United States at
least—share many outlooks on matters of religion and spirituality. For
some, this includes the general trend toward "seeking," as well as a perceived split between an inner experiential dimension (spirituality) and an
outer institutional dimension (religion).[61] However, some scholars have
identified a number of key variations between these generations. For example, Richard Flory argued that GenXers display "religious entrepre-
neurship," by which he meant that they

> are not simply religious consumers, although they are that, but also pro-
> ducers, actively creating new groups in the marketplace for themselves,
> regardless of whatever might have been provided for them by existing

religious groups. . . . Xer seeking is more than just a quest for an individual-istic spiritual experience—Xers are instead looking for and creating com-munity, belonging, and authenticity, which can only be measured within the religious community.[62]

Regardless of the extent to which such qualities may or may not be gen-erationally ascribable, they can be useful in contextualizing Burning Man, for just as Burners tend to seek personalized experiences of spirituality—the authority and authenticity of which are internally rather than exter-nally determined, and which emphasize experience over doctrine—they are also clearly religious "entrepreneurs." This can be observed in their emphasis on freeform spiritual creativity, hybridity, and "do-it-yourself" attitude. Furthermore, as I examine more fully in later chapters, *commu-nity* is undoubtedly a core element of the Burning Man experience. It is an important part of what keeps many participants coming back year af-ter year and, for some, inextricable from the aspects that render the event, in various ways, a spiritual and transformative experience.

At Burning Man all these themes and social forces are at play. Burn-ers by and large locate themselves within those elements of society that resist and reject normative religious structures. Yet for many of these in-dividuals there remains a desire for a spiritually informed life, a connec-tion to a larger, or ultimate, reality, meaning, or purpose, as well as a deepened, expanded, and reflexive sense of self. Thus, instead of adher-ing to specific religious traditions, Burners construct extremely multifac-eted experiences of spirituality unmediated by any one institution or doctrine, including those of Burning Man itself. In this process, individ-uals who are drawn to Burning Man—and who see in the event oppor-tunities to reframe their experiences of spirituality and religion—are contesting the assertion that "alternative" spiritualities, or spiritualities of "seeking," are necessarily void of a sense of either community or re-sponsibility. For many, the event is rooted in a strong sense of commu-nity and commitment while also providing license to reject "default" so-cial institutions. The example of Burning Man *challenges* the notion that the displacement of religious or spiritual impulses from normative public institutions onto alternate venues necessitates an increase in pri-vatization and individualism or a concomitant decrease in the fabric of moral communities. The spiritual questing and hybridity of Burning Man do not result in a solipsistic and disconnected individualism but rather tie individuals to expanded and deepened experiences of self within particular communities and cultural contexts.

CONCLUSION

Burners come to this festival with numerous disparate views on spirituality and religion, and this diversity of perspective is in some sense integral to the event itself. In addition to multifaceted and personal understandings about the nature of religion and spirituality, there is significant heterodoxy in participants' interpretations of their own experiences at Burning Man. Participants tend to speak of both spirituality and the experience of the festival itself as open and reflexive, emphasizing connectedness, experience, and personal authority. Yet, although many individuals locate a spiritual dimension in the event, others see such claims as running counter to their concept of the festival. Although many note similarities between Burning Man and religion, most also ultimately rebuff this label and conclude that it is something else.

In the end, the difficulty of separating out what ultimately distinguishes the institution, rituals, and ideology of Burning Man from what is typically considered "religion"—characterized, among other qualities, by institutions, rituals, and ideologies—underscores the questionable accuracy of dividing these two realms in the first place. At Burning Man, what finally matters is *how individuals frame their experiences.* Burning Man provides a domain in which participants can have experiences of connection, purpose, transformation, or simply feeling more fully human and alive, experiences that are often associated with what many call religion and spirituality. But in this context, these experiences can be interpreted or framed in whatever heterodoxic and reflexive way individuals choose. Any attempt to unequivocally quantify and untangle the problem of whether Burning Man is or isn't religion, or is or isn't spiritual, quickly becomes a kind of chicken-or-egg conundrum and is not the point. Burning Man can be whatever participants want it to be and furthermore calls the presumed stability of the very concepts of religion and spirituality into question by challenging normative assumptions about where lived religious and ritual practice is located.

People go to Burning Man to play with alternative experiences, identities, and spiritualities. In so doing, they individualistically and idiosyncratically draw on a diverse and limitless pool of global cultural resources and engage in an a la carte mixture of the world's various faith and symbol systems in order to piece together ad hoc and hybrid frameworks through which to perform their personal spiritual beliefs and aspirations. In this regard, to view oneself as spiritual but not religious is simply to adopt one set of markers among many possible ones and reflects

Burners' tendencies to embrace fluid self-descriptions rather than fixed identities. As some individuals move away from traditional religious institutions, they also seek to discover and create alternative venues in which to experience and express what they believe are more authentic or meaningful spiritualities based on practice, community, and eclecticism. Ultimately, Burning Man is available to both contain and reflect whatever desires, aspirations, or orientations diverse participants choose to express or invoke, and these notions are in turn framed within a general social movement toward spiritualities of questing, seeking, and reflexivity. In speaking to these desires, Burning Man has become a ritualized space for those who seek spirituality but not religion and thus appropriates and ritualizes symbols from a variety of global cultures.

CHAPTER 3

Ritual without Dogma

With its whimsical theme camps, quirky costumes, and interactive art-work, Burning Man teems with performance and ritual. For many par-ticipants, this profusion of artistic and creative expression is the heart and soul of the event. Numerous art installations are featured each year, often on a very large scale and with interactive elements that invite both individual and collective ritualizing. Specific ritual performances are carefully planned aspects of some artworks; others become locations for rites that are spontaneous and unpredictable. From the culminating spectacle of the Burn to intimate and personal rites created by individu-als and campmates, the blank canvas of the playa becomes a stage on which to act out a panoply of emotions, ideologies, and tensions. (See DVD.)

Just as many Burners seek to encounter a sense of spirituality apart from religion, the event is said to offer an experience of ritual without dogma. Participants are encouraged to make whatever they can or will of the event, with only minimal recourse to explicitly articulated mean-ings. As one former organizer wrote:

> Burning Man is not a religion. What self-respecting New Age cult would operate with no priests, no tithing, no doctrine, not even a shared belief in a higher power? Burning Man employs ritual, but it is ritual removed from the context of theology. Unhindered by dogma, ritual becomes a ves-sel that can be filled with direct experience. Burning Man is about having that experience, not about explaining it. In fact, if you can explain it, you're probably not paying attention.[1]

Like religion, *dogma* in this context is associated with institutionally authorized and occasionally oppressive or otherwise limiting belief systems, whereas *ritual* is thought to retain a sense of immediacy and authenticity by remaining open to personal interpretations and experiences. The rituals of Burning Man are no less mediated by a variety of cultural influences than those in traditional religious settings, but in this context there is a much greater awareness of interpretive plasticity.

Participants' views on the significance of ritual at Burning Man are typically diverse and sometimes contentious—as they are on most other topics concerning this event—and change and controversy are continuously being negotiated. For example, some of the rites and artworks discussed below are tied conceptually to one or more of the annual themes concocted by Harvey and the other organizers, and many participants are inspired by these suggested creative directions. Yet, although the annual themes have helped provoke numerous impressive works of art, other participants resist and criticize their promulgation, viewing them as attempts to delimit, constrain, or overdetermine artistic and personal expression. Burners consistently extol the event's semantic flexibility and will by and large uphold a heterodoxic ethos over any attempt to impose a unified set of meanings on the event. In their collective resistance to conformity and hierarchical authority, Burners also engage in creative critiques wherever they perceive that authenticity has waned, especially as the event has evolved and grown.

Many of the rituals, performances, and other creative works at Burning Man freely appropriate and hybridize a potentially infinite assortment of easily recognized religious symbols or other cultural motifs— from Mayan, Balinese, Islamic, or Shinto architecture to Buddhas, labyrinths, crosses, Vodou *lwa*, and many many others. (See DVD.) Very often, the traditional meanings of these symbols are transgressed, parodied, or reversed, thereby situating Burning Man within a long lineage of festivals and carnivalesque events that have been called "rituals of reversal," in which normative symbols, meanings, and hierarchies are deliberately inverted or otherwise distorted.[2] As participants play with, reshape, and sometimes ironically mock cultural sacred cows—Jesus or the American flag, for instance—the art, ritual, and performances of Burning Man serve to contest certain aspects of normative culture, thereby asserting the Burning Man festival as somehow more authentic than the default world, even while the event itself is subjected to the same critical scrutiny.

Sometimes the event's rites contain both implicit and explicit parallels to a few of the more popularly known scholarly theories of ritual. While numerous theories could be engaged to analyze the rites of Burning Man, Victor Turner's ideas about liminality and communitas, in particular, have a potent resonance. This may be driven in part by the apparently otherworldly and liminal quality of the playa itself, with Black Rock City poised distinctly "betwixt and between" its raw wilderness and domesticated civic space. In addition, participants self-consciously locate the event as marginal and extol its deliberately transgressive qualities in opposition to the default world while also celebrating community as both an ideological and a redemptive quest. While Turner's ideas by no means perfectly describe Burning Man—evinced in part by the prominence of "competing discourses" in participants' critique and contestation of various elements of the festival—something interesting, complicated, and reflexive is happening here as theories like Turner's have come to be popularized and adopted as *models* for ritualization.[3]

Participants' engagements with and narratives about ritual at Burning Man demonstrate how thoroughly religious ideas and symbols permeate our culture and are recursively mapped onto individuals and communities while at the same time rendering the semantic flexibility and instability of these concepts transparent. This can be seen in Burning Man's most prominent rituals—including the climactic burning of the Man, a series of ritualistic operas, and a succession of monumental temples, as well as a handful of smaller-scale rites and art installations—which are discussed below.

BURNING THE MAN: CELEBRATION, CATHARSIS, AND CHANGE

Undoubtedly the most prominent symbol at (and of) the festival is the Burning Man and its ceremonial conflagration. (See DVD, chaps. 1, 3, and 7.) Despite consistent maneuvers on the part of both organizers and participants to distance the icon of the Man from any specific semantic orthodoxy or hints of dogma, numerous factors render the figure highly significant. The Man can surely be said to continue in a long tradition of fiery effigies and sacrificial bonfires, even while claiming no direct ties to its predecessors. Although officially the figure is genderless, "the Man" moniker suggests patriarchal and corporate authority, rendering it a potential scapegoat for collective anxiety and anger concerning the power structures of the default world. Yet the Man also remains open to identification with personalized notions of the self, and this (if any) may be its most common association. The iconic effigy is centrally located in both time and space, indicating its primary and pivotal significance, and the element of fire operates as both a symbol and an agent of transformation. In coupling all this with the collective effervescence that erupts at its spectacular conflagration, the Man evokes a narrative of sacrifice that has the potential to generate experiences of strong emotional resonance and personal catharsis.

During the days (and even weeks) preceding the annual Burn, participants' collective level of excitement and anticipation rises, fostering heightened expectations and charging perceptions of this climactic moment with elevated significance. Come Burn night, participants may spend hours in preparation, perhaps eating a special meal with their campmates and often adorning themselves in fanciful outfits. Nearly the entire population of Black Rock City streams out to the Man, converging around its central locale (although kept at a safe distance by a crew of Rangers). The neon-lit effigy is quickly surrounded by these thousands of revelers, with an outer perimeter of parked art cars—lights flashing and stereo systems pumping. Those who can get close enough are able to witness a troupe of choreographed fire dancers, accompanied by a collective of drummers. The crowds' frenzied anticipation escalates as the Man's arms are raised, forming a distinct neon X on the horizon. This dramatic gesture of both triumph and surrender signals the official commencement of the rite, and many people begin to whoop and sporadically chant, "Burn It! Burn It!"[4] The excitement peaks as sparks fly, fireworks soar, and the figure ignites and is consumed in a blaze of glory, falling at last to the ground in a hot heaping pyre. Finally, after the towering structure collapses and the wide safety perimeter has been released, thousands converge on the bonfire to dance and celebrate through the night. (See DVD, chaps. 1 and 3.)

Some participants ritualize the Burn by tossing an object into the fire as a form of personal sacrifice, or as a way to symbolically release a burden or pain that they no longer wish to endure. As one young woman told me, "When the Man burns, I run up and throw something into the fire. Usually a letter I've written to a fallen loved one, or a letter expressing my letting go of some problems in the year past."[5] Another participant recounted the unexpected potency he and his campmates had discovered in this simple ritual act:

When we begin, as dusk falls on the night of the Burn, we begin to concentrate on what is to come and enter what some might call a sacred space. Energy is focused on a ritual that has more meaning for me than any other during the year, with the possible exception of Passover. It started by writing things that we wish to get rid of in our lives on pieces of paper, pouring in gunpowder and wrapping them around with—what else—duct tape. After the Man burned . . . we threw in the packets, and with them went whatever we had written.[6]

In other capacities beyond these personal offertory gestures, Burners unmistakably recognize, and revel in, the collective ritualism of the event. The same individual went on to describe the Burn's importance to him personally:

> In the beginning, the Burn was complete catharsis. The first time, I had no idea what to expect. For one, it was so different from the rituals that I knew—my Bar Mitzvah was nothing like this! The drums, the night, the flames, the spectacle, combined into an intoxicating whole. When the Man burned, you knew that something was happening. Shit was coming down. The old, the heavy, the burdensome, was going up in flames. The next day, where the Man had been was a flat bed of ashes, but you knew that it was to make room for the emptiness to return and hold sway for the coming year until the Man would return.[7]

This sense of cathartic release and transformative potentiality remains the dominant narrative participants ascribe to this rite. Another participant described her experience of the Burn: "It's a cleansing, it's a ritual, it's not just Burning Man, its been going on forever."[8]

As with every other aspect of this festival, the culminating rite of the Burn has changed and evolved over the years. For example, one significant change beginning in 1999 was the shift of its traditional night to Saturday. For many years after its initial move to the desert, the Burn was held on Sunday night, and attendees spent the following Monday—which has always been the annual Labor Day holiday—regrouping, packing up, and driving home. Eventually, increased attendance and increasingly stringent BLM oversight made a longer denouement and clean-up time desirable, so the Burn was moved to Saturday night. While it is still the peak—and indeed defining—rite of the entire festival, this change has somewhat diluted its significance by leaving room for another rite to displace some of the cathartic and climactic power initially associated with the Burn, as has been the case with the Temples (discussed below).

During the event's early years, it sometimes seemed like the whole city was going up in flames on the night of the Burn, as artwork everywhere was put to the torch (sometimes without the artists' permission), underscoring the anarchistic flavor of that era. As the festival matured, both externally and internally imposed regulations began to govern what can be burned and when. Many artists who design burnable art now choose to set fire to their pieces on some other night, so as to not compete with the "big" Burn or with one another, and much of the art now is not intended to be burned at all. The spectacle of Black Rock City's nightscape has become increasingly dominated by sparkling lights, electroluminescent wire, and phosphorescent glow toys—Burn night is no exception—representing an apparent turn to a technological aesthetic and away from the primal lure of fire.[9]

From year to year various enhancements have been devised to augment or modify the performance of the Burn. For example, from 1998 to 2001 the Burn was accented by four or five kerosene-powered fire cannons—designed by Jim Mason and dubbed the *Impotence Compensation Project*—which blasted 100- to 300-foot columns of flame straight up into the air, adding unmistakably to the gathered crowd's enthusiasm when ignited. Eventually, however, this practice was halted owing to safety considerations. Another prominent aspect of the Burn is the hundreds of volunteer fire performers and dancers from around the world many of whom have rehearsed for months. (See DVD, chap. 1.) Since 1998 this "Fire Conclave" has also conducted an "opening fire ceremony" at which a flame is "extracted from the sun" by means of a large hyperbolic mirror and kept burning throughout the week.[10] This flame is then used to light the fire performers' equipment, and ultimately the Man as well. With scores of fire-breathers, flaming poi-spinners, torch-juggling stilt-walkers, and numerous other fiery acts, this performance is on a scale perhaps like no other and adds to the theatrical and ritualistic air of the Burn. Yet impressive as it may be, this aspect of the Burn is not beloved by all. For many, this activity is, for all intents and purposes, peripheral to the main event as the crowd has become so large that most people cannot see the show.

Since 2001 another significant change is the elevation of the 40- to 50-foot Man on increasingly elaborate platforms, themselves 20 to 40 feet high. These platforms—each intended to reflect the annual theme—serve to augment visibility, as well as facilitate an increasingly bombastic pyrotechnic display. As a result of the increasing dominance and scale of the platforms and the amount of wood required to fabricate them, the increased heat and light generated by the augmented fuel source has greatly changed the dynamic and aesthetic of the Burn. The singular impact of the stark humanoid figure alive with flame has been diminished,

leading some participants to jokingly call this event "Burning Base."
However, another and widely celebrated result is that the towering pyre
frequently generates beautiful swirling mini-tornadoes of smoke and
dust that spiral away from the central fire—dubbed "ancestors" by
some—a phenomenon that (to my recollection) never occurred before
2001. (See DVD, chaps. 1 and 3.)

Organizers cite their impetus for introducing these platforms as
largely logistical. From 1996 to 2000 the Man was elevated off the
ground by a simple pyramid of hay bales, and before that it stood directly on the surface of the playa. But as the size of the event grew, more
and more individuals wanted to touch and interact with the Man, perhaps secreting some personal object or fetish into its framework, or inscribing a word on its wooden flesh. This began to create problems, as
many hands threatened to (and occasionally did) damage the structure,
causing technical difficulties when it came time to burn the effigy. However, the need to remove the Man from immediate access by elevating it
on a platform stands in stark contrast to the first few years on the playa,
in which all (or nearly all) participants were needed to raise the figure up
off the ground by means of winch and pulley—an activity that itself
became a central unifying ritual event. Today, the Man is set in place by
a crane, days before the gates are opened to the public.

With the introduction of these platforms, organizers strove to con-
coct various ways to foster new forms of interactivity with the Man. For
example, in 2001 the entire playa-scape was envisioned as "an enormous board game . . . [of] choice, striving, trial and transformation," with
the various art installations of the Seven Ages theme symbolizing various
life stages—the infant / cradle, the child / playground, the lover / chapel, the
soldier / coliseum, the Burning Man / wisdom, the justice / maze, and the
pantaloon / mausoleum—serving as giant game pieces.[11] (See chart 1.)
Participants who chose to play were obligated to undergo various "trials
and initiations [intended to] symbolically transform and test them" at
each of the successive stages of life symbolized by each location.[12] In so
doing, they would gain the appropriate stamps for "passports" that had
been issued at the gate, which would win them access to the *Temple of
Wisdom*, as the interior of the base on which the Man itself stood was
termed that year.

In 2002, when the theme was the Floating World, participants were
encouraged to acquire and exchange precious "gold doubloons," which
were specially minted brass coins. To gain these doubloons, one was supposed to take part in select activities—termed "rites of passage"—which

were orchestrated by select theme camps and artists.[13] One would earn a set of tokens that could then be exchanged for a doubloon that would purchase access to the *Lighthouse* tower on which the Man stood that year. (See DVD, chap. 3.) Participants were also encouraged to give the doubloons away as gifts but not barter or sell them, as the "rules" of this game stated:

> To be admitted to the *Lighthouse,* you will be asked by its Keepers to surrender your treasure. You must determine the true value of the coin that you possess. You may retain this object as a piece of property, release it for a passage upward to the Burning Man, or give it to another person as a gift. Under no circumstances, however, is it permissible to *barter or sell* this coin, nor is it acceptable to *collect more than one.* This would be unfair to other voyagers who seek treasure.[14]

Participants' responses to these games were rather mixed. Though there is no definitive count of the number of attendees who actually participated in the games, it appeared that many enthusiastically embraced them. I observed numerous people entering and exiting both the *Temple of Wisdom* and the *Lighthouse,* who therefore could be presumed to have successfully met the prescribed challenges. I also encountered a few first-time attendees in both years who had enthusiastically taken part in the games and reported having enjoyed and been challenged by them, and this had impelled them to explore things they might not otherwise have done. However, most participants I spoke with resisted being told *how* to participate and perceived the games as phony, coercive, "Disneyesque," and uncomfortably materialistic, given the quasi-monetary quality of the doubloons. For example, one woman felt that in setting forth these games the organizers were dictating a "correct" way to engage in Burning Man, whereas she believed that the event was better experienced by finding one's own way and remaining open to the unknown. She saw the games as to some extent removing the potential for random and unique discoveries (especially for first-timers).[15] In an ironic twist, doubloon distribution was purposefully subverted by one of the organization's volunteers who had been put in charge of dispensing the gold doubloons according to the stated rules of the game. However, he deliberately toyed with the rules and freely handed out numerous doubloons at random and among members of his own village—eventually leaving a large bowl of the coins on the bar of this camp's community hub—and encouraged others to disseminate them throughout Black Rock City, by whatever means they saw fit.

When I asked Harvey for his response to these explicit and implicit criticisms, he said it was entirely in keeping with his intention to inspire people to actively engage and participate in the event:

> Yes! That's what I love! They got angry! Little do they know, there are always subversive things put in these themes *to* provoke them. Art is not necessarily just blowing shit up, as the anarchists would have it. . . . I gave them a moral choice—you keep it, or you give it away, or you use it. . . . Beyond that, I didn't say anything. . . . It was just an interactive game—and people had extraordinary experiences with these things and encountered real moral quandaries, and they had to make choices about what is of value—that was the theme—what is of value and how you find it. I had my own opinion about what that meant, but I've never directly stated what my own opinion is. I was urging them to think about a spiritual lesson, that what is ultimately of value cannot be possessed.[16]

On one level these games can be understood as Harvey's artistic contribution to the event and as examples of the ritualistic, psychological, and spiritual intentionality with which he often attempts to imbue the annual themes. Yet on another level they illustrate the extent to which Burners dislike being told specifically how to participate or what the experience should mean.

In 2003 there ceased to be a ritualistic game required to gain access to the Man or its podium. Instead, the Man stood high on an elaborate Mayanesque pyramid, the *Great Temple*. Its interior, which was open to all, contained a series of altars decorated with golden flames reminiscent of Tibetan motifs, on which participants deposited numerous artifacts or offerings, such as an image of Kwan Yin, a bird's nest, a container of incense and cigarettes, a Winnie the Pooh figurine, and several iconographic representations of the Burning Man. Around the structure's exterior were a series of niches in which participants were encouraged to sit and thus embody "pantomime gods," and passersby were "invited to leave offerings as tributes" to these "living icons."[17] Some people sat in silent meditation, others offered tarot readings or otherwise issued "prophecy," some gave musical performances, and still others simply may have taken refuge from the sun. (See DVD, chap. 4.)

As a final example, during 2004's Vault of Heaven theme the Man was placed high atop an open geodesic dome called the *Observatory*. (See cover photo.) The platform's exterior was ringed with ten dioramas, each representing visions of alien worlds and futuristic scenarios in which participants were encouraged to enact interactive performances, similar to the previous year's "avatars." As the underlying concept was summarized by Harvey, "The essential secret is that aliens reproduce themselves by *absorbing the other*. What we're asking people to do is manage the (stage) space in such a way that we can create spontaneous improvisatory scenarios, and that you really don't need any preparation to do it."[18] For the most part, however, participants seemed to ignore, or to be unaware of, this injunction. When I visited the *Observatory* most of those within the diorama spaces were just chatting casually with friends. It seemed that the notion of "embodying aliens" and "absorbing others" was too abstract to take an immediate interest in. Although some individuals did take advantage of the performance spaces, most of those whom I spoke with once again disliked being told how to participate and felt no real connection with Harvey's concept (most had not even bothered to read the descriptive materials about the *Observatory*, which were available on-line before the event and handed out at the gate).[19]

Participants' responses to these transitions have been mixed. While most continue to greet the climactic Burn with considerable zeal, despite the various changes that both the ceremony and figure of the Man have undergone over time and despite the many differences of opinion about these changes, others long for what is perceived to have been a simpler time when the figure was readily accessible. It is not only longtime Burners who notice the increasingly polished and perhaps distant or disconnected tenor of the Burn. For example, one first-timer told me after the 2003 Burn that the preponderance of fire performers had made the event seem "too much like a Vegas show."[20] This surprised me, as I had come to believe that the waning interest in the Burn was a syndrome that primarily afflicted longer-term Burners. It may be that this newcomer's experience was an anomaly. Indeed, given the general enthusiasm of the crowd (and numerous testimonies), it seems clear that many participants continue to be inspired, awed, and moved by this rite. Yet the first-timers' equation of the Burn with a Las Vegas show also spoke to its increasingly professionalized aesthetic, and this in turn seems to have contributed to the Burn losing some of its visceral power.

A few participants have taken some noteworthy actions that served to critique these and other directions in which the event has moved and that also aptly illustrate the nostalgic feelings some participants have for the earlier days, alongside the realities incurred by heightened pressures from external regulatory forces. The first such action that I observed was a small-scale rite that took place in 2003 when two participants created a piece dubbed the *Early Man*. Instigated and constructed by two men known as Gomonk and Builder Ben, both of whom had attended Burning Man since the mid-1990s, this sculpture was faithfully modeled after the simpler eight-foot effigy first created by Larry Harvey and Jerry James in 1986 (fig. 3). With the help of a small crew of friends, the *Early Man* was erected on the last full day of the festival (Sunday) at the site where the much larger "new" Man and its base had burned the night before, thus symbolically invoking the rebirth of a simpler time. By the light of day, while it was unclear whether or not most observers recognized the structure's historical reference, participants readily embraced it as a ritual fetish by adorning it with a variety of small personal objects such as beads, playing cards, images of George W. Bush, and pouches.

Yet, in a rather ironic comment on the changes and increased regulations, when Ben and Gomonk attempted to burn this simple structure that evening they were cited by BLM authorities for an unplanned and unregulated burn. Both men had volunteered in different capacities for the event and were well known to Harvey and other senior organizers who were aware of and supported this homage to the initial spirit of the event. However, the *Early Man* had not made it onto the BLM's list of "approved" burns. Hence, when a warrant for a long-forgotten traffic violation (which had been paid, but late) came up in the law enforcement agency's routine search for outstanding warrants, Gomonk was arrested and taken to Lovelock, Nevada, several hours away, where he spent the night in jail before his campmates could organize his bail and release. This incident led to a new agreement between Burning Man organizers and the BLM clarifying that anyone can burn their own art, whether preregistered or not, so long as it is safely conducted and placed on a "burn platform" (constructed from sheets of corrugated steel) to prevent scaring the playa surface. (Organizers jokingly refer to this as the "Ben and Gomonk rule.")

A few years later, in 2007, a much more widely visible and controversial event took place when one individual took it upon himself to light the Man several days ahead of its scheduled Burn. This action received widespread media attention and would spark heated debate among participants.[21] For many years some Burners had joked about lighting the Man ahead of schedule in order to shake up what they felt had become the overly controlled, repetitive, and predictable nature of the Burn, but it still came as a surprise to almost everyone that someone had finally taken it upon himself to do it. Compounding the controversy,

FIGURE 3. Gomonk and Builder Ben, *Early Man*, 2003. Photo by Lee Gilmore.

the individual who eventually admitted responsibility—a man named Paul Addis—was arrested on felony arson charges immediately after his torching of the Man.[22]

Participants' reactions to this incident were mixed, to say the least. Many concluded that the act had been a violation of the community's principle of civic responsibility because the perpetrator had set fire to an artwork that was not his own. Furthermore, the act could have endangered others, as a number of people were inside the *Pavilion* below the Man when Addis scaled its supports in order to set it on fire. Some participants also felt that the perpetrator should be prosecuted and punished to the full extent of the default world's law for his transgressions.

Many others, however, applauded the preemptive Burn, viewing it as an act of symbolic reclamation, taking the Man back from the routinized bureaucracy of the Borg and restoring some of the anarchistic and prankster spirit of the old Cacophony Society. Individuals in this camp also tended to feel that the charges (and Addis's eventual sentence of 12 to 48 months in prison, plus $25,000 in restitution) were far and away in excess of an appropriate punishment or consequence for his actions.[23]

One participant I spoke with speculated that this difference in opinion seemed to be correlated with how long one had been attending Burning Man, such that those who were "newbies," or relatively new, tended to view the "early Burn" as an unforgivable crime against the community, whereas "old-timers" tended to empathize—to at least some degree—with Addis's actions.[24] To some extent, this view was borne out in my own observations of discussions about the incident on on-line forums dedicated to Burning Man, but these sentiments were by no means universal, as I also spoke with several longtime participants who condemned the "early Burn" as a farce and as the act of a mentally unstable egomaniac.[25] Other participants underscored the extent to which the early Burn (and by extension the presence or absence of the Man) was ultimately meaningless in terms of their total experience of the event that year, telling me that the early Burn had generated discussion for about a day or so before they moved on and continued to enjoy the festival as usual.

For their part, the organizers responded by building another Man, which would be burned a few days later at its traditionally sanctioned time. I was also told that Harvey's own response had been to laugh and say, "It's just lumber."[26] This second Man was constructed inside the *Pavilion* surrounding the Man's base that year and was completed by the end of the week. It was distinguished from its predecessor only by the inclusion of a small wooden cut-out of a phoenix on its face, which had been fabricated out of the charred remnants of the first Man.

Regardless of one's opinion about it, the act of burning the Man outside of its authorized ritual sacrifice made a significant statement that aroused controversy, conversations, and widespread media coverage. On the one hand, it demonstrated that the Man is not the possession of one person, or even several people; it is a public icon that belongs to all Burners, who are expressly and collectively invited to experience it as their own and to imbue it with their own meanings. On the other hand, the "early Burn" shifted the focus from the collective to the individual, as Addis—whose mugshot showed him adorned in black and red face paint, grinning widely—reaped a great deal of media attention. On the playa, the organizers attempted to turn the focus back onto the larger community by reconstructing the Man within the *Green Pavilion* that served as its platform that year.[27] The "early Burn" and the numerous discussions about it that ensued functioned as an act of emic (insider) ritual criticism—that is, a process entailing assessments of the efficacy and meaning of a given rite or ritual system—and highlighted the extent to which participants struggle with issues of authority and authenticity at the festival.[28]

Both the "early Burn" and the *Early Man* illustrate some of the tensions Burners experience between an idealized authenticity, a desire for a kind of temporary autonomous zone fully removed from the taint of the ordinary, commodified, and regulated and the reality of an event that must increasingly interact with, and at times capitulate to, the demands of the default world.[29] This longing for the idealized and romanticized "purity" of the event's earlier days—when its much smaller size and relative anonymity, away from the prying eyes of law enforcement and the mass media, fostered a greater sense of personal freedom for some participants—is a constant refrain in the public narratives surrounding this festival. This desire may be somewhat similar to those of fundamentalist religious persuasions who long for a return to what is believed to have been a simpler or more innocent cultural era, though the historical reality may not actually match their visions. Likewise, the *Early Man* spoke to a desire to re-create an imagined "good old days" that cannot in actuality ever be recaptured and that in all likelihood never really existed quite as most people might imagine it, while the "early Burn" attempted to destroy symbolically the routinized behemoth the event had become.

Both the nostalgic rite of the *Early Man* and the reactionary rite of the "early Burn" signaled a desire to recall or re-create a moment of social "anti-structure" (to use Victor Turner's term), leading inadvertently but perhaps inevitably to a crackdown by "structural" social forces. As Turner wrote, "We thus encounter the paradox that the *experience* of communitas becomes the *memory* of communitas, with the result that communitas itself in striving to replicate itself historically develops a social structure."[30] In this regard, Burning Man closely follows an arc that Turner described as spontaneous, normative, and ideological communitas.[31] At its inception in the late 1980s, friends and strangers spontaneously gathered on a San Francisco beach to create and burn an effigy for the simple and immediate joy of doing it. More recently, the event has developed a normative structure and become highly organized and regulated, morphing from its wilder and unrulier phase in order to support creative expression within a safer and more sustainable membrane. Finally, organizers also now promote an ideology of communal effort and civic responsibility among the key values encapsulated in their "Ten Principles"—and portray the event as providing a quasi-utopian social model. [32]

While Turner's models by no means perfectly mirror Burning Man and easily fracture if too rigidly applied to any context, they help to account for some of the apparent discord between the ideal and the reality encountered within the event and its rites.[33] Burners are not typically shy about unleashing all manner of critique and dissent wherever they perceive that Burning Man may fail to live up to its stated ideals, and the experience of communitas at the Burn has, for many, broken down and dissipated in numerous ways. The ritualistic, transformative, and unifying aspects of the Burn remain undeniable, yet it must also be noted that the more plainly celebratory—and perhaps more "secularly" situated—qualities of the Burn are equally evident. As with the rest of the festival, the Burn cannot be accurately considered "purely" one thing or another. Indeed, few religious and ritual traditions are without some festive or ludic features. Many medieval Christian pilgrimages, for example, were also associated with simultaneously occurring festivals, which were surely a strong component of the attraction for many pilgrims.[34] Furthermore, any attempt to strictly divorce playfulness and celebration from worship and ritual is an illusory distinction and misses a critical point. No matter how "seriously" ritual actors may comport themselves, all ritual can on some level be considered play and make-believe, and, for his part, Turner held that a playful or ludic atmosphere is one of the hallmarks of communitas.[35]

Although the immediate experience of connection and communitas at the Burn may have waned as the event has matured and grown dramatically in size, there remains a collective *desire* for this sentiment of oneness or togetherness, which still tends to peak during rites such as the Burn or, as we shall later see, the Temples. Participants also often encounter a feeling of communitas during the weeklong event, as evidenced in numerous reports of social, emotional, and cognitive liberation, alongside the generalized feeling of unity that many say they experience in being a Burner. These collective desires for authenticity and purity in the rituals of Burning Man have not been limited to the culminating Burn, as many other large-scale ritualistic performances have been both enacted and critiqued by participants. One such event that was prominent from 1996 to 2000 was a series of operas incorporating a variety of religious and mythical motifs that were orchestrated by the San Francisco–based artist Pepe Ozan and a large team of co-conspirators. (See DVD, chap. 6.)

THE OPERAS

Beginning in 1993, Ozan began sculpting conical towers during the festival made out of rebar and wire mesh and covered with dried mud from the playa's claylike surface, dubbing these "lingams," after the sacred phallic symbols of the Hindu god Shiva. These hollow spires would then be filled with wood and set aflame, forming a beautiful glowing, crackled chimney. In 1996, after a few years of progressively more complex and elaborate versions of the lingams, Ozan began to produce a series of scripted and scored operas to accompany his sculptures. These performances were traditionally held on the night before the Burning of the Man, meaning that at that time the operas were on Saturday night and came to be perceived as the festival's other "big show."

With many performers clad only in body paint and others festooned in ornate costumes, the theatrical style of the operas was highly ritualistic, and they flirted with a variety of religious and cultural symbols. For example, as described in chapter 1, *The Arrival of Empress Zoe* in 1996 was designed to complement the festival's initial hellish Inferno theme. Inspired in part by the Fertility theme in 1997, the second operatic pageant, *The Temple of Ishtar,* was meant to dramatize the sacred marriage between Ishtar, the ancient Mesopotamian Goddess of love and war, and her consort, Dumuzi.[36] The following year, *The Temple of Rudra* adopted a Hindu theme and featured insectoid figures assuming postures reminiscent of a dancing Shiva. According to its literature, this opera was loosely intended to evoke "the ancient Dravidian Fire Ceremony on the night of the final lunar eclipse of the millennium."[37]

For the 1999 opera, *Le Mystere de Papa Loko*, Ozan and a few of his associates traveled to Haiti in order to research Vodou, where they met a *manbo* (priestess) and a *houngan* (priest) who unexpectedly guided them in a weeklong initiation rite. One of these travelers, Twan, who produced the opera and related projects from 1998 to 2002, wrote of this experience: "Once the ceremony began, I was immediately struck [by] the beauty of the songs, dance, and drumming. The *sense of community was overwhelming.* Seems to me that one of the most important aspects of Voodoo is that it is the glue that holds the community together. Everyone is connected. All are one. Kinda like Burning Man."[38] His emphasis on the overwhelming sense of community is, of course, suggestive of Turner's communitas, and it is perhaps unsurprising that he also easily related this encounter to Burning Man.

Although the motifs of *Le Mystere de Papa Loko* were inspired by the myths and rituals of Haitian Vodou, it was never intended to be an authentic Vodou rite. The introduction to the opera's script, coauthored by Ozan and Christopher Fülling, a professional opera singer and director, states:

> Inspired by the clash of cultures that produced both the syncretic religions of Voodoo in Haiti and the Burning Man on the Playa, this ceremony of Initiation unleashes the mysteries of Voodoo to explore our own traumatic colonial heritage. . . . Deriving its inspiration from the Voodoo Religion, "Le Mystere de Papa Loko" is only a fantasy presented with maximum respect for Haitian culture. The use of Voodoo myths for artistic inspiration implies our veneration for the rites that serve as freedom of spiritual expression for this oppressed society.[39]

In overtly recognizing—and embracing—the syncretic cultural forces operating in the contexts of both Vodou and Burning Man, this opera sought to open up a space for dynamic cultural exchange in the context of a festival in which rampant cultural appropriation is not always acknowledged or self-aware. For the most part, the religious and mythic motifs employed in the operas were artistically or aesthetically based choices rather than intentional rituals aimed at a particular goal or actual ideal of worship. As one opera participant noted, they "may be more imitation of ritual than actual ritual," thus indicating some awareness of the dynamic tensions between mimesis, ritual authenticity, and make-believe on the part of participants.[40]

Yet in consciously playing at the slippery border between theater and worship, many performers found these rites deeply moving and transformative.[41] This was in part a result of the fact that the opera participants—numbering more than 350 at peak—typically camped together at Burning Man, which provided a sense of communal bonding. Furthermore, in some years these individuals were subdivided into "sects" that embraced select mythic identities or other roles throughout the week, sometimes initiating others into their "mysteries." For example, all *Papa Loko* performers were assigned to sects associated with the Vodou deities Ezili, Ogoun, Guede, and Couzin Azaka and the Rainbow Serpents Dambala and Aida.[42]

There appears to have been a significant difference between the insider and outsider perspectives on the operas. For those who were involved, the operas were ritually and spiritually significant; those who were not directly involved resisted becoming passive members of the audience—or dreaded "spectators." An open call for participation in the operas was propagated via e-mail and word of mouth every year, but the performances themselves were enacted only by those who committed to advance rehearsals and by and large did not invite spontaneous participation, which was necessarily limited due in part to the crowd's large size. Such was the case with the first two operas, and some Burners saw the operas as not only nonparticipatory but also too long and boring to boot.

The opera producers were not unaware of this critique, and in 1999 one of the performers satirized this perspective as he called out to the gathering crowd, "Stay away from the opera! The opera is boring!" Ozan, Fülling, and the others responded to this criticism by devising a way for the audience to interact with and contribute to the performances, thus attempting to make them more like rites in which more participants could engage. Hence, for *Le Mystere de Papa Loko,* hundreds of audience members were guided into the performance space, where they passed through a flaming "portal of life and death" between the structure's two towers, although the scope of this interactive component still remained limited due to sheer numbers.[43] (See DVD, chap. 6.)

This collective threshold crossing was no coincidence, as *Le Mystere de Papa Loko*'s creators directly and self-consciously appropriated elements of ritual theory by structuring the performance as a "rite of transformation" in which "devotees"—as performers were referred to—passed through three distinct stages.[44] According to Ozan and Fülling's script, the first was the "Requiem for Time," in which devotees were "taken out of the world of time, responsibility, and individuality."[45] The second stage was the "Breach," described as a "liminal stage [in which] the devotees are betwixt and between the positions assigned by life and society. This ambiguous state is likened to death, to being in the womb, to invisibility, to bisexuality and to darkness."[46] Finally came the "Ordeal":

> In order to emerge from the liminal stage deprived of all information, the devotees rip their clothes and throw them to the fire along with altars, flags and objects of adoration as their last step towards total liberation from the past and from their identities. They are reborn at the time of the origin of man, naked and bewildered, ready to descend into their ancestral subconscious.[47]

The language and framework here is unmistakably inspired by Turner's ideas about liminality, three-stage rites of passage, and social dramas. By engaging in explicit dialogue with ritual and performance theory, this opera provided a conspicuous example of the extent to which Turner sometimes shows up in both general and specific ways at Burning Man.

For what would be the final large-scale Burning Man opera in 2000, Ozan constructed a giant lingam and yoni (stylized female genitalia symbolizing the source of life, the lingam's female counterpart) reminiscent of his earliest such sculptures, in keeping with that year's Body theme. These were placed along a central axis—leading from Center Camp out to the Man and beyond—featuring a number of artistic representations of body parts arranged in anatomical order, evocative of kundalini chakras.[48] In an intentional move away from appropriating ritual motifs associated with specific and living religious cultures, *The Thar-Taurs of Atlan*—as the opera was called that year—invoked a fanciful Atlantian theme and took place at the foot of a large pyramidal structure placed closer in to the main camp area than the previous opera sculptures had been. The performance featured "Lunar Minotaurs and Solar Snake Priestesses" who dragged a "massive flaming Lingam across the playa to ignite the Yoni gateway."[49] After 2000, as participants' interest in these events waned, the creative energies driving them became exhausted, and the partial funding that had been provided by the Burning Man organization went to other projects, the opera was significantly scaled back and became a much less central feature of Burning Man.

However, a core community with roots in these operas continued to attend and camp together, occasionally producing smaller-scale rites and artwork on the playa and elsewhere.[50]

THE TEMPLES

The retreat of the operas inadvertently made way for another large-scale ritual event to become a beloved annual feature of the festival beginning in 2000: a succession of installations collectively called the Temples.[51] (See DVD, chap. 6.) Each of these structures would be spectacularly burned on the last night of the festival—Sunday, the night following the burning of the Man—and each became highly ritualized and deeply reverent spaces, devoted to collective mourning. Designed by David Best, an artist based in Petaluma, California, and constructed by a dedicated crew of volunteers, the first Temple incarnations were constructed of filigreed plywood cutouts left over from three-dimensional skeletal dinosaur puzzles and were visually reminiscent of Balinese or other Southeast Asian architecture. Other styles were later employed, such as the 2003 *Temple of Honor,* which was constructed of giant cardboard tubes and ornate papier-mâché and suggested an amalgamated Russian Orthodox church and Islamic mosque, with its towering, onion-shaped domes and intricate mosaic patterns. After 2004 Best decided to mostly step away from direct involvement with the Temples in order to devote his time to other projects, but the tradition was carried on by longtime Temple volunteers and other Burners.

The first Temple, 2000's *Temple of the Mind,* was roughly 20 feet in height and was to some extent a prototype of the increasingly ambitious projects these were to become. When a good friend of Best's died in an accident a few weeks before the event that year, the Temple became an impromptu memorial site. For the Seven Ages theme in 2001, Best was inspired to provide another space in which participants would be invited to remember their own beloved dead. This new and much larger installation was called the *Temple of Tears,* although participants often referred to it as the Mausoleum after the location it occupied in the thematic art layout that year and the "age" it represented: death. According to Best's vision, the *Temple of Tears* was conceived as "a place where participants can commemorate, remember, venerate, bid farewell, excoriate, exorcise, celebrate, and above all, honor those whose loss has moved them. Parents, friends, loved ones, ancestors, the unborn, those who chose to exit this plane by their hand . . . in short anyone who has had a loss and that means everyone, is welcome to pause and meditate on the meaning of pain and loss."[52] Participants were invited to inscribe memorials on the ornate walls or on wooden blocks that were placed nearby, and many individuals also left behind photos and other objects of personal significance (fig. 4). Nearly every available space on the Temple's walls was inscribed with memorials to the dead, such as "To my last baby who died, who will join two others," and "To the family I never knew."[53]

Each subsequent manifestation of the Temple was likewise designed as a chapel-like structure in which participants could congregate to honor and remember the dead. For several days during the event, participants who visited these structures discovered intensely introspective spaces devoted to remembrance and forgiving, in which the sense of grieving was palpable. People sat in corners and strolled along the walls, writing tributes, reading those of others, weeping and quietly contemplating their most personal and painful sorrows while sharing this grief publicly with others. Often, someone would be strumming a guitar or softly playing other instruments, helping to set the tone with peaceful tunes. The stated intention of these structures changed slightly over the years—for example, the *Temple of Joy* was meant to be a place "to reflect upon the gifts we have received from those we love, both living and dead, and to consider how these gifts have changed our lives"—but the focus continued to be mourning and loss: "Pilgrims to the Temple may bring tributes to the givers of these gifts, and they may inscribe messages that memorialize this passage of gifts upon its many-storied walls."[54]

In inviting participants to reflect on mortality—both through the memories of those now passed and through consideration of the inevitability of one's own demise—the Temples elicited a reverent and contemplative mood. Through the physical inscription of personal memories on the Temple's walls, and in turn through reading the inscriptions of others, participants were able to share and ritualize private feelings in public ways. The religion scholar Sarah Pike concluded, "Death rites at the Mausoleum transformed private grief and loss into public expression in ways that are generally unavailable to most contemporary Americans."[55]

Best was also often present in the Temples, fulfilling a pastoral role as he interpreted the installation for visitors, explained his intentions, and encouraged ritual activities. For example, he often led those who were gathered in a simple ritual. Pike described this as follows:

FIGURE 4. David Best, *Temple of Joy* (detail), 2002. Photo by Lee Gilmore.

Several times throughout the day Best asked Mausoleum visitors to put up
their right hands: "That's the person who committed suicide, alone and
agonized. Put your left hand close to you. That's the child who died of
leukemia, surrounded by love and support. Now move the two hands together and lift them." Best's point was that "those who died amid love will
help liberate those who died in anguish."[56]

He also comforted those who seemed in need of solace or companionship. For example, the grandmother of a friend of mine died just a few
days before the event in 2002, prompting my friend to go straight out
to the Temple on her arrival in Black Rock City. Best approached her,
presumably observing her grief, and held her while she cried her heart
out. Her partner shared in this experience with her and, recounting it
for me later, referred to the power this shared rite had also had for him,
saying, with a tinge of irony, "I miss church."[57] Many individuals were
able to find some comfort and solace in the Temples, as well in the arms
of others, often including the fatherly and quasi-priestly figure of David
Best.

On many occasions, the ritual burning of the Temple on Sunday night
has begun with a rendition of "Amazing Grace," often sung by Marisa
Lenhart, an operatically trained soprano. The crowd typically becomes
hushed as the Temple ignites, and the general tenor of participants' celebration tends to be at a lower key on Sunday than on the previous eve-
nings. This relative stillness is a stark contrast to the ebullient and boister-
ous displays of the previous night's Burn. Typically, the gathered crowd
tends to be lively and a bit impatient right up to the moment when the
Temple catches fire, at which point the several thousand people in attendance fall absolutely silent, and the only sound is that of the crackling
flame. (See DVD, chap. 6.) As the flames creep up and engulf the tower,
this silence might be punctuated by an occasional "om" or a reverent
song, intonation, or prayer, but anyone who seems disrespectful is instantly shushed by those who are nearby until the structure begins to collapse and the crowd finally begins to cheer with joy and awe. In 2002, for
example, the silence was broken only by a spontaneous performance of
"New York, New York," by a few people who were gathered near where
I stood, which I took to be a tribute to the disaster of September 11,
2001.

The Temple was host to other 9/11 memorials throughout Burning
Man in 2002. Toward the end of the event that year, a case containing
the names of each of the firefighters and other emergency workers who

died in the World Trade Towers was given a place of honor on the Temple's central altar during a special memorial ceremony—complete with a flag-draped caisson and bagpipes playing "Amazing Grace."[58] In this regard, the 2002 Temple burn served as a 9/11 memorial for the entire Black Rock City community, which seemed especially poignant as the tragedies had occurred just days after the conclusion of the 2001 Burning Man.

As Best initially sought to stretch himself artistically, the architectural style of each Temple varied from year to year, and this in turn affected the ritual mood surrounding these edifices. For example, the 2003 *Temple of Honor,* fabricated out of towering cardboard and papier-mâché tubes, with its entire surface covered in black-and-white photocopied images of ornate stars, florets, and Buddhist monks, produced an open space that drew observers' attention upward to its heights rather than instilling a sense of enclosure and safety (fig. 5; see also DVD, chap. 6). On most of the occasions that I visited the *Temple of Honor,* only a handful of people were scribbling in solitude on its walls, but for the most part people were casually chatting with one another or randomly wandering through as they might at any other large-scale installation on the playa. However, on the last day, just hours before the structure was to be burned, the tangible and often intense sense of solemnity and spirituality returned as I observed numerous individuals writing, weeping, and comforting one another, with one man strumming a guitar.

For the 2004 *Temple of Stars,* Best returned to the use of plywood puzzle remnants as construction material, although this Temple differed from previous incarnations in its enormous width and height. With a central tower ascending one hundred feet, the *Temple of Stars* featured walkways extending outward from either side of a central, two-story space, stretching a quarter of a mile in length (fig. 6). The structure required longer than usual to complete, so it was not open until late in the week. When it was finally finished, participants again gathered to leave numerous memorials within and on its walls. In 2005 and 2006 the leadership was transferred to longtime Temple volunteer Mark Grieve, whose Shinto-inspired *Temple of Dreams* in 2005 featured a collection of varying-sized huts and pagodas stained blood red, often marked by torii gates, and whose 2006 *Temple of Hope* constituted an assemblage of conical white towers. (See DVD, chap. 6.) The dispersed and exposed focal points were intended to evoke a series of decentralized ancestor shrines, once again shifting participants' interactions with these

FIGURE 5. David Best, *Temple of Honor* (detail), 2003. Photo by Lee Gilmore.

structures, although the ritual purpose and contemplative atmospere remained constant.

In some ways, the emotional potency and sense of the sacred encountered by many at the Temple has eclipsed the Burn as the most visceral large-scale rite in the event's later years. As a consequence of their focus on memory, mourning, and death, the Temples provide a poignant reminder of loss that serves to return participants to the gravity of the "real" world while also creating a powerful and accessible healing ritual that is difficult to find elsewhere. Further, given the direct invitation, participants are now much more likely to leave their personal offerings and sacrifices at the Temples rather than at the Man, as was once a common practice. That interactive and personal ritualization is explicitly encouraged at the Temples, whereas interactivity with the Man is generally restricted to the artwork of its elaborate base, also produces a more powerful, immediate, and moving experience at the Temple's bonfire than at that of the Man.

A key difference here, I believe, is that participants are given just enough direction regarding the structure's meaning to remain free to devise their own individual experiences and interpretations, unweighted by the constraints of dogma. As the burning of the Man becomes an ever more elaborate pyrotechnic spectacle, the more modest Temple burns seem to better capture and evoke the simple and direct spirit that the Burning Man previously represented to some participants. Also, as access to the Man has been restricted, participants seem to prefer the more immediate and embodied interaction and ritualization available to them through the Temples rather than the occasionally overly complex and abstract ritual modes devised by Harvey as aspects of the Man's platforms. The Temples are valued in part because they are tangibly accessible and participatory, while the Man itself now towers ever higher above the Black Rock City populace.

Finally, that the Temple burn takes place on the *last* night of the festival has shifted the temporal climax somewhat away from the Man. Many participants report that—both emotionally and aesthetically—they now prefer the quiet intensity of the Sunday night Temple burns to the sheer pyrotechnic spectacle of Saturday's Burning of the Man. On one level, this displacement is but another symptom of participants' active and ongoing critique of Burning Man's rites. Yet it also illustrates the persistence of communitas, even as the festival appears to turn increasingly from spontaneity to ideology.

FIGURE 6. David Best, *Temple of Stars*, 2004. Photo by Lee Gilmore.

VARIETIES OF RITUAL EXPERIENCE

The Burn, the operas, and the Temples are but a few of the most visible and large-scale examples of ritual at Burning Man. Many other small-scale rites enacted at the festival involve individual, personally significant acts or rites shared by groups of friends and campmates. For example, one relatively informal and unconventional rite took place among a group that I camped with during the event in 2000. Several campmates had come to feel that the infrastructure required to host a large and popular theme camp at Burning Man had grown unwieldy and unenjoyable and that the group itself had become uncomfortably large. It was determined that it was time to "kill" the camp, and a flag emblazoned with the camp logo, Motel 666, a corruption of a well-known corporate brand, was draped over an empty coffin. The group marched in a funeral procession, with a trumpet sounding "Taps," to the site where the Man had burned on the previous night, and the coffin was set down on this spot. A communion of sorts, consisting of a bottle of Jamison's Irish Whiskey and a bag of peanuts (said to have been the only food and alcohol that the original camp founders had brought with them their first year), was passed around the assembly. Individuals stepped forward one by one to say a few words about the history of the group and what "the Motel" had meant to them and to recognize some of the group's founding members who were not present. Finally, the coffin was ignited with bottle rockets. In this way campmates both reinforced their shared identity as "Moteliers" and recognized some of the tensions that had emerged in the group.

Over the years, I have both observed and heard of numerous and varied ritual activities at Burning Man, some quasi- or fully satirical, as well as others conducted in full seriousness. These have included group and individual meditation practice, Reiki attunement, yoga classes, Kabbalah classes, chakra balancing, aura cleansing, Wiccan circles, Unitarian Universalist worship services, Shabbat services, Hebraic dream interpretation, and *kecak* (more commonly advertised in this context as "Balinese Monkey chant"), along with many others. When asked if they participated in any rituals or ritual-like activities at Burning Man, participants offered a wide variety of responses. Many named events such as the Burn, the operas, and the Temples, and some mentioned popular new age practices. For example, one woman said:

> I have sought out and participated in various aspects of what I would consider the "spiritual community" at Burning Man. This includes everything

from yoga classes to Reiki, healing by people who work with energy and chakras, meditations, astrology classes, walking the labyrinth, new age teachings, [and] Kabbalah readings / teachings, and [I] had an amazing experience last year with a woman who did energy work on me and introduced me to an archway that you walk through, and it was meant to align all the strands of your DNA on a cosmic level.[59]

A few others said they participated in group rituals within their camps. For example, one man stated, "We have an opening ritual of a circle where we talk about our expectations and set a precedent for the energy in our space. We are a group of healers, and therefore we try to create a positive healing energy and environment."[60] One simple rite of sorts that I have observed and participated in celebrates the setting of the sun. One woman described this rite thus: "I applaud at the setting sun. There's this moment when the sun drops below the mountains, and lots of people take a moment to clap and whoop and holler, as if thanking it for being there and welcoming the coming night—because nighttime is extra magical on the playa."[61]

Another type of ritual occasionally performed on the playa is marriages—fully legal as well as simply celebratory. In recent years the Burning Man organization has facilitated wedding ceremonies by keeping a list of participants who are licensed to perform legal marriages in the state of Nevada and, if requested, will put engaged couples in touch with these individuals, adding a whole new spin to the cliché of running off to Nevada to get married.[62] With or without assistance from Burning Man organizers, couples have long been honoring their love and commitment in various ways on the playa. For example, in 1996 a couple who were part of Safari Camp, with whom I camped that year, celebrated their recent marriage by donning their wedding finery and "cutting a cake"—although in this instance the "cake" consisted of several large tanks of propane hidden behind a large white paper cake facade that was "cut" with shots fired from the couple's rifles. Another individual offered this story, which also indicates the extent to which the Temples are often seen to connote sacred space beyond their memorial intent:

> In 2002 my wife and I were married at the *Temple of Joy*. The year prior we had deposited ashes of her father at the *Temple of Tears*. Our marriage was a beautiful sunset ritual attended by many. As is often the case out there, everything just came together. The lamplighters escorted my bride out past the Man to the temple. A guy with an organ and amp mounted on a go-cart showed up and played the wedding march. Our

chaplain—a female friend who had just been ordained—read from the Egyptian Book of the Dead. We exchanged vows and were blessed beneath the Temple and amongst friends and people we didn't even know but who were right there with us, some in tears, as we were. It was unforgettable, and our families wished they could have been there with us. But it was so personal and real and meaningful to the two of us. Far more meaningful to us than any "normal" ceremony could have been. Burning Man has nurtured us as individuals, helped bring us closer as a couple, and sanctified our union.[63]

Another popular site for playa weddings was a monumental installation titled the *Chapel of the Burning Book* (by Finley Fryer), more commonly referred to as the *Plastic Chapel*. (See DVD, chap. 4.) Constructed of colorful, translucent, recycled, melted plastic, the *Chapel* was a twenty-foot-high cube topped with a rounded dome that appeared as a brilliant beacon on the playa as it was illuminated from within, giving the effect of stained glass. It made its first appearance at the event in 1998 and became a repeat presence in subsequent years.

In 2006 an installation called the *Conexus Cathedral* was created in order to provide an alternative ritual space. The intention was in part to allow the Temples to remain focused on mourning. Constructed of towering white spires, Gothic arches, and buttresses, the *Cathedral* was deliberately designed as an open framework to symbolize its openness to all traditions. The structure provided merely a footprint—a suggestion of ritual space that let in surrounding mountains, light, and sky rather than a definitively bounded space—so that different events could move freely through that space, including weddings, bhakti yoga classes, walking meditation sessions, a "MASSive" electronic dance celebration, and a Saturday evening Shabbat service (see chap. 5; DVD, chap. 5).

Although the majority of participants I queried stated that they took part in some form of ritual, several were adamant that they did not. Among the latter responses was this one:

No, I strongly dislike rituals and ritual-like activities. More and more stupid pseudoreligious idiots are attending [Burning Man] desperately trying to apply all the insipid labels to this experience—oh, it means this or that or a combination of all those things. Religion is the latest spoiler for me at this event, next it will be politics, and then all the kids can all know what it is about without really needing to discover anything new.[64]

Given Burners' diversity of opinion about all matters of religion, ritual, and spirituality, statements such as this reflect participants' tendencies

not only to distance Burning Man from religion but also to ascribe idealized notions of immediacy and authenticity to the event. This same
individual—one of the atheists cited in the previous chapter—went on
to say that he thought "bringing any type of codified religious experience into Burning Man with you [is to] miss the point of the event."[65]
Yet he also understood the event as "a blank slate on which to create
ourselves anew" and said, "[The experience has] stripped me down to
my core, leaving nothing but myself."[66] He condemned ritual by equating it with his negative conception of religion but nevertheless embraced
and celebrated the transformative possibilities inherent in the festival.

CONCLUSION

From the Burn to the operas, Temples, and spontaneous celebrations of
the setting sun, the various events described above put participants' understandings of ritual on display. Each instance of ritual at Burning
Man not only indicates the boundless variety of ritual expressions that
can be discovered on the playa but also reflects participants' ideas about
what ritual *is* or *should be*. In the proliferation of ritual at Burning
Man, themes such as sacrifice, play, mourning, redemption, paradox,
transformation, liminality, and communitas—which are often expressed
and developed in religious contexts—are being ritualized and displaced
onto an alternative venue. It is significant that while routinization is
often taken to be a defining feature of ritual, at Burning Man it is resisted and critiqued as a barrier to spontaneity, immediacy, and authenticity. Many Burners use this festival as a kind of theater for spirituality that avoids what they consider to be the problematic aspects of
"religion." Burning Man provides a setting in which participants have
been encouraged to express and release deep emotion, to feel bonded to
one another in community, to critique the default world through parody
and reversal, and to thereby seek both personal and collective transformation.

While the central icon of the Burning Man is burdened with no
explicitly stated or defined meaning, it invites participants to project a
host of potential meanings and interpretations—either personal or
communal—onto its naked framework, which has long served as a ves-
sel of catharsis and transformation. Later attempts to ascribe specific
significance and ritualistic interactivity to the colossal platforms on
which the polysemous Man is erected have met with mixed success, as

these and other changes have prompted some Burners to yearn for the apparent simplicity and intimacy of days gone by. Other ritualistic events such as the operas consciously have sought to create collective experiences of communitas, sometimes consciously adopting ritual frameworks from anthropological theory. Although ritual structures and assorted mythic or religious figures may have been employed largely as theatrical leitmotivs, the producers and performers themselves often experienced transformation in these "rites of passage." Yet because for most of the audience the degree of personal engagement was restricted, the success of these attempts was limited. More recently, the Temples have beautifully demonstrated the extent to which Burners will happily embrace an explicit ritual intention and even an explicit meaning, so long as that purpose rests lightly, upon itself, leaving lots of room for personal interpretations and expressions. The ritualization available through the Temples has to some extent usurped the climax associated with the Man, and, more significant, it has provided a psychological and spiritual release in a communal context that has often been absent for many individuals in contemporary society.

In each of these fiery spectacles, as well as in the smaller-scale rites explored here, an extensive range of religious symbols—as well as certain ritual theories—are creatively and reflexively performed in simultaneously obvious and subtle ways. Turner's ideas on ritual process in particular have bled into popular culture to the extent that they sometimes show up as models that outline the event's ritual contours. It is noteworthy that two of Turner's sons, Alex Turner and Rory Turner, contacted the Burning Man organization some years ago in order to find out whether or not the festival had been intentionally modeled on their father's theories.[67] At that time Harvey had not read Victor Turner, although he has since, but this story underscores the ready association of this event with Turner's most compelling ideas, and I am by no means alone in my recognition of the applicability of Turner's ideas to Burning Man and other "alternative cultural heterotopias."[68]

Turner was deeply engaged intellectually and emotionally with the concepts of liminality and communitas and perceived these processes pervading social phenomena in numerous and widely divergent cultural and historical contexts—from hippie subcultures to Roman Catholic pilgrimages. At times he appeared to have been writing more about his own Western cultural milieu than about the tribal African societies that were ostensibly his subject matter, and it is surely no coincidence that

Turner was writing some of his most important work amid the turbulent social world of the 1960s and 1970s in the United States. Much of his data emerged primarily from his fieldwork among the Ndembu of Zambia, but he also drew on the contemporary "social dramas" of the era, referring on occasion to pop-cultural themes such as "hippies" and "dharma bums," as well as to figures such as Allen Ginsberg, Bob Dylan, and Malcolm X.[69] This orientation was reflected in his conceptualization of communitas as an emanation of free expression and love and of liminality as subversive, anti-authoritarian, and anti-structural, and his repeated analogies to popular culture render his ideas especially seductive.

Ultimately, both scholarly and popular constructions of ritual's functions and capabilities must be understood as products of continuously negotiated cultural understandings, visions, and issues. In this regard, the apparent resonance between Burning Man and Turner stems in large part from the fact that members of Western cultures now often look both explicitly and implicitly to these concepts as models for what rituals *are* and how rituals *should be* when creating alternative forms of ritual expression. Recall, for example, the implicit rite of passage enacted by the first Cacophonist Burners, as they stepped across a literal threshold from one "zone" into another. Even the phrase "rite of passage," which now enjoys widespread use in the English vernacular, was first introduced by van Gennep in 1909, and in extending van Gennep's insights—and, I suspect, being more widely read in college classrooms—Turner was almost certainly a primary force behind the popularization of this term.[70] Catherine Bell, an occasional critic of Turner, noted this popular turn to ritual theories as prototypes by which to design "new" rituals:

> There are few ritual leaders and inventors these days who have not read something of the theories of Frazer, van Gennep, Eliade, Turner, or Geertz, either in an original or popularized form. Turner, in particular, by identifying a "ritual process" weaving its way through micro and macro social relations and symbol systems, has been the authority behind much American ritual invention. . . . For modern ritualists devising ecological liturgies, crafting new age harmonies, or drumming up a fire in the belly, the taken-for-granted authority to do these things and the accompanying conviction about their efficacy lie in the abstraction "ritual" that scholars have done so much to construct.[71]

In this regard, rites such as *Le Mystere de Papa Loko* not only exemplify the desire to create and experience transformative rituals at Burning

Man—often by borrowing and synthesizing elements from "non-Western" or "indigenous" religious traditions—but also supply an overt instance of the reflexive mirroring of popular ritual theories.

Other theories have also occasionally exerted a special influence on the event's plans and annual themes.[72] For example, the 1999 *Wheel of Time* description stated:

> Returning to Black Rock City after a year's absence, it sometimes feels as if one had never left the desert. Within this changeless world time seems suspended. We build the same city, we burn the same Man, and by these actions we are changed. *Ritual time is cyclical time and quite unlike the ordinary measure that divides our daily lives.* This year, as the Millennium approaches, the Burning Man Project will create such a cycle in the Black Rock Desert.[73]

By inscribing ritual time as cyclical and outside the measure of the ordinary, this passage is evocative of Mircea Eliade's notion of *illud tempus* (sacred time) and of ritual and religion as constituting an "eternal return" to this sacred temporal nexus.[74] In 2003, when the Beyond Belief theme expressly invited reflection on ritual and religious issues, another of Eliade's key concepts was referenced when the Man's central locale was labeled the "axis mundi" (world center) on a Black Rock City map, thus explicitly inscribing this long-extant correspondence and constituting another of the more obvious appeals to academic theory in devising Burning Man's ritual frameworks.[75]

Because ritual theorists such as Turner and Eliade were, on a meta-level, saying as much if not more about Western culture in general—and popular countercultures in particular—than they were about the indigenous peoples who were their supposed subjects, their ideas often speak to people embedded in alternative contexts such as Burning Man in powerful ways. In this regard, the popularization of theoretical models for ritual at Burning Man may be attributable not so much to any essential accuracy or universal applicability of these theories (although this may be partly true) but more because both Burning Man's rituals and ritual theories have emerged from—and in critical opposition to—default Western cultural contexts.

In enacting ritual without dogma, Burning Man provides spaces to ritualize a spirituality that is conceptually positioned as distinct from religion, thus calling into question both popular and scholarly understandings of what constitutes religion, spirituality, and ritual in the first place. Yet even while Burners tend to locate these understandings in opposition to those held to be endemic to default culture, a limitless host of religious

themes, cultural symbols, and even ritual theories are evoked, performed, and played with as participants negotiate and frame their experiences with this event. For many participants, these entail encounters
with community, creativity, identity, self, and other that can foster profound experiences of personal transformation.

CHAPTER 4

Desert Pilgrimage

Among the qualities of Burning Man that are shared by all (or nearly all) festival participants—the heat, the dust, the climactic rite of the Burn—there is one that is of necessity universal: the journey. Whether they join the thousands who trek over California's Sierra Nevada range from the San Francisco Bay Area, wend their way through the rain forests of the Pacific Northwest, soar by plane from the East Coast and continents abroad, or simply make the twenty-minute drive from the nearby town of Gerlach, everyone must travel to the Black Rock Desert playa to join in the event. Once within the boundaries of Black Rock City, almost everyone will visit the prominent art installations and theme camps, especially those such as the Man or the Temples that are of special ritual significance, wandering from site to site and thereby undertaking a series of internal pilgrimages. Indeed, this act of strolling or cycling about and taking in the sights is an essential part of what one *does* at Burning Man.

Opportunities for personal or social transformation are often cited as among the definitive qualities of pilgrimages, and in this regard Burning Man does not disappoint. In this collective journey to a distant wilderness, far beyond most participants' realms of ordinary experience, many individuals encounter transformations of perspective and identity that reach deeply and unexpectedly into their lives in an enduring, even permanent fashion. Whether or not transformation is the conscious intention compelling participants to make the pilgrimage to Burning Man, many of them do experience profound and real changes in their lives.

Of the hundreds of individuals I surveyed and interviewed, I was not surprised that nearly three-fourths replied affirmatively when asked, "Has Burning Man been a life- or perspective-changing experience for you?"[1] What was somewhat surprising was that a strong majority of those individuals who felt somehow transformed, more than three-fourths, referred directly or inferentially to various aspects of Burning Man's ethical framework as sources of their personal or perspectival change, the core aspects of which are signified by the terms *participation, community, radical self-expression, radical self-reliance, radical inclusivity, gifting,* and *leave no trace.*[2] In particular, respondents most frequently spoke of community, self-expression, and self-reliance—sometimes as distinct concepts but usually as interrelated themes indicating some *exchange* between self and other—as keys to their experiences of transformation through the event. Many respondents also reported that Burning Man had engendered various encounters with their sense of *self,* including increased self-knowledge, self-acceptance, self-affirmation, personal growth, challenge, expanded boundaries, opened horizons, freedom, and confidence. The challenge of surviving in the desert was another commonly cited factor, and with its vast, empty, and inhospitable terrain it is easy to see the playa as a blank slate or temporary autonomous zone on which new identities may be inscribed and where anything is conceivable. Finally, a number of respondents also spoke of creativity, art, play, ritual, and spirituality as significant elements in their transformative experiences.

Over the course of my interviews and other conversations with participants, I was repeatedly struck by the consistency with which they reflected the event's ethos to me in various ways, and no one was telling me anything about their experiences that I didn't, on some level, expect to hear. My first reaction was to assume that this simply meant my comprehension of the field was solid; I had done my homework, and my conclusions seemed reliable. Yet on reflection, I began to understand that the participants were absorbing the event's ethos and reflecting it back out onto the rest of the culture of Burning Man, where it was in turn reabsorbed and reflected. With this insight, I came to understand that Burning Man's ideology is both *performative* and *reflexive*—as these concepts are both *enacted* and rendered *efficacious*—constructing an ethos that loosely frames the festival's contexts and that participants often carry back to the default world. In this regard, participation in Burning Man often results not just in some internal sense of self-transformation but also in having an impact on how people act and interact in the larger world, as the performance of these values often serves to transform or sharpen participants' already held worldviews.[3] As the event has evolved and participants have endeavored to take the Burning Man ethos seriously by enacting the values it embodies beyond the bounds of the playa, some Burners have increasingly sought to effect meaningful changes in the default world, as well as in their own lives.

Turner saw pilgrimages, like rites of passage, as mechanisms for prompting communitas and effecting changes in status or identity, and this narrative can easily be read into Burning Man. The journey to this festival involves separation from the norms and constraints of the default world, liminality in being betwixt and between the ordinary and the outlandish on the playa, and finally aggregation in returning to the default world having integrated new insights and experiences and perhaps an altered sense of self or identity. A dialogue with some of the key characteristics Turner ascribed to pilgrimage—and how these both succeed and fail to aptly characterize Burning Man—illuminates and engages some of the festival's physical, conceptual, and transformational facets, including Burners' constructions of nature, time, civic space, social status, and gender. Event participants, of course, pride themselves on voicing discordant perspectives and alternate interpretations, and in this regard Turner's critics also provide insights into what makes Burning Man tick.

In spite of the widespread absorption and performance of the event's ethos, participants and organizers alike also note that it is not necessarily universally embraced or enacted. This has become another area that is subject to internal critique, as some participants adamantly denounce aspects of the event that they perceive as failing to live up to its stated ideals. These include controversies surrounding growth and increased regulation, the delicate balance organizers attempt to strike between commerce and commodification, and the appropriate allocation of art grants, among many other such issues. Because participants are not in agreement on these matters, organizers have sought to even more proactively promote the event's ethical principles in order to better acculturate new community members and extend the event's ideological reach into the default world. This in turn has become yet another issue subject to critique as some individuals feel that such measures are too prescriptive or dogmatic.

Finally, in exploring participants' bodily and conceptual movements to, from, and within Black Rock City, this chapter locates Burning Man in the contemporary relationships between pilgrimage (traditionally considered *sacred* quests) and tourism (typically associated with *profane* travel). Although Burning Man resists many of the banal features typically associated with blatantly commercial tourist sites—seeking to differentiate itself in part through its participatory and performative ethos—a consideration of the event's "touristic" elements reveals interesting parallels. Burners perform complex and occasionally paradoxical exchanges between imagined and reimagined *selves* and fictive or exotic *others,* which contributes to the event's potential to produce a sense of transformation.

PERFORMING SELF IN COMMUNITY

Larry Harvey has often asserted, "People often come to Burning Man to enjoy the freedom. They stay, however, and contribute more each year, because of the community."[4] And indeed, when asked whether or not they felt the event had changed their lives or perspectives on life and, if so, how, many participants mentioned or alluded to the themes of community, self-expression, and self-reliance. On a basic level, many of the individuals who attend Burning Man constitute multiple and overlapping communities that manifest in hundreds of theme camps, villages, volunteer teams, and other collectivities and that also often reflect ongoing ties and relationships that are maintained year-round. Given the geographic origin of this event, it is not surprising that many of these groups are located in the San Francisco Bay Area where they may frequently come in contact with one another through year-round events and social gatherings, although increasingly the Burning Man community extends beyond Northern California and the West Coast, reaching throughout North America, as well as Europe, Australia, New Zealand, Asia, and South Africa. For many individuals, there is also a feeling of togetherness and community within the confines of Black Rock City, as well as a shared sense of what it means to be a *participant* and hence a *Burner.* This sense of community—of a felt connection to or bond with others, despite perceived or substantive differences—is considered a quintessential aspect of the Burning Man experience, and it is a core message promoted by the organizers, who bill the event as "an experiment in temporary community."[5] This is also reflected in the event's radical inclusivity: anyone, at least in theory, is welcome to attend and participate.

Underscoring the crucial importance of community, two-thirds of all respondents to my on-line survey made some mention of this aspect of Burning Man as an important part of their experience, whether or not they personally felt they had been changed by the encounter; and of those who reported that they had been somehow transformed, almost three-fourths cited community as a source. (See DVD, chap. 1.)

These respondents used the term *community* in multiple but not mutually exclusive ways.[6] For some, it was an idea that encompassed an overarching sense of unity and solidarity in "Black Rock citizenship"; for others, it indicated a physical community—that is, the individuals who were their friends, companions, and loved ones. Many reported having discovered through Burning Man a community of new friends and like-minded others who continued as important relationships in their lives beyond the spatial and temporal confines of Black Rock City. For example, one man credited his newfound community with reinforcing his sense of identity by affirming the life choices that had placed him outside societal norms:

> It *did* restore a community to my life, which had been absent for a decade and a half. This has been a huge plus, in my experience. While I did not experience anything like the epiphanies that many other friends have, I was reminded that there are others out there who don't fit well into the constraints that mainstream society dictates. And I was both reminded and reassured to again be a part of a community where people were close, and trusting of one another, and openly emotional in situations that did *not* involve death or disaster . . . which is, all too frequently, the only time you tend to see open and honest emotion in most of our society. I'd say that I may be happier about my life and choices in part because of my Burning Man experiences, because a lot of those choices have gone contrary to what I was "supposed" to do or expected to do.[7]

For others, the sense of transformation stemmed from changes in relationships that were already rooted in their default world lives. For example:

> It's transformed my relationships, my friendships, my view of myself, my view of the world. It's opened up myriad possibilities and inspired new activities. It's the opportunity to create a community from scratch, one based on a more altruistic system than capitalism. And the freedom to be and explore whatever you want.[8]

Nearly one-fourth of respondents named more than one facet of community—connections with others, friendships, unifying or homogenizing sentiments reminiscent of communitas—as typified by the following statement:

> It has changed the way I look at myself. I can accept who I am because of it. I shed all my negative thoughts I had about myself and my image. I realized

that the kind of people who were at Burning Man were the kind of people I wanted to be like. I saw myself in them, and they recognized themselves in me. They accepted me, after I accepted myself. It has also changed my perspective on what is important in life. Survivalist events have a way of doing that. . . . Also trusting other people to help take care of me as I would take care of them. I realized that once I got there I couldn't just be a spectator. I couldn't just watch it all happen and not be a part of it. I had to open up. I had to reach out to people. . . . Granted the change would be different for everyone, but when you have to trust yourself to be responsible for yourself and your actions, your survival, both physical and emotional, and you are dealing with people who are on the same level as you are—no richer, poorer (at the moment of the event)—then you can have a real connection and friendship. Not one that takes weeks or months to build but moments.[9]

It can be seen that for this individual, it was not just a multiply understood sense of community but rather an encounter between self and community (or self and others) that had changed him.

This man was not alone in expressing this sentiment. More than one-third of respondents referred to dynamic encounters between self and other as having led to feelings of personal change. For example, another individual stated:

It certainly changed my identity—or rather, solidified it. I learned more about myself as an individual and in community. I learned that for me, the meaning of life begins with chillin' with my homies, and that that act—creating and enjoying a home and community that nourish me—is the essential starting point for anything else I hope to accomplish in the world. Burning Man helped bring about that transformation in joyful and in painful ways. Like any major change in life, and especially in forming one's identity, transformation is not a simple operation. Burning Man brought everything to extremes—heat, dry, dust, working together, working against each other, dissolution of friendships, formation of new friendships, you learn who your friends are and who is empty cargo in the desert.[10]

For others, the experience of self in community was connected to active participation in the event, leading to an increased understanding or knowledge of themselves. One woman said:

First there was kindness in the face of cluelessness, and that kindness inspired me to contribute. Through contribution came community, and my interactions with that community helped me figure out who I am and what I have to offer the world. I have the kind of friends and support that I always dreamed of having, and finally feel cared for. . . . Working with these folks has taught me so much—a greater sense of my own worth, improved communication and negotiation skills, greater respect for others' voices and ideas. You see, deep down I always hoped I was fabulous. I just didn't have much proof until Burning Man. Also, being involved with this community sparked my own creative juices.[11]

In addition to those who mentioned encounters with community, almost half traced their source of transformation through Burning Man at least in part to experiences of self-expression or self-reliance at the event. For example, many spoke of expressing themselves creatively or of being able to act with less self-restraint:

Burning Man has pretty much completely changed my life. The experience has primarily taught me that I had indeed been an artist for many years before I discovered the event but had not been allowed, either by circumstance or by others in my life, to express myself accordingly. Burning Man gave me the tools necessary to become the creative person I am and to realize that my own *radical self-expression* is a key component to the person I actually am. Or have become.[12]

Participants also spoke of the impact of radical self-reliance on their lives. One woman stated, "Burning Man's credo of radical self-reliance is something that, as a lifelong codependent, has challenged me in many ways and will hopefully make me a better, stronger person in the long run."[13] Still others said they had gained new self-reliance and personal growth through having successfully faced various challenges:

I saw that at the festival, being who you are was celebrated. It wasn't about conformity or not making waves, it was about radical self-expression. My first few years taught me to be more accepting of myself and to fly my freak flag high and proud. It also taught me that, as far as making decisions, I can play safe or take risks. And that although taking risks and pushing my boundaries a bit was more frightening and challenging, it also brought greater rewards and wonderful experiences I may not have otherwise had. That is something I try to remember every day.[14]

As already seen above, several others referred to feelings of increased self-affirmation or self-acceptance. For these individuals, the event both enabled and affirmed their unique quests to become more truly themselves. For example:

I would say Burning Man has been a life- and perspective-*affirming* experience. I have always struggled to live a lifestyle outside of the norm and have always suspected that the "norm" is not the ideal way of life. However to live outside of the norm you need to confront a lot of judgments, you need to sometimes fight to justify your way of life, yet you still need to operate within a society that has certain rules in place—many of which do

not take alternative lifestyles into consideration. . . . This puts you in a
constant state of swimming upstream, which takes a lot of energy. When
I first arrived at Burning Man I felt an immediate sense of "home." It was
a place [where I] could live by the principles I normally live by and feel total acceptance, little struggle, and it affirmed the attitudes I fight to keep in
everyday life. This not only provided a sense of freedom—existing in my
ideal community as I would have imagined it—but allowed me to further
examine my lifestyle choices. Burning Man provided a working example
of what I always suspected—that people are happiest when they can express themselves freely and enjoy the expression of others in a nurturing
nonjudgmental environment.[15]

Sometimes participants mark their sense of renewed, affirmed, or rene-
gotiated identity by adopting colorful "playa names"—Chef Juke, Evil
Pippi, Absinthia, Actiongrl, to name just a handful—some of which are
self-selected and some of which are nicknames assigned by friends and
campmates.[16] These alternate identities, which playfully signify the
changes wrought on the playa, often follow participants home. Some individuals continue to use their playa names in their day-to-day lives, thus
incorporating the experiences or ideas they denote into their whole sense
of self.

PERFORMING COMMUNITY BEYOND BURNING MAN

A significant theme voiced by nearly one-fourth of the respondents was
that of having gained a renewed hope for humanity by having witnessed
and actively participated in what seemed to them a better social model.
For example, one man stated, "Burning Man renewed my faith in my
fellow man. It showed me that people from entirely different cultures,
social settings, and economic classes can come together and create wonderful things."[17] Others thought that the event had given them a broadened perspective on human possibilities and the parameters of culture:

> Before Burning Man, I saw society as something that an individual lives
> in. After Burning Man, I see society as something more personal—that I
> am a working part of it—and that I am a small cog in a working machine.
> Even the smallest cog, when it's not participating, slows down progress. I
> find I'm more empowered and more enriched by seeing [that] my role in
> my friendships, my neighborhood, and my connections to others makes
> for a much more livable society. I found that it doesn't take much to make
> the society I live in a better place—just by making small efforts to bring
> joy, compassion, and human kindness into others' lives, I make society at
> large a much lovelier thing.[18]

Other aspects of Burning Man's ethos, such as gifting, decommodification, leave no trace, and participation, were cited as important transformative factors by over one-third of respondents. One individual mentioned several of these qualities:

> The ideals of radical inclusiveness and gifting have had a huge impact on how I live my life. I've become very aware of litter and trash. I've become more politically active, because I've learned that people are people, and life is not a spectator sport. I am less intimidated by "politicians," or performers, or actors, or whatever. I'm willing to talk to them, send them e-mail, letters, faxes, etc. I've realized that it's important to participate in the processes that greatly affect my life rather than complain uselessly about things that are happening that I don't like.[19]

Sometimes the strong emphasis on communal effort and civic responsibility fostered at the festival not only connects individuals to physical communities on the playa or feelings of personal transformation but also inspires individuals to carry the event's values into the rest of their lives by working to enact social change outside of Burning Man. Perhaps the most significant example to date took place in 2005. In the wake of the Hurricane Katrina disaster—which happened to coincide with Burning Man that year—groups of Burners traveled to the Gulf Coast immediately after the event and set up an ad hoc relief effort that came to be known as Burners without Borders.[20] (See DVD, chap. 2.) Setting up tents and shelters still dusty from the playa, more than two hundred volunteers over the course of eight months distributed food, water, and other critical supplies; demolished damaged buildings and hauled away debris; and rebuilt a Vietnamese Buddhist temple in Biloxi, Mississippi, and a home in Pearlington, Mississippi.[21] The momentum generated by these efforts would be maintained with support from the Burning Man organization, which continued to spearhead a variety of volunteer civic relief projects, including working with Habitat for Humanity in Reno, environmental cleanup and restoration projects in the San Francisco Bay Area, and building a school in Pisco, Peru, which had been devastated by an earthquake in 2007.

Other examples are the efforts of Burners located in New York City who banded together after the attacks of September 11, 2001, to assist and support rescue and cleanup crews by donating burn barrels (i.e., recycled oil drums decorated with cut patterns that are commonly used on the playa to contain fires along the Esplanade and in theme camps) to cold and grateful city workers. In 2004, when a highly contentious presidential election was to take place just two months after the Burning Man event, some participants took the opportunity to engage in voter registration and other acts of political activism. For example, one San Francisco Burner, JX Bell, organized a number of his friends and acquaintances to form what he called the Real World Greeters. Taking the Burning Man organization's Greeters model as their inspiration but reversing it, Bell and his compatriots approached participants in their cars as they slowly filed out of Black Rock City. Their message echoed the same basic themes that the Greeters employ: "You're entering into a strange new culture where you'll need to participate, express yourselves, give gifts, and leave no trace." In so doing, they also took the opportunity to direct people to voter registration information appropriate to their home states.[22]

CREATIVITY, RITUAL, AND NATURE

Although the various principles that constitute Burning Man's ethos were the predominant themes in respondents' reflections on transformation through the event, other themes emerged as well. For example, art and creativity served as catalysts for one-fourth of respondents. For some, this was tied to self-expression; for others, it came from observing and interacting with the work of others. One individual stated:

> I now look at art differently. For me, art used to be something that hung on a wall, and though it *should* be thought-provoking, there was very little interaction in it. Now I see art as all types of things—stuff people make for you, food given to you, a massage, a thought-provoking movie, etc. But it also helped me to understand that *I* could be creative, too. In the past I've always been a math-science computer nerd. Now I understand that those things can be artful, and I also have more interest in executing on my nonlinear artsy ideas.[23]

Some individuals, totaling 12 percent, specifically cited experiences of spirituality, religion, ritual, or pilgrimage as having contributed to their sense of transformation. Of those who mentioned spirituality or religion, most offered simple statements that also alluded to other themes, for example, "Burning Man for me has become a spiritual pilgrimage every year. It has renewed my faith in what humans can achieve, in terms of community."[24] Another said, "Burning Man was one of many nonreligious but spiritual activities that I have been cultivating since leaving my formal religion [Latter-day Saints] one and a half years ago. In this respect it was very powerful for me."[25] A few others specifically mentioned having been changed by an emotional catharsis in rites such as the Burn or the Temples. For example, one individual stated, "It afforded me the opportunity to ritualize a great deal of grief I had due to loss of friends from HIV. For four years after my first Burn I went to the Black Rock because I needed it. It wasn't a party for me."[26] Another individual offered this story:

> In preparing for my first Burn, I was, without really thinking about it, going through all my belongings, large and small, discarding a lot of "crap" that I didn't need or that didn't resonate with me anymore. At the end of it, I had a small pile of letters, photos, e-mail printouts, etc., that I decided to burn. . . . As the event [was] drawing to a close, I realized I still had this "stuff." I debated about throwing it into a burn barrel and just leaving it, but on the final day (Sunday), I realized where it needed to go: into the walls of the Temple. I rushed over by myself and stuffed everything into the Temple walls—it was the final hour before they closed it to prepare it for the burn. That night, I sat holding hands with two of my campmates, tears streaming down my face, as I watched it burn away all the anger, all the bad things people had said to me and I'd *kept*, like some sick testament to why I am a Bad Person. I doubt I have ever before nor will ever subsequently feel like I felt that night.[27]

The natural desert landscape and the rigors of surviving in adverse conditions were named as critical factors by 20 percent of respondents, as has already been seen in some of the excerpts above. Another participant stated:

> Every time I attend, I seem to gain a major shift in perspective. Part of it is a result of the physical environment; the stress of being in the desert and the need to focus carefully on my physical well-being sensitizes me. Emotionally, I'm in a more highly charged, "compressed" community, so my interactions with other people have a deeper impact. It's an atmosphere conducive to rapid processing, for me, as I'm in a sensitive, open space in which I feel basically safe and accepted, and able to explore my limits and boundaries. I've had really "negative" emotional experiences there, but every one has ended up being a major catalyst for growth.[28]

The shared encounters with extreme heat, cold, wind, and dust can serve as visceral reminders of the fragility of the human body. This environment can push participants to their limits, thereby establishing circumstances ripe for transformational experiences.

Although participants located the sources of their transformation in many different experiences, they collectively referenced themes that resonated with Burning Man's ethos. For many Burners, the dynamic tensions between self and community—and between self and natural environment—provided opportunities to reflect on self, identity, otherness, and the body. Through free expression, and physical and emotional challenges, many Burners have gained new perspectives on themselves, and in turn their cultural and social locations.

PILGRIMAGE AS PASSAGE?

Black Rock City, with its carefully measured streets, lampposts, "downtown" Center Camp, and other civic amenities, blends the seemingly alien nature of the playa with a para-urban setting, creating a space that is both totally other and oddly ordinary. In fulfillment of the event's "leave no trace" imperative, the city must be *completely* removed within about a month of the festival's close and re-created from scratch the following year. In producing and negotiating this aesthetic paradox betwixt and between emptiness and abundance, Black Rock City readily evokes a sense of liminality. While the threshold into the Zone has changed from a simple line etched on the cracked surface of the playa into a long line of cars marked by surly ticket takers and jovial greeters—and the sense of temporary autonomy is notably more regulated—the spatial metaphors of liminality remain pertinent in terms of participants' physical movements from home to desert and back again.

In his work on Christian pilgrimages, Turner perceived them as neatly mapped onto the threefold processes of rites of passage. Noting that the traditional liturgy and sacraments of his own Roman Catholic faith offered little in the way of the sort of liminal experiences that he identified in his fieldwork in Africa, Turner (in collaboration with his wife, Edith) looked to the phenomenon of pilgrimage in the Christian world, where he saw the processes of liminality, antistructure, and communitas in action. In the ritualized journey and hardships encountered in pilgrimages, the Turners identified "some of the attributes of liminality," including

> release from mundane structure; homogenization of status; simplicity of dress and behavior; communitas; ordeal; reflection on the meaning of basic religious and cultural values; ritualized enactment of correspondences between religious paradigms and shared human experiences; emergence of the integral person from multiple personae; movement from a mundane center to a sacred periphery which suddenly, transiently, becomes central for the individual, an axis mundi of his faith; movement itself, a symbol of communitas, which changes with time, as against stasis which represents structure; individuality posed against the institutionalized milieu; and so forth.[29]

On first reading this passage, I was struck by the number of similar qualities that can be experienced at Burning Man. The event offers a smorgasbord of shared ritualized enactments that can cultivate a strong sense of communitas. The very act of making the trip to Burning Man has certain ritualistic elements: the necessary preparations, often repeated year after year, combined with the journey to a distant and unforgiving environment converge to give participants a sense that they are performing ritual behaviors and enacting a kind of pilgrimage. Yet, on further consideration, I also began to recognize numerous ways in which Burning Man problematizes the qualities that the Turners held to be definitive of pilgrimages.

Without a doubt, Burning Man resonates in some obvious ways with the Turners' perspectives. Participants leave behind their everyday lives and mundane urban centers (separation); journey to a distant, unforgiving wilderness, where they enter into the carnivalesque setting of Black Rock City (liminality); and return home, often with changed perspectives or renewed understandings of themselves in relation to the world (aggregation). In leaving behind the default world of their daily lives—and framing their sense of separation with such language—Burners experience a release from mundane structures. This sense of release and dislocation extends to the temporal, as many individuals seek to immerse themselves in the moment and lose track of ordinary time, a collective experience that has come to be called being on playa time. They also move spatially from *center* to *periphery*—from the urban environments that most of them call home to the wilderness of the remote and inhospitable Nevada desert. Burners have even adopted their own term for the aggregation phase—*decompression*—a reference to the difficulty of reintegrating themselves into their ordinary lives after the event.[30]

Yet the separation here is not total. As different as Burning Man or the playa may be from the default world, Black Rock City consciously re-creates a familiar "civic" infrastructure, complete with streets, newspapers, and "peace officers," including representatives of external governmental agencies and its own team of Rangers. In addition, many more experienced participants bring both the comforts and the faces of home with them; they set up reasonably comfortable camps or travel and stay in air-conditioned RVs, often in the company of friends and family. In these regards, the separation from the mundane, ordinary, or default world is not as total or extreme as the Turners' model intended.

The ordeal quality of pilgrimage identified by the Turners can certainly be seen at Burning Man. Participants must be prepared to endure physical hardship and moments of trial in the harsh environment. With its extremes of heat and cold, unforgiving winds, unavoidable dust, and the persistent risk of dehydration, the environment can exact a daunting physical toll. (See DVD, chap. 1.) In addition, Burners may commit enormous amounts of time, energy, and money well above the nontrivial expense of admission and supplies in order to create elaborate art projects, costumes, and theme camps, and these "gifts" to the community can be understood as personal sacrifices.

However, these aspects of "ordeal" are mitigated by modern amenities: automobiles, ice chests, and relatively easy access to water chief among them. In this regard, I think of the pioneers on the Oregon Trail not much more than a century ago who sometimes took an ill-advised turn late in their arduous journeys through the Black Rock Desert. Some of these travelers died; others sacrificed everything but what was absolutely necessary for survival, leaving their material possessions along the trail.[31] For Burners, the trip to the playa is a choice, a vacation even, and technological advances have made surviving, even thriving, in this inhospitable place quite manageable. Indeed, part of the fun of camping on the playa may be to attempt to live as decadently and elegantly as possible in the face of the physical challenges, and while the heat, dust, wind, and occasional rainstorms may be difficult to endure, they can also be thrilling; all these are reminders that we too are subjects of nature. For example, some of my frequent campmates have instituted a ritualistic tradition fondly known as "gong camp" in which people bring out gongs, pots, pans, and other clanging noise makers and stand in the center of camp making a surreal and celebratory noise during dust storms. One participant who responded to my survey noted this *tamed* challenge: "I had *never* been to anything like it; the closest thing was Boy Scout jamborees. Same sense of exploration, *fake hardship* and self-reliance, and camaraderie."[32]

To a certain extent Burning Man invites the homogenization of status, although in this context participants' shared condition is more typically marked by flamboyant or eccentric dress and behavior than by simplicity. There is a very real sense in which the playa becomes a level playing field, as many of the standard roles individuals adhere to in the default culture fall away by means of the shared experiences of arriving at and surviving in the desert. The venerated sense of community that dominates at Burning Man includes an egalitarian idealism that manifests in feelings of connectedness, unity, and hope for humanity that are held to be absent in the default world.

Participants' notions of community, as seen in some of the narratives above, often reflect emotional sentiments of fellowship, affinity, and oneness that are among the hallmarks of communitas. But this apparent parallel between Burners' collective sense of community and Turner's communitas must be treated with caution. On a basic and pragmatic level, the term *community* is sometimes employed by Burners to refer to the physical dimensions of both person and place, whereas Turner coined the term *communitas* in part to distinguish "a modality of social relationship from an 'area of common living.' "[33]

Nor is the *homogenization* straightforward or universal here. Not only is Burning Man a heterodox community; there is an extent to which participants inevitably replicate society's class structures and other differences by what they bring with them to the desert, thus undermining the ideal of communitas. For example, some can afford to travel and stay in RVs, and others cannot; some have the resources to create large and technologically complex art projects, and others do not. The expense of the event also renders the festival mostly inaccessible to those without sufficient means, and the event is by and large—although by no means universally—attended by whites.[34] Stereotypical gender-based divisions of labor are also sometimes reproduced. Although there are, of course, *ample* exceptions to these generalizations, it has still most commonly been men who have made the big pyrotechnic art, and it has also more often been men who have built shade structures and pounded rebar stakes into the ground.[35] Even in the Burning Man organization, although both women and men work in various capacities in all the departments, men lead both the Rangers and the DPW while women manage Communications and Community Services.[36] There is also a differentiation in status on the playa between those who are more experienced or longtime Burners and first-time attendees (semidisparagingly called newbies), as well as a disparity between members of prominent and favored theme camps, that are given preferential placement along the Esplanade, and those who camp on the outskirts of Black Rock City, differences that can cause tension and territorial disputes.

Furthermore, as we have seen, Burning Man has changed a great deal as it has had to negotiate the concerns of the state, and this is certainly reflected in the qualities of liminality, communitas, and autonomy at the event, down to the event's most basic rituals. Recall, for example, the increasing distance between participants and the Man deemed necessary by the increasingly large crowds. With these changes, communitas at Burning Man has become increasingly *normative* or *ideological* rather than the ideal of free spontaneity still desired by many participants.

In Burners' condemnation of default culture, the event provides ample opportunities to reflect on the meaning of basic religious and cultural values. At Burning Man the juxtapositions of religion / spirituality, participant / spectator, self / other, and nature / culture, among others, prompt individuals to reflect on their own orientations to these concepts, ultimately encouraging an awareness of their malleability and thus supporting the Turners' assertion that pilgrimages can generate experiences of both personal and social transformation. Yet even those who have experienced profound life and perspective adjustments as novices at Burning Man often outgrow what was once a deeply radicalizing experience. For those who have become adepts in this context, the opportunities to see the world and one's position in it from a different vantage point may not be ongoing. After attending for a number years, the once-extraordinary experience can become almost routine: the festival loses some of its initial enchantment and mystery for those who know what to expect. Many longtime Burners eventually begin to criticize various aspects of the event as increasingly lacking in whatever quality of magic it was that initially, and repeatedly, drew them in the first place, and sometimes formerly avid participants burn out and choose to move on to new interests and other life experiences. Those who continue to attend year after year often do so for the sense of community it provides, and their time in Black Rock City becomes a family reunion of sorts.

For example, one participant said she decided to stop attending Burning Man because it had become "too big." "The event interferes with my appreciation for the desert environment, it's losing its impact on my psyche, and it's time to seek new perspective adjustment tools," she continued.[37] Another participant told me that he feels there are now "too many people [and] too much spectacle for the sake of spectacle. [I'm] moving on in my own life."[38] One former participant shared his lengthy critique:

> In the past tense, it was all about freedom, freedom, freedom, baby. The freedom to do what you wanted, wear what you wanted, bring what you wanted, drive what you wanted anywhere you wanted. The event was a blank slate which you could gleefully fill with whatever and whoever you could bring with you. . . . Freedom has been replaced by stifling bureaucracy, limited movement and tired formula to create what amounts to a rather controlled desert car-camping experience. The focus that it had on the small and the personal and the DIY [do-it-yourself] is mostly gone, and

it is now basically a big-ass party in the desert with way too many people
and way too many bored law enforcement personnel wandering about. For
those who enjoy Burning Man in its present form, I say, more power to
you, enjoy it by all means. . . . [B]ut for me, the things that drew me to the
event in the first place scarcely exist anymore. As someone once said, you
can't go home again. I will leave it to others. I am done with it and have
been since 2000. Time to move on.[39]

However, a woman who founded and formerly ran the Center Camp
Café saw this process as only natural. Individuals, she said, get what
they need out of the event and then reach the point where they need to
move forward and take that experience into other parts of their lives and
the rest of the world.[40] This too is an aspect of the experiences of transformation prompted by Burning Man. Although many individuals on
this pilgrimage may repeatedly experience life- or perspective-changing
encounters, it may be that these experiences cannot be reproduced in-
definitely even if the festival itself, theoretically, could.

It has been said that pilgrimage may be better understood as a realm
of competing discourses—both secular and religious.[41] Burners do indeed engage in a plethora of diverse and sometimes contradictory discourses as they seek to make sense of their individual experiences of the
event and to disrupt or reinvent traditional perceptions of community,
culture, self, ritual, and spirituality. While events such as Burning Man
may temporarily dissolve normative or default societal structures and
open up liminoid zones of freedom and autonomy—as Turner theorized—
they also reproduce and ultimately support many dominant ideologies.
More often, pilgrimages can be seen as serving multiple purposes simultaneously, and Burners tend to see their pilgrimage as being "whatever
you want it to be." Furthermore, despite the extent to which experiences
of radical life or perspective change are commonly reported by Burners,
it is important to acknowledge that approximately 10 percent of survey
respondents did not feel that the event had changed their lives in any way,
and roughly another 10 percent said that the event had changed them in
some ways but that other experiences in their lives had been more personally significant.[42]

Inevitably, the heterotopia of Burning Man imperfectly reflects the
utopian visions and aspirations expressed by both participants and organizers, as the event's core values are not universally or flawlessly embraced and enacted by all. For example, although there are occasional
acts of violence or theft—a few people have been victims of random
assaults, and bicycles in particular have been a favored target of

thieves—such occurrences remain comparatively rare among the tens of thousands of Black Rock City residents. On another level, those whose behavior is perceived as violating or undermining the event's foundational values or who are viewed as giving nothing back to the community may be seen as *spectators* by other Burners.

Thus while Burning Man is construed on the one hand as "whatever you want it to be," this is perhaps best understood as a framework for personal interpretation. As clearly evinced by the criticism lobbed by many participants, there *is* an idea of what the event *should* be, and this process too is a dialectic. As the parameters of behavior become more clearly defined and widely enacted, thus constituting an *orthopraxy* (meaning "correct practice" or "correct action") if not an *orthodoxy* ("correct doctrine" or "correct thought"), divergence from these ideals likewise comes more sharply into focus.

PILGRIMS OR TOURISTS?

Some Burners might regard themselves as pilgrims, but it is unlikely that they would want to be considered *tourists,* given the stigma attached to that term. Indeed, the term *spectator* functions here as a kind of synonym for *tourist.* Still, as Turner and Turner observed, "A tourist is half a pilgrim, if a pilgrim is half a tourist."[43] Given the realities of contemporary global travel, it is increasingly difficult to differentiate the secular tourist from the spiritual pilgrim. Burning Man both attracts and resists attracting attendees that some might consider mere spectators or tourists, and although Burners promote and practice decommodification and gifting within the bounds of Black Rock City, the event nevertheless remains embedded in global capitalist economies and can be seen as a popular commercial travel destination.

For example, in 2004 Burning Man was featured on an E! Entertainment cable television show that counted down the "top ten party spots in the world." Burning Man was listed at number 3, just behind Cancun, Mexico (popular with some college-age U.S. tourists), at number 2 and Ibiza, Spain, at number 1, which, with its innumerable nightspots, is a major international party destination. In 2002 my colleague Mark Van Proyen—who typically spends several summer weeks traveling around Europe and thus waiting on train platforms with many of those headed to and from Ibiza and other glamorous locales—reported that he was beginning to see more and more apparently young, wealthy, and fashionably attired individuals at Burning Man who looked like members of what he dubbed "the Ibiza set."[44] Such possible associations aside, there does seem to be a pronounced influx of attendees who show up very late in the week solely for the "big night" of the Burn. More than once I have observed large numbers of individuals hanging out in the Center Camp Café on Saturday afternoon who were a little too clean and well dressed to have been on the playa for more than a few hours. The Café may be a comfortable refuge for those who have come only to party for one night and who have probably not bothered to set up their own camps.[45]

Various genres of so-called electronic or techno music feature prominently in the many nighttime dance-oriented theme camps at Burning Man, and some participants are clearly drawn to Burning Man by this scene. Still, these are but one among many of the diverse subcultures and activities that can be found in Black Rock City. Many participants never partake of these venues, and some see them as antithetical to the event. There are several issues underlying these tensions, most of which can be traced to aesthetic, musical, and other lifestyle differences between various segments of the Black Rock City populace. For their part, organizers are wary of the potential legal or other consequences entailed by being too closely associated with the electronic music scene, and experience has shown them that those who attend only to party, in whatever capacity, may be less likely to uphold the ethos of Burning Man. In this regard, organizers publicly downplay and recast these elements by, for example, referring to dance camps as "large-scale sound art" and by requesting that publications geared to the international electronic dance-music subcultures refrain from listing Burning Man in their event calendars. They also dissuade prominent or internationally known deejays from promoting their attendance at Burning Man. Those who perform at the event have been told that it must be as their *gift* to the community and must not be actively publicized and certainly not charged for.[46]

With its potpourri of interactive theme camps and "attractions," another very different kind of tourist site to which Burning Man can be compared is Disneyland, and Harvey has called Burning Man "Disneyland in reverse."[47] Yet even while Burning Man seeks to be a decommodified and DIY (do-it-yourself) event, it can feel at times like the event has stumbled a bit closer to Disneyesque spectacle. For example, starting in 2003 the Artery volunteer team began offering an official "art tour" that conveys participants who sign up for this service around the playa in art cars to see the prominent art installations. I took advantage of this tour in 2004 and can attest that it was certainly convenient and that I also learned some things about the artwork that I would not have been likely to discover on my own.[48] Nevertheless, it seemed rather strange to be ferried about in a tramlike art car, listening to a guide tell us what was what via a small loudspeaker. The experience felt distinctly "touristic."

Such slippages aside, Burning Man remains in many ways a far cry from the kind of commercial tourist spectacle that is Ibiza or Disneyland. For many participants, Burning Man may be the primary annual holiday, and in a society in which many workers are allotted only two weeks of vacation per year it is perhaps remarkable that so many Burners choose to spend one of these weeks at Burning Man, which can be physically demanding "hard work." Yet they prefer this noncommodified—and hence nontouristic—experience over a more conventional and perhaps more relaxing vacation elsewhere.

Anthropological studies of tourism have often foregrounded the tension between commodification and authenticity, framing tourism as an expression of and outlet for individuals' discontent with "modern" capitalist society by way of romanticized encounters with the "premodern." For example, Dean MacCannell noted that while modern tourism depends on both the leisure time and "disposable" income provided by capitalist mechanisms, it is also seen to furnish a release from those very systems as individuals go in search of something felt to be more authentic.[49] MacCannell would go on to argue that what is at stake in the "touristic" is an experience of otherness. As cultures become increasingly commodified, the "product" that is sold to the Western tourist is an encounter with the other, such that tourism becomes a zone for the "staging of otherness."[50]

Just as Burning Man cannot be pigeonholed as essentially spiritual or religious, or for that matter as either purely pilgrimage or tourism, so too should it not be definitively labeled as either a pre- or a postmodern phenomenon. There is increasing consensus in tourism studies—as elsewhere in the scholarly world—that demarcating any essential dichotomy between "modernity" and "nonmodernity" is limiting, static, and ultimately meaningless in the contemporary globalized world.[51] Still, some of the concepts and practices generally signified by the terms *modern*, *premodern*, and *postmodern* remain readily observable cultural tropes. Through the symbolic hybridity of the event's art, theme camps, and rituals, Burners often perform romanticized conceptions of "primitive" or "exotic" others while also often parodying elements of American default culture as inauthentic or inferior.

Recall, for example, the diverse cultural motifs adopted in the operas and Temples, or *HelCo*'s sarcastic caricatures of ubiquitous corporate icons. Hybridity was also apparent in a 2003 art installation called the *Carousel Numinous,* which consisted of three carousels, each featuring a series of wooden panels painted with mutated mythological creatures: a naked Christlike sacrificial figure with a lamb's head, surrounded by corn plants with Native American motifs; a Buddha figure seated before a flaming labyrinth with wings on his head and a Kabbalistic "tree of life" formation on his chest; and a gray-green alien figure standing on top of a ouija board, with a Masonic pyramid in one hand and the other holding the hand of chimpanzee, with flying saucers and strands of DNA in the background.[52] (See DVD, chap. 2.) Another artwork from 2003 that commented on the emptiness of the default world was a piece called *Burning GreyMen,* consisting of several rigid, lemminglike lines of small gray papier-mâché men—all with receding hairlines and dressed in drab business suits—facing a central altar on which rested a hearth. Participants were invited to inscribe a burden, limitation, or conformity on a small piece of paper and affix it to one of the GreyMen before they met their fiery demise.[53] (See DVD, chap. 6.) A final example that occasionally showed up on the playa beginning in 2002 was a giant inflated Ronald McDonald figure that had been liberated from its fast-food chain and painted to resemble a golden seated "McBuddha." By comically merging an idealized Eastern aesthetic with an utterly banal American icon, this piece cleverly reversed a ubiquitous corporate brand in the guise of the quintessentially un-materialistic Buddha (fig. 7).

At Burning Man the ordinary modernity of the default world is associated with the *fake,* while the *exotic, primitive,* or *natural* remains idealized as more truly *real.* Burning Man explicitly offers itself up as an alternative to the normative, the commodified, and the institutionally religious, and what is valued in this context is an experience deemed more authentic or immediate. At the same time, participants critique Burning Man wherever they believe that it fails to authentically live up to its own utopian ideals as it is brought into increasing tension with the everyday bureaucratic and capitalistic world.

Burners' narratives reveal that in this context it is often a dialectic between communally embedded experiences of others and concomitant encounters with the self that engenders feelings of personal transformation and that can also inspire contributions to social transformation. But in this context, the other is not simply a fetishized marker of what you are not but a reflexive authentic self that you desire to become. The natural environment is also sometimes viewed as a kind of other on the playa, encounters with which were likewise said to provoke experiences of

FIGURE 7. "Ronald McBuddha" by unknown artist, 2002. Photo by
Lee Gilmore.

transformation for many Burners. By connecting with a sense of community, in being moved to reflect on oneself as reflected in others, or in
being tested by the embodied experiences of the playa, Burning Man provides models that invite participants to create and negotiate their own
frameworks of identity.

Through borrowing and mixing an enormous variety of cultural symbols that engage with exotic ideals of otherness and fictive authenticities—
which can be viewed as symptomatic of "modern" stereotypes of the
"premodern"—Burners re-create themselves as their own exotic others,
which can ironically entail or induce an experience of becoming more
authentically oneself. Paradoxically, while this hybridity creates a context considered by most participants as *more authentic,* the very appropriation and reproduction of these symbols and narratives renders
them, on a fundamental level, *inauthentic,* thus destabilizing fixed or

rigid distinctions between these concepts. As participants play with diverse cultural images and ideas—alongside various notions of cultural boundaries or authenticity—Burning Man provides a theater by which to apperceive the extent to which all cultures are constructs, thereby revealing their ultimate inherent plasticity and mutability.

CONCLUSION

Burning Man is a creature of contradictions that can facilitate significant reorientations in time and space and spark remarkable life changes. Through this pilgrimage, many participants experience something beyond the ordinary: they touch, for a moment and in their own ways, a sense of something meaningful in their lives that was missing before. Participants report numerous different perspectives on what prompted their experiences of transformation, but many referred to elements of the value system that over time has come to be established as the event's core principles. While categorically rejecting orthodoxy, participants and organizers collectively promote an orthopraxis of sorts by way of a clearly delineated ideology that encompasses personal, social, and environmental responsibility, alongside individual freedom. Even where adherence to these ideals is lacking, participants' critiques illustrate the varying degrees to which these ideals are both embraced and contested, a process stemming in part from the desire for authenticity and resistance to hierarchical authority. Many participants have been drawn to this event in the first place because, to varying extents, they already share its basic values, and in performing the ideology of Burning Man as it maps onto their personal experiences, they have helped to dialectically shape the event by collectively transmitting an ethos that capitalizes on and reinforces a nascent worldview, which can in turn engender variously located experiences of transformation.

For many survey respondents, feelings of personal transformation often emerged from or took root in encounters with *community*. The connections with others that have been forged or deepened through the festival often have meaningful and lasting impacts that transform participants' daily lives well beyond Black Rock City. Through the explicit invitation to creatively and unreservedly express themselves, many participants feel freer to continue these expressions long after the event's conclusion. Having participated in this alternative, albeit temporary, social model and having witnessed the mutability of cultural

norms, values, and symbols through this experience, some participants
are moved to continue to enact Burning Man's ideals in the default
world.

The juxtaposition between the vastness of the Black Rock Desert and
the civic circle of Black Rock City has the power to foster unique perceptions of space, land, environment, and time—both embodied and
imaginal—such that the natural world itself can be productively perceived as other. The desolate landscape invites the imagination to popu-
late its open terrain, as participants create a mind-boggling array of ex-
pressive projects, producing a stark visual contrast between geographic
emptiness and artistic abundance. The desert also evokes a potent imagery of mystery, abstraction, and limitlessness, as well as time-honored
connotations of hardship and sacrifice, creating the context for esoteric
experiences in a quasi-mythical setting. These dynamic encounters between
self and other—in tandem with embodied experiences of the desert—
coalesce to generate critical transformations for many participants, leading some to ascribe spiritual significance to the event.

Burning Man's numerous ritualistic elements—symbolic appropriation and invention, the agency and reflexivity afforded by participation,
the visceral creative and destructive forces of fire, along with the arduous journey of pilgrimage—lend themselves to experiences of transformation. In considering some of the complexities, ambiguities, and tensions between Burning Man's performance as a "sacred" pilgrimage and
its "profane" touristic elements, the event's simultaneous reflection of and
resistance to the quotidian forces of commodification and modernity becomes apparent. As actors on the global stage of travel, tourism, and intercultural exchange, Burners perform, contest, negotiate, and play with
varied notions of authenticity, otherness, and the exotic in their quests to
re-create and transform themselves.

CHAPTER 5

Media Mecca

Given its many visually and narratively compelling elements and high attendance, it is not surprising that Burning Man has been the subject of prodigious media attention. The event has been covered by large mainstream media organizations such as CNN, the Associated Press, and the BBC, as well as local news stations, newspapers, and dozens of other international outlets. It has also been visited by numerous aspiring documentary filmmakers, resulting in a few dozen completed films of differing length and quality. On occasion, parodies or other mentions of Burning Man have appeared on network sitcoms and other pop culture venues, and the event has been featured on thousands of commercial and personal Web sites.[1]

Over the years, the diverse media portrayals of Burning Man have not only helped to determine who has heard of the event and who decides to attend and why; they have also shaped both public understandings and private experiences of the event. In recognition of this powerful influence, organizers have learned to carefully manage their relations with the press so that coverage is more likely to accurately and favorably reflect on the event. As with other aspects of the festival, these efforts are founded on the principles of Burning Man's performative ethos. Members of the media are encouraged to view themselves as self-reliant and self-expressive participants rather than as detached spectators. This raises some interesting comparisons between the ethnographic practice of participant observation and the journalistic tradition of objectivity.

Cultural anthropology is traditionally based on participant observation, wherein an ethnographer becomes at once a participant in the day-to-day life of her or his subjects and an observer who maintains a critical distance. In recent decades ethnography has embraced increasingly reflexive strategies that recognize the ways in which the practice can change both the observer and the observed and that strive to more holistically situate both anthropologists and subjects in their discrete and overlapping cultural contexts. This in turn has led the discipline away from historical tendencies to stereotype ethnographic subjects as primitive, backward, or exotic objects. While visibly interactive, participatory, and reflexive media have become increasingly available through Internet technologies, the mass media still tend to fall back on well-worn patterns and stereotypes in their coverage of public events such as Burning Man. This is not necessarily the result of bad journalism; rather, this reflects the most familiar cultural categories.

As we have seen, Burning Man reflects complex notions of otherness, modernities, and spiritualities, and just as premodern or tribal icons and concepts are enlisted by Burners in their quests for immediacy and transformation, these narratives can likewise be discerned in the history of Burning Man's relations with the media. The media support the production and reproduction of these narratives by framing the event as simultaneously primitive or tribal (premodern) and technologically sophisticated (postmodern), and both Burning Man's ritualism and its demographic profile have contributed to the construction of this technopagan trope.

The mass media are complex and multifaceted institutions that constitute critical spaces for cultural production and negotiation. Yet "the media" are not simply amorphous or anonymous forces imposing a particular cultural hegemony on the masses. Rather, they are composed of and operated by men and women who are embedded in certain cultural contexts and who are thereby subject to the same sets of cultural forces and references as are those outside the media. Moreover, Burning Man's presence in and concurrent emergence with the so-called new media of the Internet has also had an important role in shaping the experiences and understandings of community and interactivity at the event. On-line media afford an increasingly visible interactivity, making it clearer than ever that the media's role in the construction of culture is not a simple one-way transmission. Rather, the media should be conceived as reflexive mechanisms that shape cultural consciousness and that in turn are shaped by culture. In this regard, Burning Man too is a hybrid reflection of countless cultural themes and traces through which participants self-consciously seek to reclaim the means of cultural production and reproduction.

Finally, it should not escape readers' attention that this book and the accompanying DVD are themselves mediated productions. As much as my aim here has been to craft a comprehensive depiction of the event, it is of course only one perspective. The textual and visual narratives presented here deliberately focus on select themes while glossing over or ignoring others. The sensorial power of moving images and sounds is explicitly intended, at least to some degree, to transport viewers onto the playa, but the act of creating a coherent visual narrative of the event carries with it the risk that its portrayal of Burning Man will be understood as unambiguously definitive or as capturing exactly what happened at any particular moment. However, experience shows that even while any given depiction of this event will certainly reveal some of its basic spirit, it will nevertheless completely miss other angles and perspectives.

MEDIA AND RITUAL FRAMES

In the past few decades several scholars have begun to examine the ritualistic aspects of the media and the various spaces of overlap and connection between the realms of media, ritual, and religion.[2] For example, James Carey notably and influentially argued that communications theorists would be well served to shift from a "transmission" view of communication to a "ritual" view, with his understanding of *communication* as entailing both "participation" and "community."[3] Others, such as Daniel Dayan and Elihu Katz, evocatively applied Turner's ritual theories in arguing that the media construct social rituals in response to significant national or international events, serving to cast public figures in mythic roles, confer legitimacy, reaffirm social values, redefine social boundaries, and inscribe memory and history (among other attributes), ultimately engendering a sense of communitas among very large audiences.[4]

Of course, the Burning Man festival is far from the scope or significance of the events with which Dayan and Katz were chiefly concerned. For example, the difference in both character and reach could be observed in 1998 when major media outlets such as CNN—which had sent a small crew to the playa that year—shelved their planned reports on Burning Man in favor of ubiquitous coverage of the death of Princess Diana, which occurred within the same week as the festival. Still, there are a few noteworthy parallels. When documentaries about the event are screened, for example, Burners in attendance often cheer at the sight of a friend or an acquaintance, or at shots of cherished art installations or ritual moments, like the Temples or the Burn—such that this shared and participatory act of viewing becomes a "community" experience, reinvig-orating a whiff of communitas.[5]

Others have looked not to the experiences of audiences but to the decisions of producers. For example, the performance theorist Richard Schechner located the ritualistic quality of "the news" in its repetitive-ness: "The ritual is in the format, in the programming, not in the content as such. The format insures that certain contents, certain classes of events, will be repeated; and repetition is a main quality of ritual. . . . Each fac-ticity is part of a sequence of similar events: this fire is followed by the next and the next; this international crisis by the next and the next."[6] These characteristics point not only to the privileging of certain *classes of events* over others but also to the ways in which certain kinds of *ideas* are privileged over others. Through these practices, the individuals who constitute the media make specific choices about which facts *and* which perspectives are selected for coverage and which are left out in any given story. These cumulative choices rely on preexisting cultural constructs and thereby come to constitute sets of rhetorical tropes to which the me-dia tend to return to time and time again in framing the ways in which "news" events are represented, communicated, and understood. Media coverage of Burning Man can likewise be seen as "ritualistic" in the fre-quent repetition of a specific set of technopagan tropes.

More recently, Nick Couldry called for a "post-Durkheimian" ap-proach to understanding the ritualistic power of the media, arguing that although the media's claim to wield a centralizing social authority is *not* as totalizing or all-encompassing as others have held it to be, the media nevertheless *claim* to wield such power and that this in itself is signifi-cant. He stated that "it is impossible to see Durkheim's image of 'primi-tive' social experience—a temporary gathering in the desert!—as anything more than a starting point for understanding the vast, dispersed complex-ity of contemporary societies, and how, if at all, they cohere" and that "there is no contemporary parallel for the Durkheimian totemic ritual in the desert where all society's central meanings and values are at stake."[7] Ironically, of course, Burning Man is another sort of "totemic ritual" and "temporary gathering in the desert," and although the ritualized negoti-ations that take place on the playa may not mediate those concepts for our *entire* society, it is nevertheless the case that any given social symbol can and will wash up on the shores of Black Rock City, where social meanings and values are constantly being contested and reinvented. Couldry also observed that in any social gathering, such as an annual music festival, one can "quickly find in people's clothes, bodily style, language and so on, traces of countless other spaces and histories, all quite independent from that gathering and not specifically intended to be expressed there."[8] Again, although not a "music festival" per se, the parallels to Burning Man are readily apparent in the multiplicity of cultural styles and traces that can be observed on the playa. Both intentionally and accidentally, Burners draw on innumerable "technological," "pagan," and other cultural sources to create, negotiate, and mediate their experiences of the event, which are in turn reflexively and indelibly represented by the mass media.

PRESS HERE

Media coverage of Burning Man has naturally increased as the event itself has grown, a phenomenon that festival organizers have successfully learned to negotiate over the years. From 1993 to 1996, a period of critical growth for the event, this task was led by a prominent Cacophony Society member, Stuart Mangrum, who also edited and managed operations for the organization's publication, the *Black Rock Gazette*. During these years it was entirely up to individual journalists and documentarians attending the event to decide whether they would check in at what was then called the Press Here trailer. As a result, organizers' perspectives on the event were sometimes left out of the stories.

Mangrum retreated from managerial responsibilities after the troubles of 1996, at which point Marian Goodell stepped in to oversee Burning Man's communications needs, a position she still held in 2010.[9] As media coverage of the event began to multiply considerably in the late 1990s, by 1998 Goodell had divided *Gazette* operations and press relations into two separate divisions so that volunteers could more readily focus on their distinctive tasks. She staffed the brand-new Media Team largely with individuals who worked professionally in press relations outside the event, as well as others who had been trained and employed as journalists, photographers, and, occasionally, ethnographers.[10] Burning Man's Media Team now works year-round and has instituted a thorough and discerning mechanism for dealing with the large number of media groups that want to cover the event.

Because the ways in which the event is portrayed often have concrete ramifications for the ways in which the event is perceived by participants, potential participants, and others, Burning Man organizers have become savvy in their relations with the media, as well as increasingly selective—as far as is both possible and prudent—of the media groups that are allowed to cover the event. Their intention is to minimize the intrusion of cameras, as well as to protect both participants and the event in general from commercial exploitation, in keeping with Burning Man's cultural ethos. For example, several attempts have been made to exploit the visually stunning imagery and edgy Burning Man "brand" in advertisements, music videos, and other commercial ventures each of which has been resisted and defeated, thanks to the LLC's trademark on the name "Burning Man."[11] Images of the event and its artwork are also protected as intellectual property and cannot be used for commercial purposes without the written permission of the organizers.

In order to enforce these policies, *all* participants—whether professional or private—who intend to capture any *moving* images must sign a use agreement form. The vast majority of these are individual Burners who simply want to shoot "home movies" in order to record their experiences and share the event with friends. These participants are asked to sign a "personal use agreement" confirming that their footage will not be put to commercial or public use and that should their objectives change, they must first contact the Burning Man organization to negotiate rights from that point forward.[12] However, all commercial and professional media outlets are required to preregister via a Web-based form that collects information about the kinds of stories and uses planned and to check in with the Media Team in person once they have arrived at Black Rock City. Contractual requirements vary depending on the outlet but generally prohibit showing participants nude or using drugs in order to protect individuals' privacy, delimit the venue(s) in which the finished product is intended to be shown in order to prevent the footage from being sold to undesirable or unauthorized outlets, request that appropriate credit be given to the artists whose work may be shown, and stipulate that some portion of any proceeds be shared with the Burning Man organization.[13]

Aside from these commercial agreements, broadcast and print news outlets are encouraged to attend. The organizers want to nurture healthy relations with the press in order to more positively mediate the event's public image and because they do not wish to be perceived as attempting to limit or regulate freedom of the press, which has the right to cover events held on public land. However, select entertainment-oriented media organizations are not welcome, chief among these being MTV, as the organizers do not want the event to be portrayed or perceived as either a "spring break-like" or "Ibiza-esque" party.[14]

The phenomenon of documentary filmmaking has been nurtured in part by the increasing affordability of high-quality digital video cameras, and it is this segment of the media that receives the most stringent scrutiny and is subject to the most restrictions by the Burning Man organization. In addition to seeking to prevent the potentially intrusive atmosphere that could be induced by too many camera crews, the organization also wishes to simply limit the number of potentially repetitive documentary films that reach the public to those that propose to tell a unique story and that are the most likely to be professionally carried out. For example, many applications from documentarians have proposed to follow and film a first-time Burner in order to capture his or her wide-eyed "rite of passage." But this angle was proposed so many times that it became something of a joke among the members of the Media Team, and very few of these kinds of proposals are approved.

On occasion, organizers will work closely with film crews whose expertise and sensitivity to the nature of the event are expected to result in widely screened and sympathetic portrayals, such as *Beyond Black Rock* (2004), which provided a "behind the scenes" look at the orchestration of the event, and *Confessions of a Burning Man* (2003), which did in fact record the adventures of a diverse group of first-time attendees. The organization will also lend extra support to one-person efforts when the "angle" seems especially interesting or unique, such as Renee Roberts's *Gifting It* (2002), which focused on Burning Man's gift economy and which received a great deal of publicity from the organization when it was released.[15]

Given the extent to which many Burners criticize the festival when they believe that it fails to live up to its ideals, it should not be surprising that some participants complain that this media relations process is overly controlling and bureaucratic.[16] Others complain that any media presence at Burning Man is tantamount to commercialization, as most media outlets rely on generating advertising revenues in order to sustain their operations and hence are seen by some Burners as profiting from this ideally decommodified event. For their part, the organization has learned several important and sometimes difficult lessons about the need to control the dispersal of or attempts to profit from images of the festival. For example, perhaps the most serious violations of privacy by a media entity at Burning Man to date occurred between 1997 and 2001 when a company called Voyeur Video issued a series of videos in which nude or partially nude female participants were intrusively filmed, without their knowledge or consent. The Burning Man organization successfully took Voyeur Video to court in 2002 to halt the sale of the videos.

Organizers have also repeatedly seen both the benefits of positive media coverage and the damage that can be done by negative reports, so they attempt to work closely with journalists. Outside perceptions have an impact on this unconventional event's ability to survive in the political climate of Nevada year after year. As one important example, in 1997 ABC's *Nightline* produced a one-hour special on Burning Man that portrayed the event in a positive light and also reported on some of the ways in which the festival was being squeezed financially by local bureaucrats. This attracted the attention of politicians at the state level and ultimately helped to ensure that the event would be allowed to continue in subsequent years. Another example of the media's substantial impact on the event, this time in a negative vein, occurred in 1999 when the Associated Press issued a story with the headline, "Drug Problem Surfaces at Burning Man," which claimed that between eighty and ninety people daily had required treatment for drug-related medical issues.[17] In fact, these numbers reflected the *total* number of daily medical incidents, the majority of which involved dehydration and miscellaneous cuts and scrapes and were not drug-related. The clinical director of REMSA later made a public statement that the reporter had misinterpreted the information he was given.[18]

Misrepresentation of the facts notwithstanding, the AP article was picked up by numerous outlets across the United States and had a direct and damaging effect on the event. The local authorities—who felt they could not afford to look "soft on drugs" in the eyes of their constituents— dramatically increased police presence at the event the next year, which not only resulted in more arrests but also contributed to a restless and potentially dangerous atmosphere brought on by participants' feelings that they were under siege. Burning Man organizers are now much more careful to correctly contextualize such information for reporters and assiduously downplay the incidence of recreational drug use at the event. Instead, the media are encouraged to explore story lines other than the obvious "sex, drugs, and rock-and-roll" angle, for example, and to instead focus on subtler (and perhaps more interesting) stories such as the event's interactions with and redefinitions of art, ritual, and culture. Since 2002 the Media and Artery Teams have collectively orchestrated an art tour for members of the media, so that they can view some of the finest art installations on the playa, as well as interview and photograph the artists with their work.[19]

Burning Man organizers' increased skill at media spin was aptly demonstrated after the 2003 event, when both print and broadcast coverage was dominated by reports of an extremely tragic accident in which a young woman lost her footing while stepping off of a slow-moving art car and was killed when she fell beneath the vehicle's wheels.[20] Whereas in the past press coverage might have portrayed such an accident in terms of irresponsibility or some inherent danger, the coverage instead stressed the entirely accidental nature of the tragedy, emphasizing that "event organizers work closely with local and federal safety officials to prevent accidents." Goodell was quoted as saying, "It is unfortunate that, despite these precautions, this unusual accident occurred."[21]

GOING NATIVE

While organizers have learned to become allies with the media, many participants continue to resist the media, perceiving it as fundamentally tied to corporate culture and as (potentially) responsible for reducing Burning Man to a commodified spectacle. The media have been viewed, to some extent correctly, as spectators at an event where participation is upheld as a key value and the motto "No Spectators" prevails. With this problematic dynamic in mind, organizers have not only instituted the registration process outlined above; they have also sought to invite the press to step outside of their usual reporting habits by calling on the event's participatory ethos. In 1998, in a unique attempt to reorient the traditional journalistic gaze toward a more reflexive practice of participant observation, the new Media Team decided to involve the press in an initiation rite. On checking in at the media tent, now officially dubbed "Media Mecca," reporters were asked to don one of a few dozen costumes that Media Team volunteers had collected for this purpose and to have their photographs taken with a Polaroid camera, which were then put on display at Media Mecca for the duration of the festival.[22] The intention was to encourage members of the media to "go native," or at least to adopt "native" dress, as well as to have the camera lens turned back on them for a change. This practice was not continued in subsequent years, having been determined to be a bit too cumbersome and perhaps confrontational when what was really needed for the media check-in process was both expediency and a welcoming attitude. However, another tradition begun that year, which continued as of 2009, was the distribution of a "press pass" with the tag line, "This pass entitles you to absolutely nothing. Immerse yourself!"[23]

The intention with these activities was to help media members become integrated into the event as full-fledged participants rather than distanced observers. As a member of the Media Team during that period, I can attest to seeing more than one reporter initially show up in khaki safari gear—resembling a stereotypical anthropologist or *National Geographic* reporter—only to come back two days later wearing nothing but a sarong and some body glitter.[24] Before 1998 many working media would come to the event only for a day, or stay in the hotel in nearby Gerlach. But from this point forward, they were not only encouraged to camp at the festival for as long as possible, they were required to do so if they wanted to secure key interviews with organizers such as Harvey. A new Media Team motto was displayed prominently on the cover of the press kit in 1999: "The best coverage of Burning Man always has been and always will be that which is profoundly personal. Immerse yourself."

In addition to pushing, and to some extent attempting to subvert, the boundaries between participant and observer (or native and outsider), the Media Team's attempts to reflexively situate the media in attendance tapped into a larger set of questions on notions of objectivity in journalism within the media itself. Michael Schudson has argued that "objectivity" should be understood to mean that

> a person's statements about the world can be trusted if they are submitted to established rules deemed legitimate by a professional community. Facts here are not aspects of the world, but consensually validated statements about it. . . . The process of news gathering itself constructs an image of reality which reinforces official viewpoints. . . . [Objectivity] is a practice rather than a belief. It is a "strategic ritual," as sociologist Gaye Tuchman puts it, which journalists use to defend themselves against mistakes and criticism.[25]

In this regard, the concept of objectivity functions as a *frame* though which the media perceives and represents events.[26] By the 1960s journalistic "objectivity" had come to be seriously questioned by many in the profession, a perspective prompted and nurtured by the larger social tensions and problems of the day. The "news" came more and more to be understood as commodity and therefore as subject to the whims and pressures of the market, as well as to the social forces of power and privilege (a critique that many Burners continue to launch against the media). One response to these observations and conflicts was the development of what was hailed as the "new journalism," characterized by narratives constructed from episodic scenes and a more subjective personal voice.[27]

As organizers hoped, some of the most thought-provoking and successful media coverage of the event does indeed come from those reporters who reflexively immerse themselves in the festival, who allow themselves to "go native" rather than remain at an artificial and self-imposed distance. For example, the *San Francisco Chronicle* reporter Robert Collier wrote a moving story about volunteering with David Best's 2001 Temple construction crew, and *Reason* magazine editor (and Burner since 1995) Brian Doherty wrote a lively and engaging history in his 2004 book, *This Is Burning Man*.[28] Although members of the media have often been seen as outsiders at the event, some of the earliest coverage was actually generated by "native" Burners who were professional journalists in the default world and who were motivated to share what they understood as a remarkable story with their readers. In particular, there was a series of early on-line *Wired* magazine articles in 1995 that set the stage for both a big cover story in the print version of *Wired* in 1996 and a coffee table collection of photographs from *HardWired*'s short-lived foray into book publishing, produced by Burners who were *Wired* employees.[29] In these regards, the boundaries between participants and observers (or insiders and outsiders) at Burning Man have always been occasionally vague and arbitrary, and in deliberately blurring these borders members of the media have encouraged to reflexively explore the frontiers of self, other, and culture alongside other participants.[30]

TROPES AND TECHNOPAGANS

Although organizers' reflexive turns and improved relations with the media have helped to reduce oversimplifications and unfavorable press, many mass media depictions of Burning Man have nevertheless tended to exoticize and sensationalize the event. This slant is in keeping with the media's propensity to focus primarily on bad news. As Schudson has observed, "News tends to emphasize conflict, dissention, and battle; out of a journalistic convention that there are two sides to any story, news heightens the appearance of conflict even in instances of relative calm."[31] Thus, even among some of the most well meaning reporters, who may even be dedicated Burners themselves or who have otherwise "gone native," the trend has been to capitalize on the more provocative or titillating aspects of the event, in keeping with the truism that stories eliciting shock and fear will sell more newspapers and airtime. By focusing on the weirdness, difference, or otherness of Burning Man, the media distance the event and its participants from what is considered normative.

One illustration of the tension between organizers' public relations efforts and journalists' interest in telling both compelling and truthful stories is the continued proclivity of many media representations to focus on sex, drugs, and rock-and-roll at the expense of other, less scandalous but perhaps equally provocative aspects of Burning Man. This is not to say that sex, drugs, and rock-and-roll are not to be found at Burning Man but rather that the media's sometimes too-singular focus on these aspects is the result of superficial impressions and not substantive examinations. For example, when I have spoken publicly about Burning Man over the years I have noticed that many individuals who have never been to the event assume that everyone, or at least a significant majority of participants, goes without clothing there. However, I have observed that though there are certainly some participants who delight in the "self-expressive" freedom to be fully or partially nude at the festival, it is by no means a majority, let alone universal, practice. While I have never attempted any systematic count, I would estimate that only approximately 10 percent or less of the population of Black Rock City is nude at any given moment. I believe that the widespread assumption that nudity is a common practice at the event says more about public preconceptions and exotic stereotypes, which have been fed by the media, than it does about what actually goes on.

Such stereotyping has certainly not escaped the notice of festival organizers. For example, in 1999 the Associated Press reported, "Organizers say they've gotten a bad rap in recent years from the media, which tends to focus on the nudity, pagan rituals, and hallucinogenic drugs that make the rounds."[32] Yet, of course, in attempting to turn the media's attention away from the ever-reliable shock value of "nudity, pagan rituals, and hallucinogenic drugs," this Burning Man spokesperson drew the reporter's attention right to it. Another instance of organizers' simultaneous resistance and capitulation to exoticizing stereotypes can be seen on one of the pages of the burningman.com Web site that is specifically directed to the media: the image selected to accompany an essay debunking the top "Media Myths" is of an individual who has painted his skin dark black and is wearing a brightly colored sarong and standing next to a cauldron of fire—giving the impression of a nonindigenous who has "gone tribal."[33] This correspondence may be entirely unintentional, but it more likely reflects a degree of sardonic acceptance and self-satire that, in its way, comments on the dynamics of the media's deployment of exoticizing tropes.

The following examples show these othering language strategies in operation and highlight the ways in which Burning Man is repeatedly painted with reference to some kind of regressive paganism or primitive tribalism while also declaring it is the ultimate technological or post-modern happening.

> The primitive survivalist aspects of the festival may seem to contrast with the digital world of its inhabitants, but Burning Man has become a pastiche of various parts of our culture and history. It has the spontaneous-gathering feel of Woodstock, the spirituality and temporary community of the Rainbow Gathering, the campiness, outrageousness and identity-transformation of the drag-queen scene, the edginess and danger of a Harley-Davidson convention and the burning and worship of, well, the ancient Druids.[34]

> It is fair to say that Burning Man is *the* influential tribal-techno-feral-pagan-digital event, happening, rave or whatever in the world. Out there in the desert, witches, warlocks and wired sorcerers use technology as if it were some electronic crystal ball. It is a living post-postmodernist Hieronymous Bosch painting with just a touch of Fellini.[35]

> It is a curious waltz between the beginning of the millennium and its end. There *is a pre-Christian paganism* that befits this ancient rock: the pilgrimage, the boulevard leading to The Man and his incineration, during which people dance and whoop in the smoke. . . . It is also about cyberspace—an assembly organised entirely through the internet. Most campers are cybergeeks; *Wired* magazine called the festival "the holiday of choice for the Digerati."[36]

As these quotations demonstrate, the media's proclivity to sensationalize Burning Man often pulls the event in two directions simultaneously—toward the primitive and the high-tech, the premodern and postmodern. To note just a few more relevant newspaper headlines and copy that drive this point home: "Tech Crowd Gets Tribal";[37] "Modern Primitive Make Burning Man Hottest Ever";[38] "a bizarre techno-primitive gathering of thousands of artists, exhibitionists, pyromaniacs and freaks";[39] "Burning Man's techno-tribalism makes Glastonbury and Woodstock look like suburban Tupperware sales";[40] and the following:

> Furrowed brows outside the press trailer: my colleagues in the media and I are finding it hard to fix a label on all this. Is it guerrilla performance art or a pyromaniacs' ball? "Mad Max" or "Priscilla, Queen of the Desert"? Is it, as previous journalists have suggested, "an atavistic, avant-garde, neo-pagan flame-back," "a post-modern carnival of the absurd," or a "post-hippie proto-apocalyptic art ritual?"

> The founder of the Burning Man, an elegantly ravaged San Francisco artist and landscape gardener named Larry Harvey, can discourse for hours on the meaning of the festival. Sitting on a deckchair in a dark suit and black hat, smoking cigarette after cigarette, he spins and weaves his theories, explaining the Burning Man in terms of post-Freudian identity crises, the demise of primitive mythocentric religions, and the sterility of

the corporate-controlled consumerism which passes for culture in America these days. "These are post-modern times," he says at one point. "Everything that's ever happened before is happening now, in one form or another, but none of it really compels us, and transforms us. We can access unimaginable quantities of information and images through the internet, we can communicate with everyone in the world, but so what? The Burning Man Festival celebrates technology as a potential tool for freedom, but it also reverts back to something primordial, prehistoric, proverbial. Throughout our evolution, in all corners of the planet, human beings have come together and gathered around fire, and this ritual still invokes a very basic, primal response."[41]

The above vignette in particular demonstrates not only the journalists' struggle to classify the event by looking to one another's explications but also Larry Harvey's own awareness of the event's paradoxical techno-pagan elements. This collective search to "fix a label" on Burning Man not only evinces a desire to define and frame this event by circumscribing it in a simplistic but catchy sound-bite; it can also be understood as part of the shared quest to discern the *meaning* of the festival, an exercise that all Burners (including, and perhaps especially, Larry Harvey) enact to some extent. Because this conversation was conveyed into the public sphere, it contributed to the persistence of the technopagan trope so prevalent in descriptions of the event, perhaps generating other buzz phrases for subsequent journalists. The Burning Man organization itself has parodied the attempt to boil the event down to a pithy adage with a feature called "The Burning Man Phrase Generator©" that appears at the bottom of the "Media Myths" page. Prefacing it for the media as "The Easy Way Out," organizers declare that if "the task of understanding Burning Man seems insuperable or inconvenient, we have prepared an easily employed device for instantly generating copy. The following Burning Man Phrase Generator© has been compiled from many reputable sources and requires no thought whatsoever."[42] My own random test of this system produced the phrases "retro-tribal-futuristic-orgy," "nerdo-druidic-underground-conspiracy," and "crypto-hipster-dada-hoedown."

Another common media theme, also highlighted in many of the examples cited above, frames the event with reference to its apparent religious or spiritual qualities. For example:

> The burning seems symbolic of many things. It could be taken as a purging, cleansing ceremony in your basic spiritual kind of way. A sort of group re-birthing if you like, but without the artsy fartsy, hippy trippy, New Agey stuff. Like its famous ancestor, Woodstock, Burning Man is

also a celebration of change, but it takes it a lot further. It is about the pulling down of old belief systems and structures, and replacing them, if only temporarily, with a new autonomous zone.[43]

The heat, the dust, the lack of water and amenities—all form a crucible where great art is created, deep connections are made and people undergo genuine spiritual transformations.[44]

The media's interest in the potential spiritual resonance of this event was perhaps most noticeable in 2003, when several reporters picked up on the Beyond Belief theme. Associated Press reporter Don Thompson called the Graduate Theological Union (where I was a student at the time) and spoke with President James Donahue, who speculated, "This can be anything from a kind of playfulness, to narcissism, to a more serious spiritual quest. . . . It is what you make of it. People bring their own interests and desires to it."[45] The article also quoted GTU professor Jerome Baggett: "The people who are going to Burning Man—Boomers and Xers—are the most educated generations in history. They're trained to question."[46] Sarah Pike (from California State University, Chico) was also quoted as stating, "It can be a religious experience, but there's no particular dogma that's adhered to. . . . This is moving for people who don't feel comfortable with organized religion."[47] Aside from the ironic and delightful happenstance that Baggett and Pike both served on my dissertation committee, these perspectives also contributed to the public positioning of Burning Man as an alternative to traditional religions. Participants likewise continue to echo this narrative, such as one individual who was quoted in this article stating, "I find Burning Man is spirituality without the church, without all the religious practices. . . . It doesn't come with any of the traditional strings attached."[48]

The media repeatedly turn toward "paganism" as the religious "type" that appears to be most clearly reflected in Burning Man's ritualism. For example, Thompson employed descriptors such as "bizarre rites," "bacchanalia," and "ancient ceremonies and symbolic sacrifices that barely echo today in modern mainstream Western religions"; and two participants were quoted as saying, "Burning Man touches something primal—it doesn't have words"; "I'm a pagan and this is a chance for me to dress in a bizarre way, but also to flaunt my paganism."[49] Michael York has contended that paganism may be best understood as a "root religion"; that is, to some extent it underlies all global religions. As we have seen, while Burning Man lacks any avowed theology and remains ideologically distanced from "religion," it nevertheless displays a number of ritualistic elements and motifs that echo this underlying root paganism in the "basic, primal response" (to borrow Harvey's own term) that the event can generate in participants' experiences. Similarly, York has argued, "Inasmuch as paganism is the root of religion, it confronts the earliest, the most immediate, and the least processed apprehensions of the sacred. This is the experiential level on which paganism in both its indigenous and contemporary forms wishes to concentrate."[50]

The media's persistent use of exoticizing, othering, and distancing strategies may limit other ways to perceive and portray the event. Of course, not every media representation of Burning Man relies on these tropes, as evinced in the *Gifting It* or *Beyond Black Rock* documentaries or the ABC *Nightline* episode, among many others. Furthermore, and especially in light of Harvey's own contributions to these themes, there are certainly numerous observable aspects of Burning Man that readily lend themselves to a technopagan narrative (see DVD, chap. 2). Participants often adopt dress that embraces what has come to be called the "modern primitive style," replete with tattoos, body piercing, and body painting that draw from a variety of global indigenous motifs and futuristic and technological images, in keeping with the high degree of cultural appropriation and hybridity this event. But while these may be among Burning Man's more visually stunning elements, they are not the only aesthetics visible at this heterogeneous festival.

CYBERGEEKS, ON-LINE COMMUNITIES, AND CULTURAL CONVERGENCES

If there is truth to the perceived "pagan" elements of Burning Man, there is also considerable ground for the "techno" half of the technopagan trope. As the media shape public perceptions and individual expectations of the event, it can also serve to attract certain populations. For example, the appearance of Burning Man on E!'s "Top Ten Parties" list in 2004 may have resulted in an upsurge in attendance by the "Ibiza set," or party seekers. Perhaps the clearest incidence of this direct effect was by way of the November 1996 *Wired* magazine cover story in which the science-fiction writer Bruce Sterling proclaimed Burning Man the "New American Holiday" for the "Digerati" (see DVD, chap. 2).[51]

Less important, perhaps, than the substance of this piece was the publication in which it appeared. It drew numerous new participants to the event from the San Francisco Bay Area and Silicon Valley "techie" communities, many of whom were awash in healthy amounts of disposable

income during the dot-com heyday of the late 1990s. This contributed
significantly to the course the event would take in those years, as demonstrated by an increase in large-scale, technologically complex, and ex-
pensively produced artwork. In addition, several high-profile high-tech
individuals are known to have attended during that period, including
Jeff Bezos, CEO of Amazon.com, and Google founders Larry Page and
Sergey Brin, among others.[52]

A good deal of media coverage about Burning Man in the late 1990s
focused on the considerable influence of the dot-com boom and culture
on the event, featuring headlines such as "Bonfire of the Techies: Hordes
of Playful Digerati Assemble for a Hallowed Annual Rite"[53] and "Geeks
at Burning Man: Or How I Spent My Summer Vacation on the Playa."[54]
When the dot-com bubble burst in 2001, the headlines shifted to "Burning Man's Dotcom Hangover"[55] and "Dot-Com Fallout Hits Burning
Man: Decline in Attendance Tied to Economic Downturn."[56] This association would continue in later years as evinced by ongoing coverage of
Burning Man and related events in tech publications such as *Wired* and
C-Net, as well as by the ongoing involvement of many Bay Area Burners
in the tech industry.

That Burning Man should be attractive to members of both the alternative and technological subcultures comes as no surprise to those familiar
with these realms. Indeed, many Burners continue to be early adopters of
new media technologies, and as early as 1996 Burning Man organizers
were attempting to webcast live from the event. The intersections and mu-
tual nativity of the alternative and techie subcultures, particularly in the
Bay Area, has been documented by Fred Turner in his examination of the
Well (which stands for "Whole Earth 'Lectronic Link"), which was an influential early on-line networking forum.[57] The Well's developer, Stewart
Brand, had previously published the popular *Whole Earth Catalogues* that
served as bibles for the countercultures of the late 1960s and early 1970s.
Burning Man had a presence on the Well by 1994 and launched its own
Web site (burningman.com) a few years later.

The Internet came to serve as an essential organizing, communications, and community-building tool for Burning Man organizers as well
as the larger Burning Man community. In addition to the burningman
.com site, numerous commercial media Web sites have produced features on Burning Man, and thousands of participants have created their
own Web sites and Web pages to showcase their photos, share their stories, and organize their theme camps. Burners all over the world stay connected year-round through numerous regional and global e-mail discussion

lists, along with on-line bulletin boards such as burningman.com's "e-playa," as well as other on-line community, social networking, or blogging Web sites such as tribe.net, livejournal.com, and facebook.com, where participants have developed Burning Man–related forums and pages. In addition, participants in the popular virtual world known as secondlife.com have held a "Burning Life" event concurrent with or shortly after the Burning Man festival since 2003, in which computer-generated avatars congregate to "burn" a digital Man on a playa-esque virtual landscape. Finally, there are numerous subscription-based e-mail discussion lists that have been popular vehicles for year-round conversations about the event and as spaces for community building, such as burnman-list@ dioxine.net, as well as several regional discussion lists hosted or supported by the organization, including newyork-list@burningman.com, burningman-list@burnaustin.org, and playadust@euroburners.org, to name just a few, and there are doubtless countless other on-line venues for Burning Man.[58] Thus, not only has Burning Man been portrayed as a playground for computer geeks, but Burners have turned to the Internet as a space in which to continue to "radically express" themselves, sharing their experiences of the event with the world through this medium and building community.

The Internet is the media sector in which the line between participant and observer may be most noticeably obscured, and both the festival and the Internet can be seen as potential zones for radical inclusivity and radical self-expression. Burning Man has likewise been compared to the Internet as an open and seemingly limitless space populated by individual nodes for creativity and community, whether theme camps or Web sites.[59] On-line media are distinguished from other forms of media in their transparent interactivity and reciprocity, as well as by the unrestricted access available to any potential user with the means to access and manipulate the technology. A renewed focus on designing interactive, participatory, and collective applications for the Internet came to be called the web 2.0 movement.[60] These tools—including open source programming, user-generated content, social networks, and blogs—increased the relative ease with which anyone could establish her or his own "media" site and thereby "talk back" to, or even supplant, the mass media. In the visibly reflexive media of the Internet, the extent to which all members of a society participate in the themes and tropes that shape constructions and experiences of culture likewise become ever more apparent. Henry Jenkins has called this process and its wide-ranging societal impacts "convergence culture," meaning a place "where old and new media collide, where grassroots and corporate media intersect, where the power of the media producer and the power of the media consumer interact in unpredictable ways."[61] According to Jenkins, this shift in the flows of media content from the top down to the bottom up is fostering a more "participatory culture" and building "collective intelligence."[62]

Burners, like many Internet participants, often use both the playa and the Internet as spaces in which to negotiate and reformulate individual and collective identities. For example, as we have seen, some Burners adopt "playa names" for use at the festival and also employ these monikers as Internet identities, such as e-mail addresses and other on-line handles, thus potentially integrating whatever qualities are felt to be represented by these nicknames across the playa, virtual, and default worlds.[63] Sherry Turkle has concluded that constructions of identity in on-line spaces exemplify the ways in which "the self is multiple and constructed by language."[64] Others have explored the Internet as a medium not only for exploring individual identities but also as spaces for community building.[65] For example, Mary Chayko has described Internet-based relationships as "sociomental," meaning "an experience of communion with another person, one that does not depend on face-to-face meetings to be initiated or maintained."[66] Burning Man, of course, is both a virtual and an "embodied" community, and many Burners who participate in Internet-based communities related to the festival endeavor to meet their on-line companions face-to-face, a fairly common occurrence among many other on-line communities and friendships, which in this case is facilitated through regional events and parties, as well as, naturally, through the Burning Man event itself.

It is tempting to borrow, yet again, the concept of liminality to describe and analyze the betwixt and betweenness of virtual realms and to compare the "experience of communion" found in some Internet-based communities with the concept of communitas. These parallels should not be stretched too thinly here, but it is still worth recalling the large-scale emanations of communitas that Dayan and Katz argued were prone to manifest through broadcast media events and rituals. While more decentralized and dispersed, it does seem that something like the bonding of communitas can occur in on-line communities as well. The immersive and consciousness-absorbing quality of these spaces can foster a sense of being freed from normative social identities, as well as of being disembodied and in between worlds, that resonates with notions of the liminoid.

Yet as with all other social and cultural contexts, on-line communities are inherently polyvocal. The Internet is simultaneously a place where genuine human ties and communities are forged and a space for multiple contested and competing voices. This is certainly apparent in Burning Man's on-line communities. While various forums have waxed and waned in popularity over the years—shifting from the old burnman-list@dioxine.com to the e-playa, tribe.net, and beyond—in each of these spaces a lively diversity of narratives and critiques proliferated, which can in turn influence the direction and nature of the event.[67] In this sense, the Internet can be a space for everyone to actively participate in what Carey termed the "the maintenance of society in time" and the "representation of shared beliefs," even while others such as Couldry have critiqued claims that the mass media wield socially unifying, centralizing, and totalizing authority.[68] Recent media scholarship is justly wary of technological determinism, whereby the media technologies themselves are presumed to utterly control the development of cultures, as well as of the methodological pitfalls of the "effects paradigm," which purports that the media's social "effects" are driven unilaterally from media producers to purely passive audiences.[69] In this vein, it is important to remember that it is not simply the case that the Internet is shaping culture but rather that it is culture that is shaping the Internet. Various cultural forces—including the interactivity and democracy of the Internet—are mutually and reflexively responsible for the evolution of cultures and "subcultures" and in turn religions and "alternative spiritualities." Burning Man's technopaganism creatively appropriates, rehearses, and negotiates symbolic resources in order to patch together do-it-yourself spiritualities, identities, and communities that are participatory, hybrid, and heterodox. In this regard, "convergence culture" is a metaphor that not only describes emerging changes between the media and the public but also may be in tune with significant cultural shifts in the way that the American public is thinking about, discussing, practicing, and imagining religions and spiritualities, especially within spaces like Burning Man.

"SHOOTING RITES"

This discussion of the intersections between Burning Man and the media would be incomplete without some reflection on my own participation in this regard. As mentioned previously, I am a former member of Burning Man's Media Team, which was an invaluable source for much of the information in this book and also meant that I had a direct hand in shaping some of the data during the years I was involved.[70] It is likewise hoped that this book and DVD will play a part in shaping public perceptions of and dialogues about the event. I should also state that I did not initially set out to produce a visual documentary when I first began my research, although I understood the tremendous potential it could have. However, I had concluded that my greater challenge was to streamline and simplify my dissertation rather than to enrich or expand it. Happily, after completing graduate school, I was encouraged to expand my work into its current form, including the supplementary DVD, and was quite fortunate that the basic resources needed to do so were readily available through my own family. My husband, Ron Meiners, had been collecting footage of the event as a personal project since he first began attending in 1998, and I was equally fortunate that my mother, Elizabeth Gilmore, has decades of professional experience with documentary video production and that she was willing to assist me in undertaking the editing of the DVD. Hence, when University of California Press expressed interest not only in my manuscript but also in possibly producing a video to accompany the text, I readily accepted the challenge because I understood the potential pedagogic and analytic benefits for students, researchers, and nonacademics alike.

Given the fact that the DVD was an afterthought, we were often limited by the footage we happened to have. We initially struggled with how to piece the odd snippets of art, ritual, and interviews captured somewhat at random over the years into a coherent narrative that would complement the text. For a brief time, we considered simply splicing together a selection of raw images, so as to perhaps create an impression of the chaos and random cultural juxtapositions that characterize the event. Ultimately, however, we created a singular and somewhat independent narrative—closely dovetailed with the text while also capable of standing alone—and structured this primarily around an interview of myself conducted with Ron's assistance. Hence, just as this text is woven from numerous different experiences filtered through my own point of view—and just as Burners patch together their experiences of the event and its meanings for their lives from the elements and moments that randomly and serendipitously present themselves—so too did we assemble the video from fragmented scraps and images not initially collected for this purpose. The final product is not perfectly polished. Shots may not always be perfectly steady, and voices may sometimes be less than perfectly clear in the cacophony of the playa. But these ostensible limitations seem appropriate to the nature of the event, which is itself far from a perfectly controlled or orchestrated happening.

Knowing that there were many aspects of the event for which we lacked footage, I sought out a few small-scale rites to shoot in order to fill some of these gaps. Perusing the 2006 *What-Where-When*—a small booklet distributed at the gate every year that lists numerous parties, performances, rituals, classes, and other events planned by participants in various theme camps—I selected a Shabbat service slated for sundown Friday at the *Conexus Cathedral* (see chap. 3). It struck me that this would provide an interesting convergence of ritual themes by simultaneously bridging Judaism, Christianity, and Burning Man in one particular moment in time and space (see DVD, chap. 5). This would prove to be an object lesson on the promise and perils of "shooting rites."[71]

I was fortunate to have the company of my niece, Yaffa. Not only was it enjoyable to share this experience with her, she was able to provide a running commentary on some of the Hebrew songs and prayers. Further contributing to this family affair, Ron graciously agreed to do the shooting so that I could participate and observe the rite in other ways. What little filming I undertook for this project convinced me that it is not my favorite role, an observation that itself entails considerable methodological consequences. When I stand behind the camera, I feel distanced from an event and less fully present and attentive; I am more focused on ensuring that I get good footage than on paying attention to the emotional and embodied atmosphere of the surrounding scene. While shooting does afford the luxury of reviewing at length and in detail what was captured by the lens, other particulars may be absent.

As described above, members of the media are expected to curtail the potential invasiveness of their cameras in their efforts to capture the event, as is explicitly stated in the press guidelines:

> One of the abiding principles of Burning Man is that participants do not interfere with the immediate experience of other participants. As a member of the media, you are expected to be respectful and comport yourself accordingly. If you do, your coverage will be far more authentic and meaningful. If any participant asks you to stop filming, you must stop immediately. If you continue to photograph or film, you face the possibility of being escorted from the event.[72]

As a onetime Media Team volunteer, I have long been a champion of these principles and was especially sensitive to such concerns after agreeing to produce a video in conjunction with this book. I was therefore very careful to identify the Shabbat's organizers ahead of time and ask their permission to shoot, which they had no problem with, nor did anyone else I spoke with.

With all this in mind, I was stunned when soon after the Shabbat service began, two men with professional still cameras jumped up on the Cathedral's altar, which was immediately behind the acting rabbi and the rest of the participants who were gathered in a circle facing her, and started snapping away. Yaffa's stubborn and solid sense of propriety prompted her to intervene. She whispered to one of the photographers, who by then was no longer perched on the high altar, asking him to please stop. Relating the conversation to me later, she told me he had responded, with an Israeli accent, "I'm a Jew, and I'm shooting this for the Jewish Museum of New York." Yaffa had replied, "That's nice. I'm also a Jew, and how would you feel if someone was doing this in your synagogue?" The photographer did not stop. At this point, Ron also decided he wouldn't stand for this guy interfering with the ritual and behaving disrespectfully to his niece, and he briefly put his camera down and stepped aside to call him on his behavior. Eventually, both offending photographers backed off, and throughout all this the service continued as though none of these distractions were taking place. There were songs, prayers, and circle dances. There was also challah that was incredibly dry from playa exposure, although Manischewitz has never tasted better than it did that evening.

Months later, in reviewing the footage we captured there, I was disappointed that very little of the conflict came across in our footage. While it showed glimpses of the intrusive photographers, the drama that I remember in that moment did not exist on video. Many professional photographers—like those we encountered at this Shabbat service—have learned that in order to capture the quality footage they require, they must not be shy about getting right up to the front line of whatever event they happen to be documenting. When shooting rites, this often means that they enter into the ritual space, such that they can become de facto actors in the rite itself. But because Ron, a former Media Team volunteer like me, was highly sensitized to minimize his interference in the immediate experience of the rite, his shooting style was much more reserved and polite. Furthermore, his impulse to intervene in the situation meant that his attention shifted from prudent observation to deliberate participation. As a result, the event as I vividly remembered it was not captured on tape. For her part, my mother's editorial sensibilities told her that the footage of the *Conexus* Shabbat wasn't particularly compelling, and she argued that we should leave this rite on the cutting room floor.

There are clearly some problematic elements to this rite, its "shooting," and its narrative. One irony is that—of the myriad performances and rituals we captured on tape—this most clearly "religious" rite comes across as not very exciting visually. It consisted largely of people standing around and singing rather than dramatically costumed characters leaping and dancing about in flames and flesh. Moreover, while I was offended by the photographer's lack of ritual courtesy, I must also admit that I was fascinated and oddly thrilled by the potentially juicy anecdote, leaving me—the ostensibly dispassionate ethnographer—in the position of having had my own family members substantially shape the data I was there allegedly only to record. My presence in this rite was on many levels rather awkward, so perhaps it is only natural if the narrative here likewise displays a certain unease and vulnerability. However, rather than erase that vulnerability from the text, I have chosen to foreground it as a problem for the reader.

The creation of an accompanying DVD entails practical methodological consequences that would not be borne by a textual narrative alone. Visual documentation of events tends to implicitly construct the appearance of reality, resulting in the impression that the whole story is accurately and completely represented. But depending on a series of decisions made both on location and in the editing suite, the visual documentation of rites can obscure, hide, or even blatantly lie, as some aspects of a given event may be faithfully reproduced while others may remain offscreen. As Grimes has written, the act of "shooting rites" does many things: it "documents, reveals, validates, publicizes, mystifies, constructs, dramatizes, violates, (dis)embodies, and complicates."[73] My own project participates in all of these consequences. As we learned at the *Conexus* Shabbat, the presence of the camera in ritual entails numerous ethical concerns for both actors and observers and can change the rite's performance. In rendering a series of disparate moments into a coherent narrative framework and in placing these in the public realm, the contents of this DVD and this text serve to reify select perspectives and occurrences— underscoring and flattering my ideas about Burning Man—while minimizing or disregarding many others.

CONCLUSION

Whether focused on Burning Man's ritual, tribal, technological, or other aspects, the event's relationships with print, broadcast, film, and online media are multifaceted. The Internet in particular has come to be fundamental to Burning Man's community-building mission—both on- and off-line—by helping participants stay connected to other Burners well be-yond the physical and temporal limitations of the event, such that the "Burning Man community" has a truly global scope. The Internet also serves to both internally and externally represent and co-create the event, as participants use on-line spaces to share, build on, and contest the experience with one another and with the rest of the world.

For their part, event organizers have invested a great deal of effort in building positive relationships with representatives of various forms of media in order to foster more sensitive portrayals of the event and thus protect it from the potentially destructive consequences of "bad press." These measures in turn shape how the event is both publicly viewed and individually experienced. It may seem incongruous that the Burning Man organization seeks to transgress many social norms while also not want-ing to be publicly portrayed as "too" transgressive or as transgressive in the wrong ways. Fundamentally, however, this impetus stems from the organizers' learned political savvy and should be understood as a re-sponse to incumbent realities of the default world that must be capitu-lated to, or at least cautiously treaded around, including the need to maintain healthy relationships with local Nevada authorities and the de-sire to protect both individuals and the event from commercial exploita-tion. Such tensions should not be surprising given that the event is a par-adoxical attempt to institutionalize a temporary autonomous zone.

By using the media to convey their unconventional social vision to a much larger audience, organizers have sought not only to manage the event's public image but also, ultimately, to use the media to influence mainstream culture. In the course of the explosive upsurge in atten-dance at the event in the mid-1990s, Harvey consciously decided that he wanted as many people as possible to experience Burning Man—despite the logistical difficulties this imposed—and in this he recognized that the media were key to spreading the message. In these regards, a central strategy for ensuring more favorable coverage of the event has been to rely on Burning Man's participatory ethos by encouraging journalists to reorient their gaze toward a more intersubjective stance, thereby gener-ating a number of more personally and contextually located perspectives on the event.

While the parallels between the media and social rituals should not be overextended, they can provide a starting point for understanding and contextualizing some of the themes and habits that the media repeatedly employ, as their representations can constitute frequently used tropes that

result from common framing practices. The free-form and dynamic syncretism of Burning Man can readily be seen as a pastiche of the "primitive" or "premodern" that is unfolding in a distinctively "high-tech" or
"postmodern" context. For Burners, both the "techno" and the "pagan"
may be viewed as more authentic options than the old or default media,
ritual, and culture, thus resonating with and reflecting participants' experiences and constructions of the festival. This process is in turn fed by
the media, generating causal and reflexive loops between individuals
and media, private and public, participants and spectators, self and other,
normative and deviant.

Burners are certainly not passive consumers of media. They constantly
debate, contest, and even mock the meanings of Burning Man, along with
the implications of various mass media portrayals of the event and each
others' interpretations.[74] In some cases, the art of Burning Man specifically comments on and parodies passive media culture, as could be seen
in a 2003 installation, *The Medium Is the Religion* (fig. 8; see also DVD,
chap. 4). Constituting a wry comment on the potential passivity and mind-
lessness of both mass media and mass religion, this piece was composed
of three rows of church pews, each with a number of television sets seated
on them, all facing an imposing podium on which sat the largest television

FIGURE 8. Irie Takeshi, *The Medium Is the Religion,* 2003. Photo by
Lee Gilmore.

set. The very acts of writing, filming, and editing likewise serve to mediate and frame certain perspectives while missing out on numerous others. Through repetition and adroit manipulation of cultural symbols, the
media, like ritual, can help to create perceptions of unity in the ways in
which social events are experienced by providing pervasive and
prescriptive—yet flexible and fluid—frameworks for understanding.

CHAPTER 6

Burn-a-lujah!

Year after year, thousands of individuals seeking a temporary alternative to the mundane routines and norms of their ordinary lives make a journey to northwestern Nevada for the Burning Man festival, where a whimsical, opulent, and chaotic stage is set on the encrusted clay and dust of the Black Rock playa. What started as a small gathering around an impromptu beach bonfire has evolved into a substantial global movement that is continuing to expand its influence as a public happening. While evading specific correlations with innumerable historical antecedents and parallels, Burning Man derives much of its resonance from a wealth of cultural sources—from mythological wicker men to contemporary culture jammers. In embarking on this laborious pilgrimage, tens of thousands of individuals descend on the desert intent on building a transient, imaginative, and flourishing civic community in the wilderness. Participants both voluntarily contribute to and vociferously critique the substantial organizational effort and infrastructure required by a festival of this size and complexity and in so doing assert their sense of ownership of the event. Within this uniquely absurd theater of the body and the mind, Burners perform a panoply of themes evoking spirituality, religion, ritual, art, hybridity, liminality, communitas, reflexivity, transformation, pilgrimage, authenticity, and otherness, to name just a few. Through these creative and sometimes contradictory enactments, Burning Man plays with and renders visible the underlying cultural construction of these and numerous other elements typically assumed to be empirical in nature.

Burning Man is at once sacred, secular, and neither. Burners desire transformative, direct, and visceral encounters that are inherently diverse and disputable as the event remains at core "whatever you want it to be." Neither Burning Man organizers nor participants consider the festival an enactment of "religion," yet at the same time both groups are likely to invoke "spirituality" as something to be discovered and embraced through the event. Burners often talk about spirituality as if it were distinguishable from religion, thus expressing their dissatisfaction with or distrust of traditional religious institutions by framing their own spiritual quests as conceptually distinct from what are viewed as default religious options. A small minority described themselves as adherents of specific religious traditions, but a larger number described themselves as spiritual but not traditionally religious. Others rejected both spirituality and religion as having significant currency in their own meaning-making processes, although some of these respondents also spoke of desires for a sense of connectedness and transformation that was similar to what others described as spirituality, seeking these experiences both in the context of Burning Man and elsewhere in their lives.

Rather than point to either "spirituality" or "religion" as essentially distinct categories or binary opposites, Burning Man, on closer examination, destabilizes these concepts, offering a window onto them as a dialectic. Religious institutions have historically been subject to innumerable critiques stemming from desires for authenticity and transformation, spawning new institutional (or anti-institutional) structures. Thus hypothetical distinctions between "religion" and "spirituality" may be more productively conceived in terms of ongoing and dialogic exchanges between individual and collective, inspiration and institution, spontaneity and liturgy, revelation and text. In this regard, the experiences held by many Burners as sacred or transformational are no less—and from their perspective, perhaps even more—genuine than many of the basic encounters that in Western cultures have long been held to be aspects of religion. Ultimately, what matters more to Burners than academic quibbles about what properly constitutes spirituality, religion, or authenticity are their own immediate and idiosyncratic experiences, their encounters with community, their cathartic and visceral rites, and the challenges met and overcome in the crucible of the desert.

Because Christianities are frequently judged by Burners, as well as other seekers of alternative spiritualities, to be irredeemably laden with repressiveness, tedium, and corruption, their quests often turn to and borrow from non-Christian sources that are considered somehow more "authentic" or to retain an ideological "purity," which in this case tends to mean Eastern or indigenous cultural and religious traditions. The extent to which participants engage in cross-cultural borrowing and hybridity renders Burning Man a kind of cultural pastiche where symbols arising out of just about any context may emerge and be offered up for interpretation and reinterpretation, as can be seen in innumerable symbolically saturated works of art, including individuals' costuming and play, which adopt, synthesize, and sometimes parody diverse religious elements. At the same time, Burning Man's most prominent rites are held to remain free of dogma or orthodoxy. Participants generate a wide variety of rituals and performances that evince this inherent heterodoxy but which also share in certain common transformational themes, such as creation, destruction, sacrifice, and redemption. The Burning Man itself evokes these narratives and serves as a primary symbol of and for the event. Other fiery works of art such as the Temples have also invited these sentiments and indeed have sometimes done so in a way that many Burners have come to perceive as more authentic or immediate than the Burning of the Man. Although sometimes the event's ritual structures have failed to achieve these desired goals—and participants typically decry rites that leave them feeling like spectators—over the years, these rites have induced palpable encounters with collective unity and individual catharsis for many Burners.

Some Burning Man rites also reflect the frameworks of classic ritual theories, which may say more about Western cultural expectations of what ritual is and what it should be than about the indigenous rites that formed the basis of many of Turner's and others' initial observations and analyses. Not only was Turner himself reflexively absorbing elements of popular culture, or countercultures, into his most provocative theorizing, his ideas have since found their way into Western cultural consciousness such that they have come to recursively influence events like Burning Man. In this way, ritual theories can be read as yet another of the cultural themes that proliferate around and inspire Burning Man.

In positioning Burning Man in ideological opposition to what is understood as the *default* worldview, Burners have evolved and embraced a set of core principles—including participation, self-expression, self-reliance, community, inclusiveness, gifting, and environmental responsibility—that many seek to actualize not only on the playa but also in the default world. When sincerely adopted, these tenets—in tandem with the challenges necessitated by the unforgiving circumstances of desert survival and the overwhelming proliferation of artistic creativity—tend to prompt self-reflection and self-examination on the part of participants, often leading to powerful and life-changing experiences. Although Burners typically eschew theological orthodoxies and fixed ideologies, this performative ethos engenders a sense of orthopraxy. Given that participants characteristically interpret their experiences of the event in a plethora of idiosyncratic and complex voices, the practice of collectivity is by no means flawless or homogeneous. Still, in seeking to make sense of these experiences, Burners recurrently spoke of various exchanges between *self* and *other* as fostering their feelings of transformation through the event. For some, this self-reflection and self-examination was inspired by newfound or reinforced communities; others emphasized their increased sense of inspiration and creativity, and still others came away with a renewed or refocused worldview, among many other possibilities. These feelings were also attributed in part to the harsh and physically demanding desert environment, which evokes potent and romantic narratives of pilgrimage, transformation, and spirituality that are deeply embedded in the Western cultural imagination. In these regards, the experience of Burning Man invites an awareness of individuals' particular positions within the constructs of normative or default culture, alongside increased understandings of the fundamental plasticity and mutability of both the self and the culture that is its context.

Burners re-create themselves, even if only temporarily, by appropriating an endless variety of cultural symbols and themes, turning in part to a romanticized premodernity as well as a futuristic postmodernity for inspiration and thereby reflect "touristic" quests for authenticity, otherness, and the exotic. This process is also mirrored in the public lens of the mass media, which has often framed the event as "technopagan." The practice of journalism bears some basic similarities to the enterprise of ethnography in the simple act of going out into the world to find human stories to tell. Yet while some journalists are concerned about the elusiveness of objectivity, by and large there remains an absence of self-reflexivity in mass media endeavors. This has an impact on the public representation of Burning Man, as the media repetitively and ritualistically tend to turn to preencoded tropes as means by which to frame their portrayals of public events. In recent years, however, the interactivity and access afforded by Internet-based media have enabled a wider public to increasingly insert its voice into the popular discourse, illustrating the extent to which the media do not simply churn out one-way authoritative transmissions but rather operate in complex, culturally embedded, and mutually influential contexts.

In bringing this book to a close, I wish to look toward some of the ways in which Burning Man's cultural reach is being creatively enacted and extended into social realms beyond Black Rock City. In particular,

the ritualistic performances and activism of a group called Reverend
Billy and the Stop Shopping Gospel Choir—both on the playa and off—
keenly reflect many of the core issues and aspirations of Burning Man.[1]
Although Reverend Billy did not emerge directly out of the Burning Man
festival, he shares and has been influenced by its ethos, and the two have
come to enjoy an important and fruitful relationship. Furthermore, this
final example allows me to conclude by looking not only toward some of
the larger potential social and political implications that may be at play
here but also back on my own experiences at Burning Man and the extent to which these have reflexively shaped my perspectives on the event.

THE TWO-THIRDS POINT IN THE NARRATIVE

Reverend Billy first appeared at Burning Man in 2003, performing on a
stage constructed especially for this purpose at the foot of the *Great
Temple* that formed the base of the Man that year. Costumed as a stereotypical evangelical preacher, complete with a clerical collar, a white
polyester sport coat, and a blond pompadour, Reverend Billy preached
in a fire-and-brimstone style about the sins of consumerism, multina-
tional corporations, war, and social hypocrisy. He was accompanied by
more than two dozen individuals dressed in bright satin robes—the Stop
Shopping Gospel Choir—singing vibrant gospel music. I later learned
that Reverend Billy, also known as Bill Talen, and his New York–based
Church of Stop Shopping were becoming increasingly visible and prominent actors in the antiwar and social justice movements—seeking to
educate the American public about the consequences of mindless consumerism, sensitizing people to consider both the origins and end-states
of products, and positioning their activism within a larger critique of
what is seen as the mind- and soul-numbing dominance of the media em-
pires that blanket the landscape and colonize our imaginations. (The
Church of Stop Shopping changed its name to the Church of Life After
Shopping, reflecting the changing economic climate and consumer ethos
resulting from the global fiscal meltdown in late 2008. But I will continue to refer to it here as the Church of Stop Shopping, since this was
the name the group performed under on the occasions described here.)

Billy's campaign first came to public attention through his penchant
for staging impromptu "retail interventions," especially targeting corporations such as Disney, Starbucks, and Wal-Mart, which are reviled
among many community activists for their exploitative labor practices

and reputations for pushing out locally owned businesses whenever they move into neighborhoods. Eventually, Billy's "strange worship" services would be joined by the Stop Shopping Gospel Choir, and together they went on to stage numerous "revival meetings" in a variety of venues across the United States, from small independent theaters in New York City to parking lots, college classrooms, street corners, and Black Rock City.[2] Billy calls upon "the God that is not a product" so as to "exorcise" cash registers, credit cards, and consumers and thereby forestall the coming "shopacalypse." In short, he seeks to—as he puts it—"put the odd back into God."

Based on a previous and brief glimpse of one of Billy's solo guerrilla "interventions" at the Disney store on Times Square, as presented in a documentary film titled *Culture Jam: Hijacking Commercial Culture*, I was expecting a cynical and caustic parody.[3] I didn't expect to like his performance, let alone be moved and inspired by it, but given the subject matter of my dissertation research, I felt obligated to see what he was all about when he and the choir first descended on the playa in 2003. My experience that night thoroughly surpassed my expectations. Picking up on that year's Beyond Belief theme, Billy repeatedly exhorted the gathered crowd to go *beyond* the limitations placed on them by the default corporate and political culture, occasionally punctuating his inspired monologue with a hearty "Burn-a-lujah!" I soon saw that although the style Billy had adopted was satirical and somewhat contrived, the message he preached was genuine and deeply felt.

The point at which this became most clear was when Billy revisited the still-painful collective memory of September 11 and spoke of the hypocrisy of the U.S. administration's response to this tragedy. Billy forcefully proclaimed, as though speaking to George W. Bush:

You *will not* return to ground zero to be reelected. Fuggitaboudit! You will not find a tall firefighter, put your arm around him and pose for the camera. Fuggitaboudit! You won't even be able to find the teleprompter that tells you what to say! Hallelujah! George *will not* return to ground zero! Fuggitaboudit! George Bush tried to persuade us that *beyond* was revenge. And now he's killed three or four times as many people as died on September 11th. He's killed many more people. And in so doing, he said that he was representing the people who died there and their relatives. That's a lie. We know what the people in the towers said in last few seconds of their lives, on the phones and in email. We know what they said to us and to their loved ones in the final seconds of their lives. They said, "I love you. I love our children. Tell them I loved our life together. And we will

see each other again." There's a kind of *beyond* going on here. Beyond the
World Trade Towers! Beyond the hatred. Let's go *beyond*. We're looking
to go tonight, children. Are you with me? Burn-a-lujah![4]

The poignancy and power of that moment touched me deeply, and I began
to sense that there was a great deal more going on here than shallow parody. As I observed this spirit also apparently moving through the crowd
around me, I began to understand that Reverend Billy was for real.

Alongside Billy's "preaching," the gospel music idiom of the Stop
Shopping Choir—backed by the Not Buying It Band—helped to create a
sense of power and unity. For example, a young African American
woman apologized for bumping into me as she danced and swayed to
the music, saying, "I went back to my childhood there!" The heritage of
gospel music and the black church is intimately embedded in the choir
through its director, James Solomon Benn. The descendant of a long line
of African Methodist Episcopal ministers and bishops, he is the first in
four generations to not follow directly in their footsteps, although he
considers his work with the Church of Stop Shopping as continuing in
that legacy.[5]

I was also delighted by the absurd yet pointed lyrics to the tunes the
choir belted out, such as "You've got to be surreal. You've got to be exor-
cised. You've got to be impossible, sometimes, to understand."[6] Another
piece—titled "The Beyond Song"—addressed the surreal emptiness of
consumerism and challenged the crowd with these lyrics:

When did I start to believe beyond you?
When did the product die on the shelf?
I think you lost us when you said—
There is nothing to love but fear itself
There is nothing to love but fear itself
You said life on earth is a network of terror
And shopping keeps the demons in the zoo
Well it's not that we're young, or we're black, or we're labor
Until you change, we're the devil to you
Until you change, we're the devil to you . . .[7]

Adding finally to the power and mystery of that evening, toward the
conclusion of the performance—which happened to be the final one in
Black Rock City that year—Reverend Billy simply walked offstage, directly through the middle of the gathered audience, and did not return.
Although this could have been a premeditated theatrical device, it seemed
that his sudden departure was unplanned. Benn and the others looked
around nervously for a bit after Billy walked away, vamping for a spell

before ultimately deciding to bring the show to a close on their own. When I interviewed Talen a few months later, he confirmed that this had been improvised, saying that he simply felt that he needed to stop saying "beyond" and just go there himself. He told me that he had headed straight out to the Temple—located, as usual, a couple hundred feet directly behind the Man, which meant that he had been gazing out at it all week long from his vantage point onstage—to spend some personal contemplative time within that hallowed space.

During our interview, Talen spoke of both Burning Man and his performance in theatrical terms, noting how these hearken back to mythic, religious, and ritualistic themes:

> It's the wandering in the desert. It's the two-thirds point in the narrative that can't make sense to the protagonist. The protagonist has to be lost. That lostness, which makes possible change, mutation, realignment, is methodically taken out of experience in our culture by advertising departments and product delivery systems because it competes with merchandising. Because it's so powerful. So corporations use storytelling primarily to sell, but they don't tell stories. A true story must have lostness, confusion, floating.[8]

When I asked him how he understood the spiritual resonance of his work, he said:

> Because the word *spiritual* is bankrupt, because of religion, because the word *religious* is bankrupt, because of churches, we tend to not return to those words. If you use old language, you can become a *Common Ground* brochure really fast. Dead language makes a dead experience. It's better in a Reverend Billy performance. . . . [I]t's better for us to walk to the edge of the abyss, beyond which is silence, and to stand there and say, "Alright, we're gonna jump." And that's the point in the sermon where I start to stutter, and I'll say, "Somebody give me an amen, help me, help me," and somebody will say, "We're with ya, we're with ya." And I haven't said anything, but we've walked to a place together.[9]

While he may be a master of the preacher's genre, Bill Talen is not ordained, or trained in ministry or liturgics, but rather has a substantial professional background in the theater.[10] The church's performances are directed by Billy's wife, Savitri Durkee. Most choir members and accompanying musicians joined the church by answering casting calls, and the Church of Stop Shopping is legally organized as a nonprofit theater company. Talen, who was raised in a Dutch Calvinist tradition, is at times suspicious of mainline religious institutions, even when their progressive politics may be aligned. Likewise, some Christians of varying political and theological orientations that I have spoken with about Billy have expressed their dislike and distrust of his work, taking offense at his sarcastic appropriation of the preacher's mantle and collar. But as Reverend Billy's public profile has grown, some Christians have come to celebrate the Church of Stop Shopping's work and see its parallels to their own traditions. For example, Walter Brueggemann wrote, "Rev. Billy is a faithful prophetic figure who stands in direct continuity with ancient prophets in Israel and in continuity with the great prophetic figures of U.S. history who have incessantly called our society back to its core human passions of justice and compassion."[11]

Billy considers his work "postreligious," but his cheeky public persona and ritual performances transcend one-dimensional satire. By simultaneously exploiting and reinventing the evangelical revival motif, combined with the deep sincerity of their message, the Church of Stop Shopping deliberately blurs the lines between irony and spirituality, thereby destabilizing normative assumptions about the nature of religion, spirituality, ritual, and theater. Billy has elsewhere made use of the ambiguity, paradox, and marginality that comes with his role as preacher. For example, for a February 2005 protest against a new Starbucks branch at Cooper Union in New York City, his press agent sent this informative e-mail:

> Originally, the land was leased by the city to the college rent-free in perpetuity, with the stipulation the college use it for "educational purposes only." Giuliani and Cooper Union achieved classic, Orwellian doublespeak in deeming a transnational coffee shop "educational." *If Starbucks is a study hall, Reverend Billy is a fake preacher!!!*[12]

Clearly, the Church of Stop Shopping does not think Starbucks is an appropriate study hall, and in the implicit message that Reverend Billy is not a fake preacher, they challenged the stability of the categories "preacher" and "religion" and indeed the notion of "authenticity." Through their exploitation of select Christian symbols and ritual modes and their core commitment to social justice and public activism, Reverend Billy and the Church of Stop Shopping—like Burning Man—are part of larger cultural trends that displace and redefine collective notions of where religious and spiritual experience is located.

A couple of years later, in 2005, Billy and a few choir members returned to Burning Man and led an impromptu memorial service at the Temple for the victims of Hurricane Katrina, which had devastated the Gulf Coast just days before (see DVD, chaps. 2 and 4). Approaching the Temple to the strains of New Orleans's famous anthem, "When the

Saints Come Marching In," Billy called for participants to contribute funds for humanitarian relief that were being collected by Burning Man organizers in Center Camp. (These efforts in support of Katrina victims would soon lead to the establishment of Burners without Borders.) Addressing the crowd from a double-decker art bus created by David Best, decorated with scraps of cut-out wood in the style of Best's earliest Burning Man Temples, Billy spoke movingly of life, death, and ritual:

> Throughout the week I know many of you—I know I have—brought to the Temple our artifacts, our pictures, our fragments of conversation, our shared dreams, with people that passed this year, and I know that to simply walk through this dusty red Temple is to feel the accumulated power of the conversation, the prayer, that we're sharing with our loved ones over the week. And the Temple has the pictures and notes—our memories of our loved ones. And we will ask the earth and the sky to take those memories up and out. And we know that we will join those memories when we become ashes and smoke ourselves.
>
> We have a way of dealing with death on the playa. At the end of the week, we burn a collective individual and feel our own deaths in last night's burn. . . . We instantly humanize this. Each of us knows we will have that moment ourselves, and that the people we love the most in the world—we will be holding their hands as they have that moment, and someone will hold our hands. We practice life and death together, don't we here? Because life, we learn here, has death in it. And if there is one thing that the second line of a funeral in New Orleans teaches us—there is life in death and death in life. And the way that we've learned here at the Burn—when we have the silence of our loved ones speak to us from beyond the flames here—that thing that we've learned about finding life in death, so that the new spirit can be among us, so that we can do our work and then in our death lend what life we've lived to the next generation.
>
> But the people of New Orleans, really—that is our sister city, what teaches us to be Burners more than Mardi Gras? Amen! . . . I don't know if you've noticed over the last day or two but [in Center Camp] they have been meeting, meeting, meeting, nonstop setting up a structure to receive energy. A lot of us here on the playa have things we can do—have skill sets that are *bizarre* [laughter]—but those skill sets might be very much to the point at this time. There are people who solve the problem of our waterlessness here who might be able to help the people who are flooded by Katrina there. We have a lot of work to do. Let's listen to the New Orleans people who have passed, the ones who are suffering. Somehow they will get their message to us, just as our loved ones who go up in the Temple will over the next year tell us, give their lives, teach us and direct us and comfort us. Amen. Bring the troops home.[13]

He then surprised the gathered crowd by handing off his bullhorn to Joan Baez—who just happened to be in attendance at Burning Man that year. Baez stepped up to do what she has done for decades, inspiring the crowd by leading a rendition of "Amazing Grace."

Reverend Billy's performances at Burning Man have been criticized by some participants for some of the same reasons that Ozan's operas were in their day—as being shows for spectators. However, a distinctly interactive flavor can permeate the crowd during Reverend Billy's performances, aided, I believe, by the gospel and evangelical ritual style in which the tradition of call and response fosters an inherent turn toward the participatory. Billy's larger body of work has also been criticized by some I've spoken with who feel that he is literally "preaching to the choir," because most of the people who attend his shows and his actions almost certainly already share Billy's left progressive politics. On this point, I agree that for those not already sympathetic to his message, his street activism may come across as invasive and sanctimonious. But at the same time his work is intended to jolt the public out of its habitual materialism while also serving to energize and inspire those working to "take back" the default culture from the clutches of corporate consumerism, letting individuals and communities know that they are not alone in their alienation. Speaking for myself, there was something in that first performance I saw in 2003 that touched me on a deep level. Perhaps the sense of transformative magic I felt that night stemmed from what Talen called "the edge of the abyss, beyond which is silence," and "the sense of lostness" that was necessary to bring about change. In that palpable liminality, I "walked to a place" with Reverend Billy. I felt connected to those around me, I felt connected to and activated by a deeper truth. I was, in a word, *inspired*.

Reverend Billy's self-conscious appropriation of the evangelical motif saps it of its traditional associations while usurping and realigning those symbols in service of a sincere spiritual critique. The gospel theme of the church's music also conveys an effective ritual style, one that has a powerful cultural resonance for many. Yet another read on Reverend Billy's gospel is that it is actually a profoundly Christian message, based as it is on the ideals of love, compassion, fellowship, and the importance of looking beyond material wealth as an ultimate value. In harnessing this ritual mode, Billy and the choir—like Burning Man—step into a place that resides on the border between the silly and the serious. There is a power in that liminal space—something capable of touching people deeply, something that can begin to break down the barriers between everyday banality and the magic of a perhaps more inspired and sustainable way of life. In so doing, the Church of Stop Shopping (or, as it is now known, the Church of Life After Shopping) seeks to aid in decolonizing the public imagination by challenging expectations and assumptions about the nature and location of religious experience.

SIFTING THROUGH THE ASHES

When ritual tools are skillfully employed and the lines between audience and performer are artfully blurred, really good theater can—like a really good Burning Man experience—change the course of human lives and cultures. In both the Church of Stop Shopping/Life After Shopping and Burning Man there is a deliberate refusal to unquestioningly accept a dominant ideology or dogma, as well as a refusal to be spoon-fed a predigested experience. There are also conscious inversions and reinventions of traditional ritual frameworks—whether adopting a gospel, pagan, or any other motif from the intercultural stew pot of symbols and possibilities—but which continue to resonate with transformative power, even while the content of these ritual containers may be altered.

In Reverend Billy's performances and activist interventions emerge many of the themes that are so intrinsic to Burning Man: spirituality absented from religion; ritual absented from dogma; performativity, ideology, and ethos; multicultural and hybrid religious symbols; immediacy and transformation; anticommodification sentiments; corporate mass media tropes; and utopian discourses of social protest. If Reverend Billy's creative appropriation of the evangelical motif serves to destabilize religion and spirituality, then Burning Man's ritual pastiche—which draws from an infinitely larger pool of cultural resources—cracks these categories wide open by inviting all participants to redefine and reinvent their relationships with concepts such as religion, spirituality, ritual, art, authenticity—among the many others explored here—but on their own terms and by means of their own performative engagements. (See DVD, chap. 7.) The dynamic and creative deployment of religious discourses and ritual symbols in surprising and compelling new ways at Burning Man—and elsewhere in North American society and culture—illustrates how themes such as transformation and redemption that have traditionally been expressed and developed in "religious" contexts are also experienced and ritualized in "alternative" venues such as Burning Man, which many participants understand as a theater for spirituality, self-expression, communal bonding, and cultural transformation.

When I interviewed Larry Harvey, he spoke of his hope that this event might actually change the world in tangible and pragmatic ways, and he asked me to at least consider that this might be possible. The Burning Man organization *is* actively seeking to propagate its social model and ideology by supporting a growing regional network and various Burning Man-esque spin-off events, as well as by such endeavors as Burners without Borders that contribute in pragmatic ways to civic and humanitarian needs in the default world. These endeavors aim to proactively spread the gospel of Burning Man by inspiring ever more individuals to embrace the event's ethos, including those who may never make the journey to Black Rock City. Although on a broad cultural scale it is too early to tell what the true long-term social influence, if any, of this event will be, it does seem clear that Burning Man has had a measure of social impact through its transformative effects on individuals and specific communities, as well as on occasion through its public outreach efforts.

In its countercultural critiques, Burning Man draws on the long-standing mode of the carnivalesque, as is evident not only in the event's festal atmosphere but also in its attempts to momentarily break down rigid hierarchical boundaries and default cultural hegemonies. Such recurring attempts to create idealized public realms have emerged once more through the Burning Man festival, conceived in this instance as a temporary autonomous zone where participants seek to perform a utopian social model, even, paradoxically, while attempting to institutionalize this quasi-anarchic autonomy. In the multiplicity of discourses that thrive around this event and the common criticisms of the event's inevitable failures to live up to its ideals, Burning Man may be better understood as a heterotopia. It should also be remembered that the realization of utopia (literally, both "good place" and "no place") as a steady state is by definition an impossibility. Rather it is the *quest* for freedom, justice, and authenticity that is significant, and Burning Man has, in its own eclectic way, sought to participate in this grand human endeavor.

In the end, I would like to posit that there *is,* in fact, something unhealthy and inauthentic lying at the heart of what Burners describe as the default world, which is part of what drives many participants to seek satisfaction on the playa. Through this festival participants have been able to ritualize and reinvigorate their lives in ways that are felt to counter the oppressive tendencies and discourses of our society, and through these performative engagements with Burning Man's endless creative and symbolic diversity, participants seek to redefine and re-create their lives in both temporary and enduring ways. It may well be that, for some, the transformative experiences rooted in Burning Man are superficial and as transitory as Black Rock City itself. But it is also the case that many Burners ultimately seek to bring their playa experiences back out into the rest of the world with them and increasingly strive to re-create the default world in the image of Burning Man by enacting these values in the social realms that touch their daily lives. For my part, I have been participating in both the Burning Man event and the communities that have grown up around it for well over a decade, and these varied experiences—ultimately including the years of effort that have gone into writing this book—have changed the course of my life and my self-image in more ways than I can begin to count. Similarly, by offering the gift of my labor through this book and DVD, perhaps my own perspectives may in some way touch the broader world.

Let's face it. Burning Man is chock-a-block full of compelling, provocative, and weird things, and there are doubtless as many ways to frame these expressions as there are Burners. Given my own interests, I have chosen to look at the event's religious and ritual referents. The Burning Man festival can bring about numerous moments of wonder, joy, and fascination—as well as revulsion, disgust, and heartbreak. The environment—both the natural desert and the hyper-freak show that is Black Rock City—can bring out the best and the worst in people. Attempting to boil down this event into some singular meaning would obscure the richer and far more complex multiplicity that gives the event its flavor, heart, and soul. This book has sought to discover a few among many possible truths about Burning Man by examining its playful and inventive ritualizing alongside participants' narratives about spirituality and transformation. By providing a unique forum in which to negotiate a wide variety of themes and ideals, this festival renders the boundaries between the sacred and the secular—along with a host of other conceptual dichotomies—utterly ambiguous. Yet in explicitly inviting participants to project their own meanings and intentions onto the event's ample ritual frameworks, Burning Man provides an exemplary and magical space to ritualize and be transformed.

Demography: The Face
of the Festival

This brief characterization of Burners' gender, age, and ethnic and economic backgrounds is derived primarily from annual surveys taken by the Burning Man organization in 2001, 2003, and 2004, the key years of my study. A questionnaire was distributed to the Black Rock City populace at the gate, and attendees were encouraged to drop off completed forms in Center Camp. In 2001 and 2003 this form was also made available on-line after the event. Finally, the results were summarized and made available on-line as part of the organization's annual reports.[1] Organizers did not state how many participants responded to their poll in 2001, but in 2003, of approximately 31,000 participants, 5,102 responses, or roughly 16 percent, were received. In 2004, 4,676 participants of an estimated 35,400 attendees responded, representing 13 percent of the population that year.

Another source of data is my on-line survey, conducted in summer 2004 (see Appendix 2). I received a total of 315 responses, which represented approximately 1 percent of that year's total attendance of 35,644. Although not designed to capture a statistically significant or appropriately weighted and randomized portrait of Burner demography—but rather to qualitatively flesh out my portrait of Burners' sentiments on questions of spirituality, religion, ritual, and transformation—I kept track of respondents' demographic characteristics and tallied the results.[2] These data are summarized below and compared to the Burning Man organization's census findings where possible.

---

1. Burning Man continued to take a "census" of the Black Rock City populace from 2005 through at least 2009. Ongoing results can be found in "Afterburn Reports," available at http://afterburn.burningman.com; accessed September 23, 2009.

2. Many of the field interviewees were approached because I already had reason to believe they would tell an interesting story or because they simply seemed approachable on a hot, dusty afternoon, so I do not include their demographic characteristics in my summaries here.

SUMMARY OF FINDINGS

Both the Burning Man organization's annual census reports and my survey results indicate that there is a somewhat higher percentage of males at the event. In
my survey 54 percent identified themselves as male and 44 percent female; fewer
than 1 percent replied "other," and another 1 percent declined to provide that information.[3] The Burning Man organization also found that there tend to be more
males than females at the event: in 2001, 64 percent reported they were male, 34
percent female, and 2 percent declined to state; in 2003, 57 percent reported they
were male, 42 percent female, 0 percent as transgender, and 1 percent declined
to state in 2003; in 2004, 57 reported they were male, 41 percent female, 1 percent transgender, and 1 percent provided no answer.

I also queried survey respondents about their sexual identity but did not define
these categories, preferring instead to allow individuals to select their own ter-
minology. Thus while most stated they were "hetero," "straight," "bi," "queer," or
another relatively easily interpretable—and hence categorizable—response, a number of replies were impossible to classify. (I see this as entirely in keeping with the
fluidity of identity and resistance to normativity that is so prevalent among the
Burning Man populace.) Hence the numbers in this regard broke down more or
less as follows: 40 percent heterosexual male; 24 percent heterosexual female; 5
percent bisexual male; 15 percent bisexual female; 3 percent gay male; 2 percent
gay female; 7 percent inscrutable; 4 percent no response.

The Burning Man organization's census in both 2003 and 2004 also queried
participants about sexual orientation but did not separately track gender. In
2003, 77 percent identified themselves as "heterosexual," 7 percent as "homo-
sexual," and 16 percent as "bisexual." In 2004, 70 percent reported they were
"straight," 8 percent "gay," and 18 percent "bisexual"; 4 percent offered no
or unclear responses. I know of no widely agreed upon statistics indicating the
relative percentages of gay, lesbian, bisexual, and transgender (GLBT) individuals across the U.S. population, but based on the (albeit long-disputed) average
of 10 percent cited in the classic Kinsey study, it seems likely that the numbers of
GLBT individuals at Burning Man is probably on a par with or slightly higher
than the national average. It is also noteworthy that in both my survey and the
Burning Man organization's, the number of those who said they were bisexual
seemed fairly high.

The age and generational ranges of respondents to my survey were provided in
chapter 2 and are repeated here for ease of comparison with the Burning Man organization's findings. My survey respondents ranged in age from 17 to 66, with a
median age of 37.5 (table 2). The Burning Man organization also queried participants about their age in their 2003 and 2004 surveys, as summarized in table 3
below. All these figures indicate that the majority of participants are members of
what has been called Generation X (i.e., born between 1965 and 1980), and a significant number are Baby Boomers (i.e., born between 1945 and 1965).

3. I had provided check boxes for Female, Male, FTM, MTF, and Other. Only one respondent checked MTF, one checked Other, and three declined to state.

TABLE 2
Age of Respondents at Time of Survey

Age	Percentage
17–19	1
20–29	20
30–39	42
40–49	24
50–59	11
60–66	2

TABLE 3
Burning Man Organization Data on Participants' Ages

2003	
Age	Percentage
18–21	3
22–25	10
26–30	22
31–39	37
41–50	17
51–60	9
61–70	2
Over 71 or under 18	<1

2004	
Age	Percentage
Under 21	4
21–30	30
31–40	36
41–50	18
51–60	9
61–70	2
Over 70	0

Economic and class indicators can be gleaned to a limited extent from queries about annual income, as well as from questions concerning how much money individual participants spent preparing for the event. I did not include this question in my research, but in 2003 and 2004 the Burning Man organization's census asked respondents about annual income, making a distinction between personal and household income in 2003 but not in 2004, as summarized in tables 4 and 5. It is also noteworthy that in 2004, 34 percent of respondents to the Burning Man organization's survey indicated that they were home owners, 60 percent said they were not, and 6 percent declined to state. It is also interesting to look at how much money participants spent on their Burning Man experience, which may provide an indication of the extent of economic class diversity on the playa. According to the Burning Man organization's 2003 census, participants typically spent several hundred dollars or more in preparation for the event that year, as summarized in table 6.

In 2004 the Burning Man organization did not report differences in amount spent but asked participants how much they spent on supplies and activities in preparation for the festival. On average participants spent a total $1,148: an average of $234 on tickets, $374 on travel, $285 on survival expenses, $313 on "fun supplies," and $290 on "other expenses." Given the inconsistencies from year to year, as well as the lack of other indicators, it is difficult to know how to interpret these findings, although it appears that most, but by no means all, Burners could be considered middle class. My informal observations also indicate that most participants are probably of middle-class backgrounds and means.

As to the ethnicity of Burning Man participants, the organization did not include questions on this in any of the annual surveys considered here. However, it can be readily observed at the event that most attendees are of predominantly European ancestry (i.e., white), and this was confirmed by the respondents to my survey. I intentionally left this question (simply phrased "ethnicity") open-ended so that individuals could define their identities themselves. Of these, 61 percent specifically stated that they were "Caucasian" or "white," 5 percent stated that they were an unspecified European mix or named a general European region (usually northern or western), and 12 percent defined their ancestry specifically, including Irish, Scottish, English, French, Italian, Spanish, Dutch, Norwegian, Swedish, German, Austrian, Czech, Hungarian, Russian, Croatian, and Polish (in various combinations, as well as singular affiliations). Finally, 3 percent indicated that they were "white/Jewish."

Only 6 percent of respondents indicated they were people of color; of these, nine individuals stated that they were Latino/a, Hispanic, or Mexican American; six stated that they were Asian; one stated he was Middle Eastern, one stated that he was Assyrian, and one stated that he was Native American. Another 7 percent of respondents indicated they were of mixed European and non-European ethnicity; of these, nearly half stated that they were of both European and Native American ancestry (often but not always naming a specific tribal affiliation), while others gave the following descriptions indicating an admixture of heritages: "Vietnamese/Caucasian mutt (warbaby)," "Celtic/Cantonese/Latina," "half honky, half camel jockey," "Japanese Honky," "Egyptian/Irish American," "African/Norwegian American," "half white and half Afghan," "white/Middle

TABLE 4

Burning Man Organization Data on Participants' Income, 2003

Annual Income	Personal (%)	Household (%)
Under $15,000	12	6
$15,001–$25,000	12	7
$25,001–$50,000	31	21
$50,001– $75,000	19	19
$75,001–$100,000	10	15
$100,001–$200,000	8	17
Over $200,001	2	5
Declined to state	6	10

TABLE 5

Burning Man Organization Data on Participants'
Income, 2004

Annual Income	Percentage
Under $15,000	18
$15,000–$24,999	13
$25,000–$49,999	24
$50,000–$74,999	14
$75,000–$99,999	9
$100,000 or more	11
Declined to state	11

TABLE 6

Burning Man Organization Data on Participants'
Amounts Spent on the Event, 2003

Amount Spent	Percentage
Over $3,000	4
$1,000–$3,000	18
$751–$1,000	17
$501–$750	24
$201–$500	31
$101–$200	4
$51–$100	1
<$20	<1

TABLE 7
Location of Survey Respondents

State, Region, or Nation	Number	State, Region, or Nation	Number
Arizona	15	Massachusetts	2
Australia	1	Minnesota	3
California, Central	15	Missouri	2
California, Northern	81	New Jersey	4
California, Southern	38	New Mexico	4
Canada, Alberta	8	Nevada	23
Canada, British Columbia	3	North Carolina	1
Canada, Manitoba	1	New York	14
Canada, Ontario	1	Oregon	12
Canada, province not specified	2	Pennsylvania	5
Colorado	16	Texas	13
Georgia	1	United Kingdom	4
Hawaii	2	Utah	2
Idaho	2	Virginia	1
Illinois	8	Washington	14
Ireland	1	Wisconsin	3
		(Not stated)	13

TABLE 8
Survey Respondents' Years Attended Burning Man

Years Attended	Total Number
1991	1
1992	7
1993	10
1994	18
1995	29
1996	43
1997	58
1998	84
1999	115
2000	135
2001	163
2002	201
2003	231
2004	248

East," "white/Hispanic," "black/white," and "Black/Caucasian." Finally, eleven individuals declined to state, and twelve individuals gave replies that could not be categorized, including four who simply stated that they were "American," two who stated that they were "human," and two who stated that they were "earthlings," as well as a variety of inscrutable replies such as "Capitalist."

As to the significance of the fact that this event appears to appeal mainly to those of European American heritage, some commentary seems warranted. Larry Harvey's gloss on the general scarcity of color in the Burner populace is that many white people in the United States have a sense that something is lacking in their own cultural experiences and that Burning Man fulfills that desire. To put it another way, there is a sense in which the false homogenization and cultural normativity of "whiteness" has resulted in a perceived absence of cultural uniqueness or of shared cultural rituals for many European Americans. This may indeed account, at least in part, for the general ethnic demography of Black Rock City. Burning Man is attractive to those whose "culture" is the norm, or default, and who also in various ways find themselves in opposition to that norm and its perceived deficiencies. Furthermore, as can be witnessed in the event's hybridity, it may also be that white Americans feel more implicit privilege moving into and appropriating realms of cultural difference.

In another area of particular interest to this study, the Burning Man organization asked participants in 2004 whether or not they felt that the event was a spiritual experience for them. Of the total 4,676 respondents, 2,020 stated that they "agreed," 1,515 "strongly agreed," 235 "disagreed," 103 "strongly disagreed," 621 stated no opinion, and 802 gave no or unclear responses. In 2001 the Burning Man organization also queried respondents as to whether or not they thought Burning Man had changed their lives and found that roughly 60 percent reported having a life-changing experience. My own findings in both of these regards are summarized and examined at length in chapters 2 and 5 and need not be repeated here.

Finally, my survey collected data on respondents' geographic locations and the number of years attended. Table 7 summarizes the states, provinces, or nations that survey respondents cited as "where they lived (when not in Black Rock City)." The number of survey respondents who attended Burning Man in specific years is summarized in table 8.

APPENDIX 2

On-Line Survey

LETTER POSTED TO ON-LINE BURNING MAN COMMUNITIES

(Sent July 20, 2004)

Greetings Burners Everywhere!

I'm seeking Burning Man participants to contribute to my ethnographic survey on spirituality and religion at the Burning Man festival. I hope to gather a wide variety of ideas on these subjects—from *all* perspectives. Why? Well, the parallels between Burning Man and "religion" have been noted by many folks over the years, but so far no one has undertaken a serious study of this association. I seek to fill that gap.

A bit about me—I'm a doctoral candidate at the Graduate Theological Union in Berkeley and I'm writing my dissertation on Burning Man. I've been coming to Burning Man since 1996, and so have been a participant first and a participant observer second. I volunteered for several years with the Media Team and have camped with the Blue Light District on and off since 1997.

I hope you will take a few moments to complete this questionnaire. I estimate this will take approximately 20–30 minutes. Your identity will remain anonymous in any printed materials resulting from this survey, unless you specifically state that it is okay to refer to you by the name you provide. And please feel free to forward this far and wide.

With much gratitude,

Lee Gilmore, burningsurvey@randomgroup.com

OFFICIAL CONSENT FORM

I am asking you to participate in an on-line survey about your own experiences at or in connection with the Burning Man festival. I am conducting this research for my dissertation. I estimate this process will take approximately 20–30 minutes.

If you provide me with an e-mail address, I may decide to contact you with a few follow-up questions. Any e-mail address or other contact information you provide will be used for no other purpose.

There is no known risk to you by participating in this survey. A potential benefit of participating in this survey is that you may find the content to be an interesting opportunity to reflect on your personal experiences.

Your identity will kept completely confidential and anonymous, unless you explicitly indicate otherwise. If you would prefer that I refer to you in print by either your legal name or a chosen alias, please indicate so at the top of the survey form (on the next page).

You are of course free not to answer any specific question and are free to withdraw from this survey at any time. If you wish to discuss this survey with me, please feel free to contact me at burningsurvey@randomgroup.com.

I retain all intellectual and commercial rights to the material in this survey but freely consent to give you free access to cite or quote the material for your own purposes.

By clicking on the link below, you indicate that you have been informed of my purposes for conducting this survey, that you fully understand your rights and responsibilities in connection to this research, and that you voluntarily consent to participate in this survey. (This link will take you to the survey itself.) *I agree to these terms.*

BURNING MAN SURVEY

(In July 2004 this survey was posted to eplaya.burningman.com, bm.tribe.net, www.livejournal.com/community/burning_man, and burnman-list@dioxine.net; and also distributed to a number of the Burning Man organization's "regional" contacts, with the assistance of senior staff member Andie Grace. These questions were a streamlined version of the questions I used as a guide for field interviews, although those often became more conversational and veered occasionally onto other topics as indicated by participants' interests.)

Name you wish to use in connection with this survey? (playa name or legal name or whatever else you prefer—none is also okay)

Is it okay to call you by this name if I decide to quote you in print? (if you prefer to remain anonymous, I will assign a pseudonym) Yes No

E-mail address? (I swear on a stack of *Survival Guides* that I will *not* share this with anyone or sign you up for any spam. This is only so that I am able to send a few follow-up questions if that seems pertinent.)

How did you first hear about Burning Man, and why did you decide to go?

Have you been to any other events or festivals similar in some way to Burning Man (including but not limited to regional burns)? If so, what was different or similar about those events for you?

Has Burning Man been a life- or perspective-changing experience for you? If so, please say more about how that transpired for you. Why do you think Burning Man brought about that transformation?

Do you participate in any rituals, ritual-like activities, or performances at Burning Man?

In general, do you consider yourself a religious or spiritual person? Please say more about what that means to you, why you do or do not. What has been your religious/spiritual background?

Do you think Burning Man is a religious or spiritual event? Why or why not?

What does Burning Man mean to you?

Anything else you want to add?

Finally, some simple demographic questions:
Age:
Gender: [Male] [Female] [MTF] [FTM] [Other]
Sexual identity/orientation:
Ethnicity:
Occupation:
Where do you live (when not in Black Rock City)?
Do you affiliate with a particular theme camp(s)/village(s) or other group(s), & if so which one(s)?
How did you find out about this survey?
Years attended?

1986	1987	1988	1989	1990	1991	1992
1993	1994	1995	1996	1997	1998	1999
2000	2001	2002	2003	2004 (plan to attend)		

Thank you!!!

APPENDIX 3

Burning Man Organization
Mission Statement

Our mission is to produce the annual event known as "Burning Man" and to guide, nurture and protect the more permanent community created by its culture. Our intention is to generate a society that connects each individual to his or her creative powers, to participation in community, to the larger realm of civic life, and to the even greater world of nature that exists beyond society. We believe that the experience of Burning Man can produce positive spiritual change in the world. To this end, it is equally important that we communicate with one another, with the citizens of Black Rock City and with the community of Burning Man wherever it may arise. Burning Man is radically inclusive, and its meaning is potentially accessible to anyone. The touchstone of value in our culture will always be immediacy: experience before theory, moral relationships before politics, survival before services, roles before jobs, embodied ritual before symbolism, work before vested interest, participant support before sponsorship. Finally, in order to accomplish these ends, Burning Man must endure as a self-supporting enterprise that is capable of sustaining the lives of those who dedicate themselves to its work. From this devotion spring those duties that we owe to one another. We will always burn the Man.[1]

1. Available at www.burningman.com/whatisburningman/about_burningman/mission .html; accessed January 5, 2009.

Notes

INTRODUCTION

1. See, among other sources, Bellah et al., *Habits of the Heart;* Ellwood, *Alternative Altars;* Fuller, *Spiritual, but Not Religious;* Kripal, *Esalen;* Lynch, *The New Spirituality;* Roof, *Spiritual Marketplace;* Schmidt, *Restless Souls;* Wuthnow, *After Heaven.*

2. Fuller, *Spiritual, but Not Religious,* 6. Also see Green, "The American Religious Landscape and Political Attitudes."

3. For example, I have found that many of my students consider themselves spiritual but not religious while simultaneously retaining an identity as Christian or Catholic. The sociologist Jerome Baggett also discovered this parlance was in high usage among a diverse cross section of Catholic parishioners in the San Francisco Bay Area (pers. com., March 2005).

4. Lévi-Strauss, *The Savage Mind,* 17.

5. This choice is also made in part out of respect for the Burning Man organization, which prefers that public representations of the event do not foreground the practice of consuming licit or illicit drugs. There are both pragmatic and ideological reasons for this policy, which are discussed in more detail in chapter 5. The final reason that I opted to leave this aspect of the event aside is because these are not practices that I indulge in, and hence I lack the insider's perspective and interest that has been key to my other insights regarding the event.

6. This village was, and continues to be, called the Blue Light District (or the BLD) for no particular or literal reason.

7. I remained minimally involved for a few years as the "academic liaison," meaning that from time to time I responded to e-mail queries sent to the Burning Man organization from other academics. I should also state that the most personally significant result of my stint with the Media Team has been my marriage to another (also now former) volunteer from that group.

8. Special thanks are due to my nieces Yaffa and Shaina Meiners for sharing this observation with me. I later learned that the phrase was cited as a "Yippie Proverb" by Abbie Hoffman, who wrote, "Free speech is the right to shout 'theater' in a crowded fire." See Hoffman, *Steal This Book.*

9. See, among others, Clifford, *Writing Culture;* Behar, *The Vulnerable Observer;* and Davies, *Reflexive Ethnography.*

10. These findings are summarized in Appendix 1, and specifics about my survey are given in Appendix 2.

11. Select sources from Victor Turner that I primarily draw on here are *The Ritual Process; Dramas, Fields, and Metaphors; From Ritual to Theatre; The Anthropology of Performance;* and Turner and Turner, *Image and Pilgrimage in Christian Culture.*

12. Van Gennep, *The Rites of Passage.*

13. Turner is by no means without important critics, and my strategic applications of his ideas are modified by more recent contributions to ritual studies, looking particularly to Ronald L. Grimes's conception of ritual as an analytic construct and a "tool to think by," as well as Catherine Bell's understanding of ritual as a reified scholarly construction. See especially Grimes's *Beginnings in Ritual Studies; Ritual Criticism; Deeply into the Bone;* and *Rite Out of Place;* and Bell's *Ritual Theory / Ritual Practice* and *Ritual.*

14. A longer discussion of my thoughts on Turner can be found in Gilmore, "Of Ordeals and Operas."

15. In addition to the support and guidance provided by my editors at UC Press, my coproducers and collaborators on this project have been Elizabeth Gilmore and Ron Meiners, my mother and my husband, respectively. I am also indebted to Ron Grimes, who encouraged me to take on this project in the first place.

1. INTO THE ZONE

1. Doherty, *This Is Burning Man,* 26–27. A great deal more about the early history of Burning Man can be found in Doherty's book.

2. Larry Harvey, "La Vie Bohéme: A History of Burning Man," available at www.burningman.com/whatisburningman/lectures/la_vie2.html; accessed January 5, 2009.

3. For one recollection of this event, see Dawn Stott, "Summer of 1989," available at http://people.tribe.net/amanda_peckinpaw/blog/733c2c21-f075-40e7-aab8-a6757a9604c0; accessed January 5, 2009.

4. This date was selected in large part because of the basic convenience afforded by the three-day Labor Day weekend, as well as because the playa surface—which becomes a shallow, muddy lakebed with the annual winter rains and snow—is completely dry by the end of summer.

5. I have on rare occasion seen a few insects out there and once even saw a very lost looking seagull, although none of these are indigenous to the playa. It is likely that the insects blew in from the nearby hills, and the seagull probably hailed from Pyramid Lake, about fifty miles south of Gerlach. For more on the geography of the Black Rock Desert, see Goin and Starrs, *Black Rock.*

6. According to Doherty, "The notion of the 'Cacophony Zone Trip' was derived from Andrei Tarkovsky's *Stalker,* a beloved art-school film that features a mysterious Zone that looks like the rest of the world but in which bizarre, inexplicable things occur." See Doherty, *This Is Burning Man,* 49.

7. Michael Michael, *Rough Draft,* 1990.

8. Brill, "The First Year in the Desert."

9. See Turner, *The Ritual Process; Dramas, Fields, and Metaphors; From Ritual to Theatre;* and *Anthropology of Performance;* and Turner and Turner, *Image and Pilgrimage in Christian Culture;* van Gennep, *Rites of Passage.*

10. Bey, *T.A.Z.,* 101.

11. Ibid., 99.

12. Ibid.

13. Foucault, "Of Other Spaces."

14. See Caesar, *Caesar's War Commentaries,* 104. There is archaeological evidence that the ancient Celts may have practiced human sacrifice on rare occasions, based largely on remains found in peat bogs and other burial sites across northern Europe. However, the historical evidence for "wicker men" is based solely on literary sources such as Caesar as well as Strabo's *Geography,* which have long been considered potentially sensationalized propaganda. See also Green, "Humans as Ritual Victims in the Later Prehistory of Western Europe."

15. See Frazer, *The Golden Bough.*

16. For example, see Hutton, *The Stations of the Sun.* For contemporary studies of Guy Fawkes Day, see Santino, *Halloween and Other Festivals of Death and Life.*

17. Directed by Robin Hardy. A remake of this film, directed by Neil LaBute, was released in summer 2006.

18. See www.thewickermanfestival.co.uk; accessed January 5, 2009.

19. Also held annually in Edinburgh, Scotland, is the Beltane Fire Festival, a public event commemorating the May 1 feast of Beltane. This event doesn't feature a burning effigy but does showcase hundreds of fire performers, and given its "tribalesque" look and feel, its visual similarity to some aspects of Burning Man is striking. See www.beltane.org; accessed January 5, 2009.

20. One source on Ram-lila festivals is Schechner, *The Future of Ritual,* 131–83.

21. Organizers state that Shuster's "inspiration for Zozobra came from the Holy Week celebrations of the Yaqui Indians of Mexico; an effigy of Judas, filled with firecrackers, was led around the village on a donkey and later burned." See "Zozobra-history," available at www.zozobra.com/history.html; accessed January 5, 2009. However, the authenticity of this lineage is contested by some members of the local community, who view Zozobra as "an Anglo attempt to secularize the Fiesta, to push in on and take over a Spanish event, a real and quasi-religious ceremony celebrating the Spanish conquest of New Mexico." See Hockett, "Men of Fire." Hockett also states that a counter-festival in a predominantly Latin neighborhood in nearby Albuquerque—called the Festival de Otoño (Autumn)—has converged with the ritualistic burning of another effigy figure called Kookooee (or el Cucui), who represents a folkloric bogeyman that appears throughout diverse

Hispanic cultures. For an earlier study of the Santa Fe Fiesta, see Grimes, *Symbol and Conquest.*

22. Little is publicly known about the origins of this farcical rite, although some Masonic influence likely exists. The Bohemian Grove encampment and the Cremation of Care were surreptitiously videotaped in 2000 by "conspiracy theorist" Alex Jones for a documentary titled *Dark Secrets: Inside Bohemian Grove.* Copies of this film can be obtained from www.infowars.com/bg1.html; accessed January 5, 2009.

23. Harvey, "Media Myths." Former organizer John Law disputes Harvey's contention that he had not seen *The Wicker Man* film before the first Burn in 1986. See Law v. Harvey, Mikel, Paper Man, LLC, and Black Rock City, LLC, U.S. District Court, Northern District of California (available at http://laughingsquid.com/other/john_law_burning_man_complaint.pdf; accessed January 5, 2009). Rather than engage in a protracted and almost certainly unprovable discursion into either side of this allegation, I have opted in this matter—as well as in other potentially contested points regarding the event's origins—to accept Harvey's most popularly accepted version, along with that provided by Doherty.

24. Calling itself "a non-organization of non-members," the Rainbow Gathering typically eschews the National Forest Service's permit process and thus differs greatly in this respect from Burning Man's rigorous attempts to remain within the letter of the law. See Niman, *People of the Rainbow;* see also www.welcomehome.org/rainbow/index.html; accessed January 5, 2009.

25. See Pike, *Earthly Bodies / Magical Selves.*

26. For more on some of these events, see St John, *Technomad.* See also Sylvan, *Trance Formation.*

27. See www.burningflipside.com; http://playadelfuego.org; www.midwest burners.com; www.toast-town.org; www.element11.org; www.apogaea.com; www.massiveburn.org; www.burningmanportland.com; all accessed January 5, 2009.

28. "Culture jamming" can also refer somewhat more narrowly to a form of media activism that seeks to turn mass media messages and images on their head in order to produce biting and ironic commentary on the social condition of consumerism. See, e.g., Lasn, *Culture Jam.*

29. Selected sources on these movements are, respectively, Kachur, *Displaying the Marvelous;* Debord, *The Society of the Spectacle;* McDonough, *Guy Debord and the Situationist International;* Baudrillard, *Simulacra and Simulation;* Kaprow, *Essays on the Blurring of Art and Life;* Perry, *On the Bus;* Hoffman, *Steal This Book;* Hill and Thornley, *Principia Discordia.*

30. "San Francisco Suicide Club," available at www.suicideclub.com; accessed January 5, 2009. Former club members later summarized the group's "hystery" writing: "On January 2, 1977, gale warnings were issued in San Francisco, and, at midnight, four friends unexplainedly found themselves holding onto handrails as 20 foot waves broke over them. Afterwards, they agreed they wanted to explore other such experiences in a larger group of friends. The *Suicide Club* was chosen as a name, based on the Robert Louis Stevenson story of a club that gamed at midnight, the losers forfeiting their lives. The name was chosen to

alienate and frighten people away. It was offered in the Spring '77 catalog of
Communiversity, a San Francisco Alternative University without fees. . . . The
Club [had] two annual events: A Champagne Dinner on the Golden Gate Bridge
on the last Friday of February and a massive treasure hunt taking place amidst
the chaos of the Chinese New Years Parade comprised of opposing teams, culminating in a water balloon and pie fight at the final destination on the last Saturday of February." See "San Francisco Suicide Club—Cacophony," available
at www.suicideclub.com/cacophony/cacophony.html; accessed January 5, 2009.
The Chinese New Year Treasure Hunt has survived to become a relatively well
known and beloved San Francisco tradition, and the practice of bridge climbing
continued into the 1990s, although the political climate post–September 11, 2001,
finally made such adventures unfeasible.

31. For more on the Billboard Liberation Front, see www.billboardliberation
.com; accessed January 5, 2009.

32. The San Francisco Cacophony Society is still in existence, although in a
reduced and decentralized form, and also has lodges in Portland, Seattle, Denver,
and Los Angeles, among other locations. See www.cacophony.org/lodges.html;
accessed January 5, 2009.

33. See www.zpub.com/caco/caco1.html; and www.cacophony.org; both
accessed January 5, 2009.

34. See www.santarchy.com; accessed January 5, 2009. Another route of Ca-
cophony's larger cultural influence was through the success of the film *Fight
Club,* based on a novel by the Portland Cacophonist Chuck Palahniuk. The story's
"Project Mayhem" was loosely based on the Cacophony Society, although in a
much darker and more violent guise than is the actual nature of the Cacophony
Society. See Palahniuk, *Fight Club.*

35. For yearly population statistics, see "Burning Man Timeline," www.burning
man.com/whatisburningman/about_burningman/bm_timeline.html; accessed January 5, 2009.

36. Burning Man Project, *Burning Man Survival Guide,* 1996.

37. One prominent member of the Burning Man community—Michael Hopkins, better known as Flash—dressed up and enacted the role of "Papa Satan" as
a washed-up corporate executive whose position was now imperiled by the in-
cursions of the behemoth HelCo.

38. Designed by the Seeman art collective, led by Kal Spelletich. These corporate behemoths were mocked when each of these pieces, including a 30-foot
papier-mâché skyscraper, was set aflame in a sensational performance that cul-
minated in John Law's rapid flight down the tower via zip-cord as the structure
began to catch fire.

39. This was the first in a series of ritualistic and religiously thematic operas produced by Ozan and associates that were prominent features at Burning Man from 1996 to 2000. Ozan began creating art on the playa in 1993
with a series of *Fire Lingams* and the subsequent opera sets or sculptures
were elaborations on these. These performances are discussed more fully in
chapter 3.

40. In early 2007 John Law sued both Larry Harvey and Michael Michael
over the right to control the "Burning Man" trademark, to which he still had a

legal claim. This case was eventually settled, and Law relinquished his interest in the trademark. For more background and participant reaction to this suit, see Beale, "John Law Sues His Former Burning Man Partners."

41. Harvey and these compatriots chose to form an LLC rather than a non-profit or other type of fiscal entity so that they could collectively maintain more direct control over the event; a nonprofit structure would have required a board of outsiders to oversee the activities of the organizers and staff, a prospect they did not see as in the best interest of the event. Other former LLC members include attorney Carole Morrell, businessman Andy Pector, and event producer Joegh Bullock. Morrell and Pector both left the LLC in 1998; Bullock, in 1999. Bullock continues to produce Burning Man community parties and other assorted events in the San Francisco Bay Area. See www.burningman.com/whatisburningman/people/project_bio.html; accessed January 5, 2009. For more on the organization behind Burning Man, see Chen, *Enabling Creative Chaos.*

42. See Northrup, "Kaleidoscopic Cortege." The U.S. art car community first coalesced in Houston, where they continue to hold annual gatherings as part of a celebration of folk art called the Orange Show. There is also now an annual exhibition of art cars in Northern California. See www.orangeshow.org/artcar.html; and http://artcarfest.com; both accessed January 5, 2009.

43. Also in 1997, pending a BLM-mandated environmental impact review, the event relocated temporarily to privately owned land on the nearby, smaller Hualapai playa. After engaging in a number of sometimes-contentious negotiations with various local agencies, the event was permitted to return to the Black Rock playa in 1998, where it has continued to take place ever since. This has been made possible in part by paying the BLM over half a million dollars annually, based on a per-person per-day usage fee, since 2000.

44. For example, in 2003 when the theme was Beyond Belief, slogans included the following: "I'll believe in you" (Lewis Carroll); "Religion is the sigh of the oppressed creature, the heart of a heartless world, and the soul of soulless conditions. It is the opium of the people" (Karl Marx); "Set souls on fire" (St. Therese of Lisieux); and "The awareness of emptiness brings forth a heart of compassion" (Gary Snyder). Other signs are more pragmatic, intended to establish some of the ground rules for behavior, such as those that admonish drivers to slow down to five miles per hour and leave no trace. Beginning in 2003, first-time attendees were encouraged to step out of their vehicles at the Greeter's station and onto a waiting platform to ring a bell, a rite of passage declaring their intention to participate.

45. The Burning Man organization makes a small number of low-cost "scholarship" tickets available every year.

46. Harvey has joked on occasion that the event provides an opportunity for everyone to experience being a "starving artist" who sacrifices everything for their art.

47. See "Burning Man Timeline."

48. This entails surveying and marking out the city's streets, laying out a subterranean generator grid, and constructing simple wooden structures for the organization's own needs in Center Camp. A skeleton DPW crew lives year-round in Gerlach in order to maintain a nearby storage depot called Black Rock

Station, and many volunteers also stay behind for weeks after the festival's conclusion to help clean up.

49. See www.pissclear.org; accessed January 5, 2009; and Roberts, *Burning Man Live*. *The Spock Science Monitor* also began contributing its own acerbic brand of wit to Black Rock City in 2002; see www.pigdog.org/features/ssm2002/ ssm2002.htm; accessed January 5, 2009.

50. For more on this aspect of Burning Man, see St John, *Technomad*; and Sylvan, *Trance Formation*.

51. In 1999 this "alpha" street was called Mercury (with subsequent streets named sequentially Venus, Earth, etc.), and in 2000 the first street was named Head Way, in keeping with the Body theme. But many participants continued to call this main causeway the Esplanade, and organizers returned to this designation in 2001. See www.burningman.com/whatisburningman/1999/99_brc_map.html; www.burningman.com/whatisburningman/2000/00_brc_map.html; and www .burningman.com/whatisburningman/2001/01_brc_map.html; accessed September 13, 2009.

52. An exception was in 2002, when—in keeping with that year's nautical Floating World theme—the longitudinal streets were named after degrees in a circle—180°, 195°, 210°, etc. However, many participants found this system confusing such that subsequent years have returned to the more immediately intuitive clock-face model. See www.burningman.com/whatisburningman/2002/ 02_brc_map.html; accessed September 13, 2009.

53. These installations are mapped—both in advance and on-site—by a volunteer team called the Artery, which ensures that projects are appropriately placed so as to not unduly distract from one another.

54. Interview with Larry Harvey, January 8, 2005.

55. Eliade, *The Myth of the Eternal Return*.

56. Although several of the organizers provide input into this process, it is chiefly guided by Harvey, who carefully designs, considers, and articulates the artistic themes, elaborating and delineating the underlying concepts in each annual event's promotional literature.

57. See www.burningman.com/whatisburningman/2000/00_body_map.html; accessed September 13, 2009.

58. *Ukiyo-e* was a popular artistic style of the classical Edo period (1600s–1867) in Japan. The concept of the floating world was based on Buddhist notions of the transience of worldly affairs and evoked a sense of liminality in its reference to the ultimately illusory pleasures of urban life. See Kita et al., *The Floating World of Ukiyo-e*.

59. See www.burning.man.com/whatisburningman/2003; www.burningman .com/whatisburningman/2004; www.burningman.com/whatisburningman/2005; accessed September 13, 2009.

60. See www.burningman.com/whatisburningman/2006; www.burningman .com/whatisburningman/2007; www.burningman.com/whatisburningman/2008; www.burningman.com/whatisburningman/2009; accessed September 13, 2009.

61. "Ten Principles," available at www.burningman.com/whatisburningman/ about_burningman/principles.html; accessed January 5, 2009.

62. "Survival Guide," available at www.burningman.com/preparation/event
_survival; accessed January 5, 2009. This document is mailed out in advance of
the event to all ticket holders and is distributed at the gate to those who purchase
their tickets on-site.

63. For the full text of these rules, see "Participant Responsibilities," available
at www.burningman.com/preparation/event_survival/participant_responsibilities
.html; accessed January 5, 2009.

64. This newsletter is titled *The Jackrabbit Speaks* and is the organizers' primary communications vehicle.

65. I have been told that some participants—especially those whose liveli-
hoods are sustained by selling food, crafts, and other goods as they travel an annual
festival circuit—find this ban on vending bothersome and limiting. However, I have
never heard any participants say that they wished they could sell or buy things at
Burning Man. Sarah Pike, pers. com., January 2005.

66. Hyde, *The Gift*. Hyde was in turn influenced by Marcel Mauss's classic
study of gift-giving as a traditional means of economic exchange and as a mechanism by which social capital was exchanged and accrued in archaic societies.
Although Mauss's original study was not necessarily intended as a form of cultural criticism, Hyde drew on those ideas to articulate and position his concept
in opposition to the commodification of art and in turn culture. See Mauss, *The
Gift*.

67. For more on the organization's finances, see "Afterburn Reports," available at http://afterburn.burningman.com; accessed January 5, 2009. Other sources
of income include a small percentage of any profits earned by those who produce
videos or photographs of the event for commercial sale and a very small number of
site fees paid by some large, well-heeled media production companies.

68. "Marketplace," available at http://marketplace.burningman.com; accessed January 5, 2009. Also see "Larry Harvey's 1998 Speech," available at www
.burningman.com/whatisburningman/1998/98_speech_1.html; accessed January
5, 2009.

69. See chapter 5 for more discussion of these efforts.

70. Robert V. Kozinets, "Can Consumers Escape the Market?" See also
Kozinets and Sherry, "Welcome to the Black Rock Café."

71. "Participate In Burning Man!" available at www.burningman.com/
participate; accessed January 5, 2009.

72. Darryl Van Rhey, "The Meaning of Participation: An Interview with
Larry Harvey," in *The Official Journal of the Burning Man Project* (summer
2000); available at www.burningman.com/whatisburningman/2000/oon_letter
_sum_1.html; accessed January 5, 2009. (Darryl Van Rhey is an anagram and the
nom de plume of Larry Harvey).

73. Michael Michael, *Rough Draft*, 1990.

2. "SPIRITUAL, BUT NOT RELIGIOUS"?

1. See Christine Kristen, "Burning Man," *Raw Vision* 57 (winter 2006):
28–37.

2. "Mission Statement," available at www.burningman.com/whatisburning man/about_burningman/mission.html; accessed January 5, 2009. The complete Mission Statement is given in Appendix 3.

3. Harvey, "Media Myths."

4. For example, Talal Asad argued, "There cannot be a universal definition of religion, not only because its constituent elements and relationships are histori-cally specific, but because that definition is itself the historical product of discur-sive processes," and further that "the theoretical search for an essence of religion invites us to separate it conceptually from the domain of power." See Asad, *Genealogies of Religion,* 29. Asad was here specifically critiquing Clifford Geertz's definition of religion in *The Interpretation of Cultures,* 90. See also Smith, "Reli-gion, Religions, Religious."

5. David Chidester's treatment of "religion" in his study of religion in Amer-ican popular culture is somewhat similar in that he is interested in "how the term has actually been used by people to make sense out of their lives," such that "the meaning of the term *religion* is determined by usage." See Chidester, *Authentic Fakes,* 17.

6. Of those in my extended community who affiliate with and practice a spe-cific religious tradition, the majority are Jews.

7. In order to take advantage of these networks, I created a Web-based sur-vey and solicited Burners' responses by publicizing it on various on-line discus-sion boards and e-mail lists. In addition, the Burning Man organization for-warded my appeal to its network of regional contacts. I received a total of 315 responses to this survey, representing approximately 1 percent of that year's total attendance of 35,644. Combined with field interviews conducted from 2001 to 2004 and a small pilot e-mail survey conducted in 2001, my total sample was 336. See Appendix 2 for the on-line survey and more specific information about where it was distributed. The demographic characteristics of survey respon-dents are summarized in Appendix 1.

8. Although the specific phrasing of this and other questions doubtless col-ored individuals' responses, after careful consideration and experimentation in field interviews and the pilot e-mail survey, I concluded that it was effective for eliciting the type of information that I was interested in while minimizing the potential for misunderstandings.

9. Most responses reflected these general dispositions, but some responses (totaling 7 percent) were ambiguous, difficult to interpret, clearly sarcastic, or otherwise impossible to categorize. A handful of individuals (less than 1 percent) declined to respond to this question.

10. The full context of an individual's worldview can hardly be adequately communicated in either an off-the-cuff e-mail response or a onetime conversa-tion, and individuals' personal identities, orientations, and underlying experi-ences are surely much subtler and more complex than these short statements indicate. Furthermore, given the self-selected nature of on-line survey respon-dents, many of those who participated may have done so *because* they had a favorable inclination toward the subject matter. The opposite may be equally true: some of those who rejected the notion that Burning Man is in some way a

spiritual or religious event may have been similarly motivated to respond. At the
least, it seems reasonable to assume that those who participated in the on-line
survey often did so because they felt they had something to say on the matter.

11. E-mail interview with James, March 30, 2001. All names given here are
those participants requested I use; hence some may be legal names, some may be
nicknames (or playa names), and some may be pseudonyms fashioned only for
participation in this study. A handful of participants asked to remain anonymous,
in which case I assigned a numeric identity for them. I also retained some stylis-
tic quirks in both e-mail responses and verbal replies, although I corrected spelling
and minor grammatical errors.

12. Field interview with Julie, August 30, 2003.

13. Response to on-line survey from Sorren, July 20, 2004.

14. Response to on-line survey from Shawnrif, July 22, 2004.

15. Response to on-line survey from Carmen, July 22, 2004.

16. Response to on-line survey from inferna kittybean, July 20, 2004.

17. Response to on-line survey from James L. Bianchi, July 20, 2004.

18. Response to on-line survey from loraculora, July 20, 2004.

19. Response to on-line survey from Madame_Antibody, July 20, 2004.

20. Interestingly, the number of respondents who cited affiliations with specific Christian or Jewish denominations (totaling 16 Christians and 3 Jews) was
slightly higher than the number who named less "mainstream" affiliations, such
as Buddhism and contemporary Paganism (4 Buddhists, 8 Pagans, and a few others such as Taoists and Hindus). Also, many more participants than I included in
this grouping stated a Jewish identity or background, but most of these individuals made it clear that they saw this as a more secular or cultural affiliation. It is
also noteworthy that when Jewish imagery and ritual show up at Burning Man,
it most often seems to be brought by Jews engaged in creative renewals or re-
constructions of their tradition—such as was the case with the BRCJCC theme
camp and a Shabbat service I attended at the *Conexus Cathedral* in 2006 (chap.
5; see also DVD, chap. 5). This seems attributable to the fact that Judaism remains a minority religion in the United States and hence lacks the stigma that
Burners from Christian backgrounds tend to associate with Christian religions.

21. There was also one respondent who stated, "I'm a serious muslim . . .
heh . . . but BM is in line with Allah so its all good" (response to on-line survey
from Japhy, August 2, 2004). The same individual gave his ethnicity as "half
white and half afghan," but given the sarcastic tone I read in his first response, I
included his reply in the unclassifiable group. It is also noteworthy that Islamic
imagery or practice is almost never found at Burning Man, possibly because of
the prevailing cultural tensions between and stereotypes surrounding "Islam"
and "the West," as well as the relatively few Muslims (or those of Muslim de-
scent) who attend the event.

22. Field interview with Jay Michaelson, September 4, 2004.

23. Field interview with Rachel, August 31, 2002.

24. Response to on-line survey from Burnzie, August 2, 2004.

25. E-mail interview with Michael Ackblom, March 30, 2001.

26. Randy Bohlender, "The Redefinition of My Personal Concept of Weird,"
available at www.next-wave.org/oct00/burningman.htm; accessed June 7, 2007.

27. Ibid.

28. Field interview with Randy Bohlender, September 2, 2004.

29. Randy Bohlender, "A Pastor on the Playa? Why I Go to Burning Man," available at http://www.burningman.com/blackrockcity_yearround/written _reflections/pastor_on_the_playa.html; accessed January 5, 2009.

30. Field interview with Priscilla Queen of Persistence, August 29, 2002; response to on-line survey from Agrazeone, July 20, 2004; response to on-line survey from Jocko, July 20, 2004; response to on-line survey from Charles Gadeken, July 21, 2004; response to on-line survey from anonymous respondent (#264), July 29, 2004; response to on-line survey from Rex, August 8, 2004.

31. Response to on-line survey from anonymous respondent (#154), July 21, 2004.

32. Response to on-line survey from Electro Pimp Daddy, July 20, 2004.

33. Response to on-line survey from St. Vincent Harvestore, July 20, 2004.

34. Response to on-line survey from anonymous respondent (#12), July 20, 2004.

35. E-mail interview with Argyre, March 30, 2001.

36. Response to on-line survey from Kitte Ka'at, July 20, 2004.

37. Response to on-line survey from Julie, July 21, 2004.

38. Response to on-line survey from Juicy Mermaid, July 21, 2004.

39. Response to on-line survey from Jessica, July 20, 2004.

40. Response to on-line survey from sunnay, July 24, 2004.

41. Response to on-line survey from Edie Kaboom, July 20, 2004. Original emphasis.

42. Response to on-line survey from Player, July 20, 2004.

43. Response to on-line survey from Rick Brown, July 20, 2004; response to on-line survey from Jarjar, July 20, 2004.

44. Response to on-line survey from Mr. Freeze, July 31, 2004.

45. Response to on-line survey from bc, July 20, 2004.

46. Response to on-line survey from aerialbear, July 21, 2004.

47. Response to on-line survey from Mixtress Pinky, July 21, 2004.

48. Response to on-line survey from evonne, July 20, 2004. Original emphasis.

49. Response to on-line survey from Cait, July 21, 2004.

50. Response to on-line survey from Charles Gadeken, July 20, 2004.

51. Response to on-line survey from Sensei, July 23, 2004.

52. Response to on-line survey from queer orange voodoo, July 20, 2004.

53. Weber, *The Protestant Ethic and the Spirit of Capitalism.*

54. Gallup Organization, "2006 Gallup Poll: Religion," available at www .galluppoll.com/content/default.aspx?ci=1690; accessed February 23, 2007.

55. The Association of Religion Data Archives, "2004 General Social Survey," available at www.thearda.com/Archive/Files/Codebooks/GSS2004_CB.asp; accessed February 23, 2007; and Baylor Institute for Studies of Religion, "2006 Baylor Surveys of Religion," available at www.baylor.edu/isreligion/index.php?id= 40634; accessed February 23, 2007. See also Gallup and Lindsay, *Surveying the Religious Landscape,* 2; and Roof, *Spiritual Marketplace,* 36.

56. For example, the historian Jon Butler found that Christianity initially attracted a very slim percentage of adherents in the nation's colonial, revolutionary,

and postrevolutionary periods and that beliefs and practices concerning magic and the occult thrived in early periods of U.S. history. These continued into the nineteenth century as spiritualism, New Thought, and other alternative religious movements, which have continued to influence spiritual and religious beliefs and practices into the present. See Butler, *Awash in a Sea of Faith*. For another example, the sociologists Roger Finke and Rodney Stark concluded from their examination of the history of "corporate" (i.e., institutional) U.S. religions that the perceived "eruption" of new and alternative religious movements since the 1960s is in fact "far better characterized by stability and continuity. Although significant changes have occurred, or at least been recently recognized, they were the result not of sudden eruptions but of gradual, long-term, linear shifts." See Finke and Stark, *The Churching of America, 1776–1990*, 239.

57. Bellah and colleagues termed this trend "Sheilaism," after the pseudonym of one of their interviewees, who described her religious orientation with this oft-cited statement: "I believe in God. I'm not a religious fanatic. I can't remember the last time I went to church. My faith has carried me a long way. It's Sheilaism. Just my own little voice." See Bellah et al., *Habits of the Heart*, 221.

58. As an alternative to either the rootless "spirituality of seeking" or rigid "spirituality of dwelling" (which he felt lacked the fluidity and negotiability necessitated by our constantly and rapidly shifting social landscape), Wuthnow proposed a "spirituality of practice" that would embrace the deeper sense of community and commitment implicit in a spirituality of dwelling while also welcoming the freedoms and inspirations of a spirituality of seeking. See Wuthnow, *After Heaven*.

59. Roof, *Spiritual Marketplace*, 203.

60. The demographic constituency of survey respondents is summarized and compared to survey data from other sources in Appendix 1.

61. In an earlier publication, Roof proposed a distinction between spirituality and religion, which he framed in terms of spirit and institution: "*Spirit* is the inner, experiential aspect of religion; *institution* is the outer, established form of religion." He went on to state that for the majority of respondents to his survey, "to be religious conveys an institutional connotation. . . . To be spiritual, in contrast, is more personal and has to do with the deepest motivations of life. . . . Religion . . . is doctrine and tradition, and spirituality is more immediate and experiential." See Roof, *Generation of Seekers*, 30, 76–78; original emphasis. Robert Fuller—who estimated that roughly 19 percent of the U.S. population would describe themselves as "spiritual, but not religious"—echoed this sentiment in maintaining that for the individuals he studied, the term *religious* has come to be associated with the *public* sphere, while the term *spirituality* is increasingly thought to refer to the realm of *private* experience. He argued that a specifically spiritual orientation "consists of attitudes, ideas, lifestyles, and specific practices based upon a conviction (1) that the visible world is part of a more spiritual universe from which it draws its chief significance, and (2) that union or harmonious relation with this 'spiritual more' is our true end." See Fuller, *Spiritual, but Not Religious*, 5–6, 8.

62. Flory, "Conclusion," 244.

3. RITUAL WITHOUT DOGMA

1. Stuart Mangrum, "What Is Burning Man?" (1998 Summer Newsletter), available at www.burningman.com/whatisburningman/1998/98n_letter_sum_1 .html; accessed January 5, 2009. Mangrum was director of communications (or, as he termed his role, Minister of Propaganda) for the Burning Man Project from 1993 to 1996.

2. For other considerations of festivals as "rites of reversal" or "inversion," see, among others, Bell, *Ritual*, 120–28; and Falassi, *Time out of Time*, 1–10.

3. For an important critique of the alleged universal applicability of Turner's key theories based on the existence of "competing discourses" in various pilgrimage sites, see Eade and Sallnow, *Contesting the Sacred*, 5.

4. In 2002 I heard a woman nearby shouting, in all apparent earnestness, "USA! USA!" though this was a rather uncharacteristic form of expression. Perhaps it can be interpreted as a reaction to the increasing professionalism of the attendant fireworks display, rendering the event more like a Fourth of July celebration. Or perhaps it was a response to the increased political concerns that were in evidence that first year after 9/11. Or perhaps she just represented one of the unpredictable anomalies that give Burning Man its mystery.

5. Response to on-line survey from Inferna Kittybean, July 20, 2004.

6. E-mail correspondence with Jeff Herzbach, November 13, 2000.

7. Ibid.

8. Field interview with Julie, August 30, 2003.

9. Erik Davis writes of this as "the cult of flicker." See Davis, "Beyond Belief," 16–40.

10. "Afterburn Report 2001: Fire Conclave," available at http://afterburn .burningman.com/01/art/fire_conclave.html; accessed January 5, 2009.

11. "2001 Theme: The Seven Ages," available at www.burningman.com/whatis burningman/2001/01_theme.html; accessed January 5, 2009. The Seven Ages theme was modeled on a passage from Shakespeare's *As You Like It*, act 2, scene 7: "All the world's a stage, / And all the men and women merely players: / They have their exits and their entrances; / And one man in his time plays many parts, / His acts being seven ages." See George Lyman Kittredge, ed., *As You Like It* (Lexington, MA: Xerox College Publishing, 1967), 44.

12. "2001 Theme: The Seven Ages."

13. "2002 Theme: The Floating World."

14. Ibid. Original emphasis.

15. KS, pers. com., August 2002.

16. Interview with Larry Harvey, January 8, 2005.

17. "2003 Art Theme: Beyond Belief," available at www.burningman.com/ whatisburningman/2003/03_theme.html; accessed January 5, 2009.

18. Landberg, "Interactivity in the Observatory," 1. Emphasis added.

19. I did witness a few performances in the *Observatory* that appeared to embrace its abstract intention. One was a man clad in a monkish brown robe and hood that concealed his face, with a rubber snake wound aound his neck, sitting lotus-style. He uttered dark pronouncements about humanity, addiction,

and God, saying, for example, "We're all just God's little crack babies." (I later saw this man sitting silently in front of the Temple.) Another intriguing use of the space was provided by bodies inhabiting a large orange sack. Individuals, duos, or groups inside the sack animated the stretchy fabric as a large gelatinous blob by pushing their faces and bodies against the fabric. Occasionally they drew unsuspecting observers in through an opening, where, for a time, they became assimilated into the superorganism. Other participants used the space for somewhat more conventional musical performances, but it often seemed that the most frequent use of the dioramas was as places in which to hang out. I also saw a man with a can of Budweiser in his hand, stumbling about and mumbling belligerently, though I couldn't be sure that his behavior wasn't meant to be taken as some form of dada performance art.

20. TH, pers. com., August 30, 2003.

21. For the most extensive coverage and summary of many other media reports, see Scott Beale, "Burning Man Set on Fire Early Due to Arson," available at http://laughingsquid.com/burning-man-set-on-fire-early-arson-is-to-blame; accessed January 5, 2009.

22. In June 2008 Addis pled guilty to the lesser felony charges of damaging property. His sentence generated intense debate among Burners as well. See http://laughingsquid.com/paul-addis-pleads-guilty-to-burning-man-2007-arson-charges; and http://blog.burningman.com/?p=1988; both accessed January 5, 2009.

23. Paul Addis was paroled in June 2009 and released in September 2009. Arrested in late October 2007 and held without release until his parole, he served a total of twenty-two months. Amacker Bullwinkle, pers. com., September 15, 2009.

24. Patrice Mackey, pers. com., September 2007.

25. See especially www.bm.tribe.net; accessed January 5, 2009.

26. Mark Van Proyen, pers. com., September 2007.

27. The Man that year was mounted above a structure called the *Green Pavilion*, in which a number of environmentally friendly projects using art and technology were showcased—in keeping with the Green Man theme. The *Pavilion* had already been the subject of much controversy in the months preceding that year's festival, because some participants felt that the organizers' invitation to green and alternative energy businesses to exhibit some their projects in the *Pavilion* was tantamount to commodification, even though those businesses were strictly forbidden from advertising or otherwise branding their products on the playa. (See Taylor, "Burning Man Grows Up"). Because of the early Burn and the organizers' decision to use the *Pavilion* space as a worksite in which to rebuild the Man, the *Pavilion* ended up being closed for most of the week.

28. Grimes defines ritual criticism as "the interpretation of a rite or ritual system with a view to implicating its practice." See Grimes, *Ritual Criticism*, 16.

29. See Bey, *T.A.Z.*

30. Turner, *From Ritual to Theatre*, 47. Original emphasis.

31. Turner and Turner, *Image and Pilgrimage*, 252.

32. See "Ten Principles," available at www.burningman.com/whatisburning man/about_burningman/principles.html; accessed January 5, 2009.

33. It has been argued that Turner too often attempted to universally ascribe the qualities of liminality and communitas to the rituals he studied most closely—that is, rites of passage and pilgrimages—without sufficient attention to the ways in which these frameworks may, at various times and in various contexts, break down or be inapplicable in the idealized ways that he was sometimes prone to advance. See, e.g., Eade and Sallnow, *Contesting the Sacred;* Grimes, *Ritual Criticism;* Bell, *Ritual Theory/Ritual Practice;* Sax, *Mountain Goddess;* and Bynum, "Women's Stories, Women's Symbols."

34. Turner and Turner, *Image and Pilgrimage,* 36.

35. Turner, *From Ritual to Theatre,* 32. Turner called this the *subjunctive mood* of ritual—that is, "always concerned with 'wish, desire, possibility, or hypothesis'; it is a world 'as if' not 'it *is* so' " (83).

36. The libretto was based on translations of ancient Sumerian and Akkadian hymns to the Goddess Inanna/Ishtar. See Wolkstein and Kramer, *Inanna, Queen of Heaven and Earth.*

37. "The Temple of Rudra: Opera 1998," available at www.burningmanopera .org/opera98/opera98.html; accessed January 5, 2009.

38. Twan, "Mystical Journey," available at www.burningmanopera.org/history/ opera_99/page_1/mystical/mystical.html; accessed January 5, 2009. Original emphasis.

39. Christopher Fülling and Pepe Ozan, "Le Mystere de Papa Loko: Opera 1999," available at www.burningmanopera.org/opera99/script.html; accessed January 5, 2009.

40. Response to on-line survey from anonymous respondent (#24), July 20, 2004.

41. Christopher Fülling, pers. com., March 5, 2007.

42. See Fülling and Ozan, "Le Mystere de Papa Loko: Opera 1999."

43. Ibid.

44. Ibid. This language was introduced into the script by Fülling, who holds a B.A. in anthropology and studied with Mady Schutzman, a former student of Turner's colleague Richard Schechner, while earning his M.F.A. Christopher Fülling, pers. com., March 27, 2005.

45. Ibid.

46. Ibid.

47. Ibid.

48. "2000 Art Theme: The Body," available at www.burningman.com/whatis burningman/2000/00_theme.html; accessed June 15, 2007.

49. Ibid.

50. For later examples of Ozan's and the opera contingency's contributions to Burning Man, see www.burningmanopera.org; accessed June 15, 2007. In 2009 a new "Burning Opera" premiered in San Francisco titled *How to Survive the Apocalypse:* "a Burning Man–inspired theatrical freak-out that combines rock opera, vaudeville, and a Dionysian revival show that is just as inspired and terrified by current events as you are" and that "aims to communicate the

culture of Burning Man to wider audiences." Directed by Christopher Fülling, scored by Mark Nichols, with a libretto by Erik Davis, and produced by Dana Harrison, this project began after Ron Meiners and I randomly encountered Nichols on the playa one morning in 2006. Meiners is to be credited with spearheading initial efforts to turn that conversation into reality by recruiting Fülling, Davis, Harrison, and others to join in the project. As of this writing, it is hoped that this new opera will be staged in various cities.

51. These were titled in sequence: *Temple of the Mind* (2000); *Temple of Tears* (2001); *Temple of Joy* (2002); *Temple of Honor* (2003); *Temple of Stars* (2004); *Temple of Dreams* (2005); *Temple of Hope* (2006); *Temple of Forgiveness* (2007); *Basura Sagrada* (2008); *Fire of Fires* (2009).

52. David Best and Jack Haye, "Temple of Memory," available at www .burningman.com/whatisburningman/2001/01_art_theme.html#mausoleum; accessed January 5, 2009.

53. Collier, "Building a Community for Grieving at Burning Man"; and personal inscription.

54. David Best, "Temple of Joy," available at www.burningman.com/ whatisburningman/2002/02_art_theme.html; accessed January 5, 2009.

55. Pike, "No Novenas for the Dead," 198.

56. Ibid., 197.

57. BC and DJ, pers. com., August 2002.

58. See Poseidon Rex, "BRC Honors Emergency Heroes," *Black Rock Gazette* 11, no. 46 (September 1, 2002, Exodus ed.): 1.

59. Response to on-line survey from Danielle French, July 20, 2004.

60. Response to on-line survey from Michel "Maquette" Reeverts, July 22, 2004.

61. Response to on-line survey from Technopatra, July 22, 2004.

62. See "Getting Married at Burning Man," available at www.burningman .com/preparation/event_survival/weddings.html; accessed January 5, 2009.

63. Response to on-line survey from Chris Arkenberg, July 30, 2004.

64. Response to on-line survey from Charles Gadeken, July 21, 2004.

65. Response to on-line survey from Charles Gadeken, November 30, 2004.

66. Ibid. Between 1996 and 2002 Gadeken installed a series of 100- to 300-foot-long canvas paintings on the playa, each of which was created with the help of his community of friends in the Illumination Village theme camp and ceremonially burned at some point during the event. See www.burningart.com; accessed November 26, 2008.

67. Interview with Larry Harvey, January 8, 2005. Also Rory Turner and Alex Turner, pers. com., March 22, 2005.

68. St John, "Alternative Cultural Heterotopia and the Liminoid Body." See also Bowditch, "Temple of Tears"; Pike, "Desert Goddesses and Apocalyptic Art"; Hockett, "Burning Man as Ethnographic Experience"; Hockett, "Reckoning Ritual and Counterculture in the Burning Man Community"; Kozinets, "Can Consumers Escape the Market?"

69. Turner, *Ritual Process*, 113; see also Turner, *Dramas, Fields, and Metaphors*, 168–69. Ron Grimes, once a student of Turner's, also noted this intellectual

exchange: "Some would say Turner absorbed it from his students in the 1960s; others would say his students of the 1960s absorbed it from him. The truth is probably that the relations between culture and counterculture are circular, or systematic." See Grimes, *Ritual Criticism*, 21.

70. Van Gennep, *The Rites of Passage*.

71. Bell, *Ritual*, 263–64.

72. Harvey credited Mircea Eliade as well as William James and Heinz Kohut as influences. Interview with Larry Harvey, January 8, 2005.

73. "1999 Art Theme: The Wheel of Time," available at www.burningman .com/whatisburningman/1999/99_theme.html; accessed January 5, 2009. Emphasis added.

74. See Eliade, *The Myth of the Eternal Return*.

75. "2003 Art Theme: Beyond Belief," available at www.burningman.com/ whatisburningman/2003/03_theme.html.

4. DESERT PILGRIMAGE

1. I phrased the question this way because I wanted to encourage participants to think of "transformation" broadly, recognizing that individuals probably would have different understandings of this term. I also asked respondents to say more about how these changes had transpired for them and why they thought Burning Man brought about that transformation. See Appendix 2.

2. These values, along with immediacy, decommodification, and responsibility, reflect Burning Man's "Ten Principles." See chapter 1 for more on these concepts.

3. I am influenced here by Geertz's perspectives on ethos and worldview as synthesized through rituals and symbols, as well as Bell's critique of this theory. See Geertz, *Interpretation of Cultures*, 126–27; Bell, *Ritual Theory / Ritual Practice*, 20–31.

4. "Afterburn Report 2001: Future Vision," available at http://afterburn .burningman.com/01/future.html. See also Larry Harvey with the Very Rev. Alan Jones, "The Forum at Grace Cathedral: Radical Ritual," available at www .gracecathedral.org/enrichment/forum/for_20010520.shtml; both accessed January 5, 2009; and at "Awe to Action Conference," San Francisco, July 10, 2004.

5. "Culture in Black Rock City," available at www.burningman.com/ preparation/event_survival/culture_in_brc.html; accessed January 5, 2009.

6. As with other aspects of participants' experiences at and conceptions of Burning Man—such as their views on religion and spirituality—these narratives tended to display certain common tendencies and themes while remaining varied and individualistic, as befits the heterogeneous nature of the event. However, nearly two-thirds of respondents (59 percent) referenced more than one common theme in explaining their understandings of how and why they felt Burning Man had changed them. Thus it should be noted that any percentages given here reflect the total number of respondents who voiced these particular orientations rather than any particular typology.

7. E-mail from Argyre, March 30, 2001. Original emphasis.

8. Response to on-line survey from Playapus, July 16, 2004.

9. Response to on-line survey from Silken Tofu, August 11, 2004.

10. Response to on-line survey from Emily, July 21, 2004.

11. Response to on-line survey from technopatra, July 22, 2004.

12. Response to on-line survey from Captain Conundrum, July 25, 2004. Original emphasis.

13. Response to on-line survey from PurpleKoosh, July 20, 2004.

14. Response to on-line survey from mstyckle, July 16, 2004.

15. Response to on-line survey from Danielle French, July 20, 2004. Original emphasis.

16. Those who volunteer for the organization are explicitly invited to create playa names for themselves, which are used as radio handles for internal communication during the event.

17. Response to on-line survey from Rockstar, July 21, 2004.

18. Response to on-line survey from Edie Kaboom, July 20, 2004.

19. Response to on-line survey from Trouble, July 22, 2004.

20. See www.burnerswithoutborders.org; accessed June 20, 2007.

21. These efforts were initially dubbed the "Temple to Temple" project because several members of the Temple construction crew were among the first to be involved. See "Burning Man and Hurricane Katrina," www.burningman.com/blackrockcity_yearround/misc/katrina_thumper.html; accessed January 5, 2009.

22. Another creative voter registration effort was spearheaded in 2004 by a New York Burner called Lady Merv, who drove a bus painted to look like a bald eagle across the country to the event, spelling out the word *vote* on the map, charting her progress on a Web site, and registering voters along the way.

23. Response to on-line survey from Nelzibub, July 20, 2004. Original emphasis.

24. Response to on-line survey from twistedcat, July 20, 2004.

25. Response to on-line survey from cenglewood, September 9, 2004.

26. Response to on-line survey from Isotopia, August 8, 2004.

27. Response to on-line survey from lady god diva flamma, July 23, 2004. Original emphasis.

28. Response to on-line survey from Cait, July 21, 2004.

29. Turner and Turner, *Image and Pilgrimage,* 34.

30. To assist in this transition, the San Francisco-based Burner community and several regional ones host "decompression parties" in the weeks after the event.

31. The Black Rock Desert was declared a National Conservation Area in 2000 in part as a recognition of the historical value of these trails, which are several miles away from the part of playa where Burning Man takes place. This is intentional on the part of the BLM in its mandate to protect historic sites. See "Black Rock Desert-High Rock Canyon Emigrant Trails National Conservation Area Act of 2000," available at www.nv.blm.gov/Winnemucca/blackrock/NCA%20Act%20of%202000.pdf; accessed January 5, 2009.

32. Response to on-line survey from John Juan, July 20, 2004. Original emphasis.

33. Turner, *Ritual Process,* 96.

34. For more on Burner demography, see Appendix 1.

35. A prominent exception is an artists' collective called the Flaming Lotus Girls, founded by women but whose membership now includes both women and men. The collective has designed and built large-scale pyrotechnic art for Burning Man since 2000. See www.flaminglotus.com; accessed June 20, 2007.

36. A research team from the women's studies, sociology, and social psychology departments at the University of Nevada, Reno, attended Burning Man in 2005 to study gender roles at the event. The team administered the *Bem Sex Role Inventory (BSRI)* and found that men enjoyed a higher degree of "erotic plasticity"—meaning that they felt freer to express a variety of gendered and sexual traits—in this context than in the default culture. Mary White Stewart, Jaime Anstee, Sean P. O'Hair, Maia Finholm, and Monica McNeely, "The Burning Man's Man: Temporary Autonomy and Emerging Gender Norms," paper presented at the National Women's Studies Association, June 17, 2006.

37. E-mail from Sena, March 30, 2001.

38. E-mail from Michael Ackblom, March 30, 2001.

39. Response to on-line survey from St. Vincent Harvestore, July 20, 2004.

40. P Segal, pers. com., October 2001. When the Café was run by P, it was called the Café Temp Perdu, in honor of her favorite author, Marcel Proust.

41. Eade and Sallnow, *Contesting the Sacred,* 5.

42. Two percent of respondents declined to respond to this question.

43. Turner and Turner, *Image and Pilgrimage,* 20.

44. Mark Van Proyen, pers. com., August 2002.

45. Graham St John also speculated that some art cars and camps were becoming more like "VIP lounges." Personal correspondence, March 7, 2007.

46. For more on electronic dance music culture at Burning Man and elsewhere, see St John, *Technomad*. For more on the tensions between different subcultures at Burning Man, see Steven T. Jones, "Burner Season," *San Francisco Bay Guardian,* June 14, 2005; available at www.sfbg.com/39/37/cover_barsclubs_burningman.html; accessed January 5, 2009.

47. Weiners and Plunkett, *Burning Man,* n.p.

48. I should also mention that several of those who took advantage of this tour with me were individuals with limited mobility, as a result of injury or disability, who otherwise might have had a difficult time seeing the artworks, which are dispersed across a few square miles of open space.

49. See MacCannell, *The Tourist*. MacCannell later clarified his argument, saying that tourists know that the experience is a kind of "fake authenticity" but desire it nevertheless. Dean MacCannell, presentation at the Tourism Studies Working Group, University of California, Berkeley, February 13, 2004.

50. MacCannell, "Remarks on the Commodification of Cultures"; MacCannell, *The Tourist,* 84.

51. For example, the sociologist Kevin Meethan argued:

> The development of tourism analysis needs to proceed beyond static concepts that reduce complexity to an essential either/or choice, modernity versus the primitive, the inauthentic versus the authentic, the local versus the global.... The central problem here, I would suggest, is a result of seeing modernity as an end product or a steady state, as being that which "we" have, and "others" should avoid. In turn,

this can imply a static model of equilibrium in which cultures are classified as either modern or non-modern, and the intrusion of the former into the latter through the medium of tourism can only result in destabilisation and the erosion of authentic ways of life. (*Tourism in Global Society*, 15, 165)

Curiously, what initially drew me to Meethan's book was not its content but its cover, which features a photograph of Pepe Ozan's 1996 *City of Dis* (see DVD, chap. 6). However, the text makes no mention of Burning Man, not even in the photo caption on the book jacket. When I queried Meethan about this choice he simply told me that he had found the image, initially clipped from the *Independent* newspaper, "strong and strange," and when the painting he had suggested for the cover was unavailable, he presented this photograph to his publisher as an alternative (personal correspondence, Kevin Meethan, October 26, 2003). I cannot help but read his ironic choice as reflecting the notion that Burning Man, or at least one its key early images, exemplifies touristic quests for a romanticized premodernity but one that has emerged in a distinctly modern (or "postmodern") milieu.

52. See Jenny Bird and John Mosbaugh, "Carousel Numinous," available at www.burningman.com/whatisburningman/2003/03_art_theme4.html#carousel; accessed January 5, 2009.

53. See Dadara, "Burning GreyMen," available at www.burningman.com/whatisburningman/2003/03_art_theme4.html#greymen; accessed January 5, 2009.

5. MEDIA MECCA

1. Examples here are *Malcolm in the Middle, Reno 911, The Simpsons, South Park,* and the *Colbert Report,* among many others.

2. See, among others, Hoover and Lundby, *Rethinking Media, Religion, and Culture;* Hoover and Clark, *Practicing Religion in the Age of the Media;* and Clark, *Religion, Media, and the Marketplace.*

3. Carey, *Communication as Culture.*

4. See Dayan and Katz, *Media Events.* Dayan and Katz were careful to differentiate between "ceremonial" media events—which they categorized as contests, conquests, and coronations—and "news" media events that might also enthrall national or international audiences, noting, for example, that they were "interested here in the Kennedy funeral—a great ceremonial event—and not the Kennedy assassination—a great news event" (9).

5. When I screened rough cuts of the DVD for a handful of friends, they had much the same responses.

6. Schechner, *Between Theater and Anthropology,* 315. See also Grimes, "Ritual and the Media," 226–27. Grimes has argued that the metaphorical linkages between media and ritual need to be treated with caution:

The equating strategy (media = ritual) has limited utility. It turns heads, it attracts attention, but the shock value is short-lived. . . . If in the long run there is nothing more to say than "Media activity is ritual activity," each idea loses its capacity to provoke interesting perspectives on the other, because there is insufficient tension between them. . . . Scholars need to ask not just whether some aspect of media is ritual, but in what respect it is ritual. Do we treat something as ritualistic because

it is formulaic? Because it is repetitive? Because it is religious? In short, what definition of ritual do we imply by our claims?

7. Couldry, *Media Rituals,* 8–9. Durkheim understood rituals as systems of
belief and practice that unite individuals in moral communities by constructing
and mediating collectively held beliefs. See Durkheim, *The Elementary Forms of
Religious Life.*

8. Couldry, *Media Rituals,* 8–9.

9. Mangrum returned to write articles for the *Black Rock Gazette* in 1998
but has since withdrawn completely from any staff or volunteer role, although
he continued to attend as a participant in later years.

10. I wrote for the *Gazette* in 1997 and was a member of the Media Team
from 1998 to 2001. I was not the only scholar with some ethnographic training
who joined the Media Team at that time. Others were Karie Henderson, who completed a visual anthropology senior thesis at the University of California, Santa
Cruz, and Katherine Chen, who was completing her sociology Ph.D. at Harvard by
conducting a study of volunteerism at Burning Man. See Chen, *Enabling Creative
Chaos.*

11. A semi–pro bono attorney is retained to defend these rights, although some
usages of "Burning Man" for commercial purposes slip through. For example, a
2007 Microsoft television ad briefly referred to the event in order to parody relations between a father desperately trying to seem "hip" to his young Microsoft-using
son. Needless to say, many participants were outraged, but the organization chose
not to take action, stating that the advertisement fell under "fair use." In early 2007
control of this trademark was disputed in a lawsuit filed by John Law against the
BRC LLC and his former partners, Harvey and Michael. For more on this suit, see
chapter 1, note 39.

12. It does not actually matter that some participants inevitably capture moving images without signing a personal or other use agreement, as the fact that
organization has consistently articulated this policy renders it legally binding.

13. The DVD that accompanies this text was subject to and abided by these
requirements.

14. MTV's sister channel, VH1, coproduced a documentary series, *The
Drug Years,* that traced the history and cultural impact of illicit drug use in the
United States and featured a short clip of the Burning Man festival at the end of
the last episode. Organizers had not approved of this project and were not even
aware of it until it aired in mid-2006. However, they were unable to retroac-
tively censure the series because the producers had acquired old footage of Burning Man that predated the organization's current media policies.

15. For more information on these films, see, respectively, www.goneoffdeep
.com; www.burningmanconfessions.com; and www.giftingit.com; all accessed
January 5, 2009.

16. In 2009, the Electronic Frontier Foundation (EFF), which is dedicated to
"defending free speech, privacy, innovation, and consumer rights" on the Internet,
took the Burning Man organization to task for its image rights policy, which
stipulates, "No use of images, film, or video obtained at the event may be made
without prior written permission from Burning Man, other than personal use."

See www.eff.org/about; and http://tickets2.burningman.com/info.php?i=2386; both accessed September 20, 2009. The EFF critiqued Burning Man's policy as damaging to free speech and as counter to the event's stated goals to "celebrate our individuality, creativity and free spirit." Andie Grace responded for the Burning Man organization:

> Just like the EFF, we honestly seek to think outside old paradigms and boxes of "creative property" in the digital age, but we view Black Rock City through a more complicated lens, and our view of issues facing creative ownership is not rendered in extremes of black and white. To us, the rights of the individual participant to privacy while in Black Rock City in this unique environment for free expression— and our philosophical desire to maintain it out of reach of those who would exploit that expression just to sell cars or soft drinks—happens to come first.
>
> In fact, there are but two essential reasons we maintain these increased controls on behalf of our community: to protect our participants so that images that violate their privacy are not displayed, and to prevent companies from using Burning Man to sell products.

For the full text of this exchange, see Corynne McSherry, "Snatching Rights on the Playa," *Electronic Frontier Foundation* (August 12, 2009); available at www.eff.org/deeplinks/2009/08/snatching-rights-playa; and Andie Grace, " 'Snatching Digital Rights' or Protecting Our Culture? Burning Man and the EFF," *The Burning Blog* (August 14, 2009); available at http://blog.burningman .com/?p=4599; both accessed September 20, 2009.

17. Martin Griffith, "Drug Problem Surfaces at Burning Man Festival," Associated Press, September 4, 1999.

18. See Lessley Anderson, "Burning Spin: Organizers of the Burning Man Festival Pull out All the Stops to Control the Press—and It's a Good Thing They Do," *San Francisco Weekly,* August 28, 2002.

19. The art tour that I took in 2004 (see chap. 4) grew out of this tour led by Media Team staff members for media professionals covering the event.

20. This incident, combined with increasing problems resulting from the rising numbers of art cars, led to changes in the internal administrative oversight of art cars starting in 2004. A much stricter "registration" process was implemented in order to limit the number of vehicles on the playa. Although many participants had complained about the growing art car problem, this new process was also controversial. Some participants felt that the new policies were too restrictive, once again demonstrating the multiplicity of participants' perspectives on the event.

21. Goldston, "Family Comes to Terms with Belmont Woman's Death at Burning Man Fest."

22. The "Media Mecca" moniker for the media registration tent replaced the "Press Here" slogan in 1998 for its evocation of the idea that all members of the media should go there at least once during their visit to Black Rock City. I feel I should add that I suggested this title to the team, after overhearing the phrase spoken in passing by someone else. It struck me as an apt description for the on-playa home of the Media Team, and the rest of the team at that time enthusiastically agreed.

23. Other admonitions were occasionally added, such as the 2002 version, which read: "This pass entitles you to nothing in particular, but instead should serve as a reminder to move beyond the constraints of analyzing perception to the joy of experiencing."

24. *National Geographic* sent a small team to the event in 2000, as part of a larger story on the BLM. This issue featured an image of a costumed woman from Burning Man on the cover. See Mitchell, "Public Lands."

25. Schudson, *Discovering the News*, 7, 185–86. Schudson traced the "ideal of objectivity" in the media to the Associated Press's origin in 1848, but it wasn't until after World War I that journalists began to question the nature of vested interests, propaganda, and their own potential collusion with these forces, such that they collectively began to strive for "objectivity."

26. See Goffman, *Frame Analysis;* and Gitlin, *The Whole World Is Watching.* Gitlin defined media frames as "little tacit theories about what exists, what happens, . . . what matters[,] . . . persistent patterns of cognition, interpretation, and presentation, of selection, emphasis, and exclusion, by which symbol handlers routinely organize discourse, whether verbal or visual" (6–7).

27. See, e.g., Wolfe, *The New Journalism*. The tradition and sentiments of "new journalism" live on today: I encountered at least one young journalist who declared in his Media Team registration that he planned to write a "new journalism" piece.

28. See Collier, "Building a Community for Grieving at Burning Man"; and Doherty, *This Is Burning Man.*

29. See Janelle Brown, "Quest for Fire: Playing with Matches at the Burning Man Festival," *HotWired,* September 8, 1995; (was) available at http://hotwired .wired.com/road/95/36/index5a.html; accessed February 21, 2005; and Weiners and Plunkett, *Burning Man.*

30. Jeremy Hockett argued that for *all* attendees Burning Man can be "understood as occasioning an 'ethnographic ritual' that invites participant observation, as individuals are encouraged to reflect on their own culture and their own roles in constructing that culture." For example, Hockett observed that many participants seem compelled to write down their stories and share them with the world (thus enacting the "-graphy" component of "ethnography") on e-mail lists, on-line bulletin boards, or their own Web sites. See Hockett, "Burning Man as Ethnographic Experience," 75–76.

31. Schudson, *The Sociology of News*, 50.

32. Sonner, "Burning Man Drawing 20,000 to Nevada's Black Rock Desert."

33. See Harvey, "Media Myths."

34. Colton, "America's Hottest Festival."

35. Priedite, "Where High-Tech Meets Low Life and Many a Wood Man Has Met His Match."

36. Vulliamy, "Anarchy Rules at Wildest Party on Earth."

37. Hua, "Tech Crowd Gets Tribal."

38. Whiting, "Modern Primitive Make Burning Man Hottest Ever."

39. Upledger, "The Burning Man Experience."

40. Vulliamy, "Anarchy Rules at Wildest Party on Earth," 8.

41. Grant, "Ten Thousand Go Mad in Nevada."

42. Harvey, "Media Myths."

43. Priedite, "Where High-Tech Meets Low Life."

44. Martin, "Burning Man Organizers Grow Hot under the Collar over Rising Federal Fees to Use Black Rock Desert for Festival."

45. Thompson, "Burning Man Festival a Focus for Parties, Religious Yearning."

46. Ibid.

47. Ibid.

48. Ibid.

49. Ibid.

50. York, *Pagan Theology,* 167. Another Pagan scholar, Chas Clifton, has similarly speculated that "a Pagan theologian like Michael York, with his position that 'Paganism is [a] root religion,' could argue that Burning Man undoubtedly contains Pagan cultic elements at an almost unconscious level." See Chas Clifton, "Pastors on the Playa," in *Letter from Hardscrabble Creek (a Pagan Writer's Blog);* available at www.chasclifton.com/archive/2004_11_01_archive .html; accessed January 5, 2009.

51. Bruce Sterling, "Greetings from Burning Man," *Wired* 4.11 (November 1996): 196–206, 274. Also available at www.wired.com/wired/archive/4.11/ burningman.html; accessed January 5, 2009.

52. Google first began to incorporate seasonal themes in its logo when Page and Brin made their own pilgrimage to the event in 1999. See www.npr.org/templates/ story/story.php?storyId=1521761; and www.google.com/intl/en/holidaylogos99 .html; both accessed January 5, 2009.

53. Kelly, "Bonfire of the Techies."

54. Joyce Slaton, "Geeks At Burning Man: Or How I Spent My Summer Vacation on the Playa," *SFGate* (September 8, 1999); available from www.sfgate .com/cgi-bin/article.cgi?f=/g/a/1999/09/08/burningman.dtl; accessed January 5, 2009.

55. Werde, "Burning Man's Dotcom Hangover."

56. Sullivan, "Dot-Com Fallout Hits Burning Man."

57. Turner, *Counterculture to Cyberculture.*

58. Although it is largely inactive as of this writing, burnman-list@dioxine .net—founded and hosted by Burner Eric Pouyoul since 1994—was once a key on-line presence for the event and its "official" e-mail list in the mid- to late 1990s. It was also an important community and research resource for me when I first began to attend and study the event.

59. This concept has been expressed in personal communications from Ron Meiners, Bruce Damer, and Mark Pesce, among others. Another source for this analogy can be found in the transcript of Larry Harvey, "Burning Man and Cyberspace (9th Annual Be-In, January 1997)," available at www.burningman.com/ whatisburningman/people/cyber.html; accessed January 5, 2009.

60. In addition to blogs, the on-line applications Wikipedia, Flickr, YouTube, Facebook, and MySpace are just a handful of the most popular sites that were held to exemplify "web 2.0," although this has been a contested term among

engineers and entrepreneurs. See, e.g., Tim O'Reilly, "What Is Web 2.0: Design Patterns and Business Models for the Next Generation of Software," available at www.oreillynet.com/pub/a/oreilly/tim/news/2005/09/30/what-is-web-20.html; accessed January 5, 2009.

61. Jenkins, *Convergence Culture*, 259–60.

62. Ibid., 2.

63. For example, many respondents to my on-line survey chose to use their playa names and/or on-line aliases in their replies.

64. Turkle, *Life on the Screen*, 17.

65. See, among many others, Rheingold, *The Virtual Community;* Smith and Kollock, *Communities in Cyberspace;* and Dawson and Cowan, *Religion Online.*

66. Chayko, *Connecting*, 1–2.

67. For example, in late 2004 and early 2005 a group calling itself "Borg2" challenged the Burning Man organization's art granting process, demanding greater transparency and democracy. This effort was largely organized and driven on-line, relying extensively on the tribe.net community forums. Although the campaign did not succeed in its quest to effect changes in the BMorg's art granting process, it did succeed in raising funds for artwork and reduced complacency about the process on the part of both participants and organizers. See www .whatiamupto.com/BORG2/index.html; accessed January 5, 2009.

68. Carey, *Communication as Culture*, 18; and Couldry, *Media Rituals.*

69. See, e.g., Hoover, *Religion in the Media Age.*

70. In other regards, too, my long involvement with the event has sometimes meant that my perspectives and analyses have, sometimes unwittingly, filtered into others' representations of Burning Man. For example, in his book, *Authentic Fakes,* David Chidester cited Larry Harvey as stating, "Burning Man brings together art, performance, fire, and temporary community to create what has been called 'ritual without dogma.' " When I initially (re)read those words they struck me as oddly familiar, so I Googled them. Sure enough, though the quotation draws on terms and phrases that Harvey had used, I actually wrote that sentence in 1999 when, while employed at Grace Cathedral in San Francisco, I arranged to have Harvey speak at the weekly public conversation program I coproduced. See "Larry Harvey at Grace Cathedral: 'Radical Ritual,' " available at www.burningman.com/blackrockcity_yearround/jrs/vol05/jrs_v05_i13.html; accessed January 5, 2009; and Chidester, *Authentic Fakes,* 196. See also DVD, chap. 1.

71. Grimes, *Rite Out of Place*, 27.

72. See "Rights and Responsibilities for Media and Participants," available at www.burningman.com/press/pressRandR.html; accessed January 5, 2009.

73. Grimes, *Rite Out of Place*, 38.

74. For example, in summer 2007 a vigorous debate broke out among Burners on the tribe.net forums in response to a *Business 2.0* article that covered the efforts of Burning Man organizers to "Green the Burn" in part by inviting alternative energy businesses to display their wares at the event that year in a large "pavilion" located at the base of the Man. Although organizers were clear that no "branding"

or other direct product promotion would be allowed at the festival site, some participants were outraged by this apparent transgression of the event's core decommodification principle, but others thought that the controversy had less to do with any actual breach of the festival's ethos and more to do with the language employed by the journalist (and longtime Burner) Chris Taylor in framing the article to the business readership of that magazine. See Chris Taylor, "Burning Man Grows Up," *Business 2.0,* July 3, 2007, 66–70; and "Green Man Pavilion," available at www.burningman.com/environment/pavilion_invitation.html; accessed January 5, 2009.

6. BURN-A-LUJAH!

1. For more information and background on Reverend Billy, see his books and Web site: Talen [Reverend Billy], *What Would Jesus Buy?;* Talen, *What Should I Do If Reverend Billy Is in My Store?;* and www.revbilly.com; accessed January 5, 2009.

2. Specific venues have ranged from a spectacular art deco Spiegeltent to the parish hall of St. Mark's (Episcopal) Church-in-the-Bowery. Their public demonstrations have included "prayer meetings" in front of Ground Zero in New York in advance of the 2004 Republican Convention, as well as various rallies in support of union labor, anti-sweatshop legislation, and other progressive causes. In late 2005 Reverend Billy took his "gospel" on the road with a cross-country bus tour from Manhattan to the Mall of America in Minnesota and ending up at Disneyland just before Christmas. This tour was filmed for a documentary about Reverend Billy titled *What Would Jesus Buy,* directed by Rob VanAlkemade and produced by Morgan Spurlock, released in late 2007. See http://wwjbmovie.com; accessed January 5, 2009.

3. Directed by Jill Sharpe. See www.culturejamthefilm.com; accessed January 5, 2009.

4. Performance of Reverend Billy and the Stop Shopping Gospel Choir, August 29, 2003.

5. Interview with James Solomon Benn, June 5, 2005.

6. Composed by Bill Talen and Benny Key, performance of Reverend Billy and the Stop Shopping Gospel Choir, August 29, 2003. Recordings of these songs have since been made available on CD: *Reverend Billy and the Church of Stop Shopping* (Tomato Records / The Egge Company, New York, 2004).

7. Ibid.

8. Interview with Bill Talen, October 16, 2003.

9. Ibid. *Common Ground* is a monthly newspaper that publishes listings of New Age goods and services.

10. From the mid-1980s through the early 1990s Talen codirected a successful and well-respected San Francisco theater company, Life on the Water. When the company folded, he moved to New York, where he eventually reinvented himself as "Reverend Billy." He was inspired in part by his friend and mentor the Rev. Sidney Lanier, an Episcopal priest (and cousin of Tennessee Williams) with long ties to the New York theater community whose parish, St. Clement's in Hell's Kitchen, serves part-time as a theater for which Talen became the house manager.

11. See Walter Brueggemann, "What Would Jesus Buy?" *Sojourners* (November 2007); available at www.sojo.net/index.cfm?action=magazine.article& issue=sojo711&article=071110. Accessed January 5, 2009.

12. E-mail from Michael O'Neil, February 23, 2005. (Sent to revbilly-discuss@ lists.riseup.net.) Emphasis added.

13. Performance of Reverend Billy and the Stop Shopping Gospel Choir, September 4, 2005.

Bibliography

Asad, Talal. *Genealogies of Religion: Discipline and Reasons of Power in Christianity and Islam*. Baltimore: Johns Hopkins University Press, 1993.

Baudrillard, Jean. *Simulacra and Simulation*. Translated by Sheila Faria Glaser. Ann Arbor: University of Michigan Press, 1994.

Beale, Scott. "John Law Sues His Former Burning Man Partners." Available at http://laughingsquid.com/john-law-sues-his-former-burning-man-partners.

Behar, Ruth. *The Vulnerable Observer: Anthropology That Breaks Your Heart*. Boston: Beacon Press, 1996.

Bell, Catherine. *Ritual Theory / Ritual Practice*. New York: Oxford University Press, 1992.

———. *Ritual: Perspectives and Dimensions*. Oxford: Oxford University Press, 1997.

Bellah, Robert, et al. *Habits of the Heart: Individualism and Commitment in American Life*. Berkeley: University of California Press, 1985.

Bey, Hakim. *T.A.Z.: The Temporary Autonomous Zone, Ontological Anarchy, Poetic Terrorism*. Brooklyn, NY: Autonomedia, 1991.

Bowditch, Rachel. "Temple of Tears: Revitalizing and Inventing Ritual in the Burning Man Community in Black Rock Desert, Nevada." *Journal of Religion and Theatre* 6, no. 2 (fall 2007): 140–54.

———. *On the Edge of Utopia: Performance and Ritual at Burning Man*. Chicago: Seagull Books, 2010.

Brill, Louis. "The First Year in the Desert." Available at www.burningman.com/whatisburningman/1986_1996/firstyears.html; accessed January 5, 2009.

Butler, Jon. *Awash in a Sea of Faith: Christianizing the American People*. Cambridge, MA: Harvard University Press, 1990.

Bynum, Caroline Walker. "Women's Stories, Women's Symbols: A Critique of Victor Turner's Theory of Liminality." In *Anthropology and the Study of Religion*, edited by Ronald L. Moore and Frank E. Reynolds, 105–25. Chicago: Center for the Scientific Study of Religion, 1984.

Caesar, Julius. *Caesar's War Commentaries*. Edited and translated by John War-
rington. New York: E. P. Dutton, 1953.

Carey, James. *Communication as Culture: Essays on Media and Society*. New
York: Routledge, 2009.

Chayko, Mary. *Connecting: How We Form Social Bonds and Communities in
the Internet Age*. Albany: State University of New York Press, 2002.

Chen, Katherine K. *Enabling Creative Chaos: The Organization behind the
Burning Man Event*. Chicago: University of Chicago Press, 2009.

Chidester, David. *Authentic Fakes: Religion and American Popular Culture*.
Berkeley: University of California Press, 2005.

Clark, Lynn Schofield, ed. *Religion, Media, and the Marketplace*. New Brunswick,
NJ: Rutgers University Press, 2007.

Clifford, James. *Writing Culture: The Poetics and Politics of Ethnography*.
Berkeley: University of California Press, 1986.

Colton, Michael. "America's Hottest Festival; An Eclectic Arts Event Draws
15,000 to the Nevada Desert in August. Call it 'Weirdstock.'" *Washington
Post*, August 27, 1997, D01.

Couldry, Nick. *Media Rituals: A Critical Approach*. London: Routledge, 2003.

Davies, Charlotte Aull. *Reflexive Ethnography: A Guide to Researching Selves
and Others*. New York: Routledge, 1999.

Davis, Erik. "Beyond Belief: The Cults of Burning Man." In *AfterBurn: Reflections on Burning Man*, edited by Lee Gilmore and Mark Van Proyen, 16–40.
Albuquerque: University of New Mexico Press, 2005.

Dawson, Lorne L., and Douglas E. Cowan, eds. *Religion Online: Finding Faith
on the Internet*. New York: Routledge, 2004.

Dayan, Daniel, and Elihu Katz. *Media Events: The Live Broadcasting of History*. Cambridge, MA: Harvard University Press, 1994.

Debord, Guy. *The Society of the Spectacle*. New York: Zone Books, 1994.

Doherty, Brian. *This Is Burning Man: The Rise of a New American Underground*. New York: Little, Brown, 2004.

Durkheim, Emile. *The Elementary Forms of Religious Life*. Translated by Karen
E. Fields. New York: Free Press, 1995 [1912].

Eade, John, and Michael Sallnow, eds. *Contesting the Sacred: The Anthropology of Christian Pilgrimage*. London: Routledge, 1991.

Eliade, Mircea. *The Myth of the Eternal Return: Or, Cosmos and History*. Princeton: Princeton University Press, 1954.

Ellwood, Robert S., Jr. *Alternative Altars: Unconventional and Eastern Spirituality in America*. Chicago: University of Chicago Press, 1978.

Falassi, Alessandro, ed. *Time Out of Time: Essays on the Festival*. Albuquerque:
University of New Mexico Press, 1987.

Finke, Roger, and Rodney Stark. *The Churching of America, 1776–1990: Win-
ners and Losers in Our Religious Economy*. New Brunswick, NJ: Rutgers
University Press, 1992.

Flory, Richard W. "Conclusion: Toward a Theory of Generation X Religion." In
GenX Religion, edited by Richard W. Flory and Donald E. Miller. New York:
Routledge, 2000.

Flory, Richard W., and Donald E. Miller, eds. *GenX Religion*. New York: Rout-
ledge, 2000.
Foucault, Michel. "Of Other Spaces." Available at http://foucault.info/documents/
heteroTopia/foucault.heteroTopia.en.html; accessed January 5, 2009.
Frazer, James George. *The Golden Bough: A Study in Magic and Religion*.
Abridged ed. New York: Collier Books Macmillan, 1922.
Fuller, Robert C. *Spiritual, but Not Religious: Understanding Unchurched Amer-
ica*. New York: Oxford University Press, 2001.
Gallup, George, Jr., and D. Michael Lindsay. *Surveying the Religious Land-
scape: Trends in U.S. Belief*. Harrisburg, PA: Morehouse Publishing, 1999.
Geertz, Clifford. *The Interpretation of Cultures*. New York: Basic Books,
1973.
Gilmore, Lee. "Embers, Dust, and Ashes: Pilgrimage and Healing at the Burning
Man Festival." In *Pilgrimage and Healing*, edited by Jill Dubisch and Michael
Winkelman, 155–77. Tucson: University of Arizona Press, 2005.
———. "Fires of the Heart: Ritual, Pilgrimage, and Transformation at the Burn-
ing Man Festival." In *AfterBurn: Reflections on Burning Man*, edited by Lee
Gilmore and Mark Van Proyen, 43–62. Albuquerque: University of New
Mexico Press, 2005.
———. "Desert Pilgrimage: Liminality, Transformation, and the Other at the
Burning Man Festival." In *On the Road to Being There: Studies in Pilgrim-
age and Tourism in Late Modernity*, edited by William H. Swatos, 125–58.
Leiden: Brill, 2006.
———. "Media Mecca: Tensions, Tropes, and Techno-pagans at the Burning
Man Festival." In *Religion, Media, and the Marketplace*, edited by Lynn
Schofield Clark, 249–79. Piscataway, NJ: Rutgers University Press, 2007.
———. "Of Ordeals and Operas: Reflexive Ritualizing at the Burning Man Fes-
tival." In *Victor Turner and Contemporary Cultural Performance*, edited by
Graham St John, 211–26. New York: Berghahn, 2008.
Gilmore, Lee, and Mark Van Proyen, eds. *AfterBurn: Reflections on Burning
Man*. Albuquerque: University of New Mexico Press, 2005.
Gitlin, Todd. *The Whole World Is Watching: Mass Media in the Making and
Unmaking of the New Left*. Berkeley: University of California Press, 1980.
Goffman, Erving. *Frame Analysis: An Essay on the Organization of Experience*.
New York: Harper and Row, 1974.
Goin, Peter, and Paul F. Starrs. *Black Rock*. Reno: University of Nevada Press,
2005.
Goldston, Linda. "Family Comes to Terms with Belmont Woman's Death at
Burning Man Fest." *San Jose Mercury News*, September 1, 2003.
Graburn, Nelson H. H. "Secular Ritual: A General Theory of Tourism." In *Hosts
and Guests Revisited: Tourism Issues of the Twenty-first Century*, edited by
Valerie L. Smith and Maryann Brent, 42–50. New York: Cognizant Commu-
nications Corp., 2001.
Grant, Richard. "Ten Thousand Go Mad in Nevada; Once a year, Califor-
nians head for the desert for four days of art, sex, guns and primal ritual.
Richard Grant goes feral at the Burning Man Festival, while a 40ft effigy

(and much else) goes up in smoke." *Independent* (London), November 17, 1996, 10.

Green, John C. "The American Religious Landscape and Political Attitudes: A Baseline for 2004." Pew Forum on Religion and Public Life. Available at http://pewforum.org/publications/surveys/green-full.pdf; accessed January 5, 2009.

Green, Miranda J. "Humans as Ritual Victims in the Later Prehistory of Western Europe." *Oxford Journal of Archaeology* 17, no. 2 (1998): 169–89.

Grimes, Ronald L. *Symbol and Conquest: Public Ritual and Drama in Santa Fe, New Mexico.* Ithaca, NY: Cornell University Press, 1976.

———. *Ritual Criticism: Case Studies in Its Practice, Essays on Its Theory.* Columbia: University of South Carolina Press, 1990.

———. *Beginnings in Ritual Studies.* Columbia: University of South Carolina Press, 1995 [1982].

———, ed. *Readings in Ritual Studies.* Upper Saddle River, NJ: Prentice Hall, 1996.

———. *Deeply into the Bone: Re-Inventing Rites of Passage.* Berkeley: University of California Press, 2000.

———. "Ritual and the Media." In *Practicing Religion in the Age of the Media: Explorations in Media, Religion, and Culture,* edited by Stewart M. Hoover and Lynn Schofield Clark, 219–34. New York: Columbia University Press, 2002.

———. *Rite out of Place: Ritual, Media, and the Arts.* New York: Oxford University Press, 2006.

Harvey, Larry. "Media Myths: Setting the Record Straight on Burning Man Myths (and a few new ideas)." Available at www.burningman.com/press/myths.html; accessed June 4, 2007.

Hill, Greg, and Kerry Thornley (aka Malaclypse the Younger and Omar Khayyam Ravenhurst). *Principia Discordia: Or How I Found Goddess and What I Did to Her When I Found Her.* Port Townsend, WA: Loompanics, 1980.

Hockett, Jeremy. "Reckoning Ritual and Counterculture in the Burning Man Community: Communication, Ethnography and the Self in Reflexive Modernism." Ph.D. dissertation, University of New Mexico, 2004.

———. "Burning Man as Ethnographic Experience: Participant Observation and the Study of Self." In *AfterBurn: Reflections on Burning Man,* edited by Lee Gilmore and Mark Van Proyen, 65–84. Albuquerque: University of New Mexico Press, 2005.

———. "Men of Fire: Three Burning Rituals of Rebirth and Renewal, Questions of Authenticity." Available at www.msu.edu/~hockettj/MenofFire.html; accessed January 5, 2009.

Hoffman, Abbie. *Steal This Book.* New York: Pirate Editions, 1971.

Hoover, Stewart M. *Religion in the Media Age.* New York: Routledge, 2006.

Hoover, Stewart M., and Knut Lundby, eds. *Rethinking Media, Religion, and Culture.* Thousand Oaks, CA: Sage, 1997.

Hoover, Stewart M., and Lynn Schofield Clark, eds. *Practicing Religion in the Age of the Media: Explorations in Media, Religion, and Culture.* New York: Columbia University Press, 2002.

Hua, Vanessa. "Tech Crowd Gets Tribal: Burning Man Draws Ardent Souls, 25,000 Gather to Form a Brief, Manic, Doomed Community." *San Francisco Examiner,* September 3, 2000.

Hutton, Ronald. *The Stations of the Sun: A History of the Ritual Year in Great Britain.* Oxford: Oxford University Press, 1996.

Hyde, Lewis. *The Gift: Imagination and the Erotic Life of Property.* New York: Random House, 1983.

Ivakhiv, Adrian. *Claiming Sacred Ground: Pilgrims and Politics at Glastonbury and Sedona.* Bloomington: Indiana University Press, 2001.

Jenkins, Henry. *Convergence Culture: Where Old and New Media Collide.* New York: New York University Press, 2006.

Kachur, Lewis. *Displaying the Marvelous: Marcel Duchamp, Salvador Dalí, and Surrealist Exhibition Installations.* Cambridge, MA: MIT Press, 2001.

Kaprow, Allan. *Essays on the Blurring of Art and Life.* Berkeley: University of California Press, 2003.

Kelly, Kevin. "Bonfire of The Techies: Hordes of Playful Digerati Assemble for a Hallowed Annual Rite." *Time Magazine,* August 25, 1997.

Kita, Sandy, et al. *The Floating World of Ukiyo-e: Shadows, Dreams, and Substance.* New York: Harry N. Abrams in association with the Library of Congress, 2001.

Kittredge, George Lyman, ed. *As You Like It.* Lexington, MA: Xerox College Publishing, 1967.

Kozinets, Robert V. "Can Consumers Escape the Market? Emancipatory Illuminations from Burning Man." *Journal of Consumer Research* 29 (June 2002): 20–36.

Kozinets, Robert V., and John F. Sherry Jr. "Welcome to the Black Rock Café." In *AfterBurn: Reflections on Burning Man,* edited by Lee Gilmore and Mark Van Proyen, 87–106. Albuquerque: University of New Mexico Press, 2005.

Kreuter, Holly, ed. *Drama in the Desert: The Sights and Sounds of Burning Man.* San Francisco: Raised Barn Press, 2002.

Kripal, Jeffrey J. *Esalen: America and the Religion of No Religion.* Chicago: University of Chicago Press, 2007.

Kristen, Christine. "Burning Man." *Raw Vision* 57 (winter 2006): 28–37.

Landberg, Leslie. "Interactivity in the Observatory." *Black Rock Gazette* 13, no. 53 (Gate ed.): 1.

Lasn, Kalle. *Culture Jam: The Uncooling of America™.* New York: Eagle Brook/William Morrow, 1999.

Lévi-Strauss, Claude. *The Savage Mind.* Chicago: University of Chicago Press, 1962.

Lippard, Lucy. *On the Beaten Track: Tourism, Art and Place.* New York: New Press, 1999.

Lynch, Gordon. *The New Spirituality: An Introduction to Progressive Belief in the Twenty-first Century.* London: I. B. Tauris, 2007.

MacCannell, Dean. *The Tourist: A New Theory of the Leisure Class.* Berkeley: University of California Press, 1999 [1976].

———. "Remarks on the Commodification of Cultures." In *Hosts and Guests Revisited: Tourism Issues of the Twenty-first Century,* edited by Valene L.

Smith and Maryann Brent, 380–90. New York: Cognizant Communications
Corp., 2001.

Martin, Glen. "Burning Man Organizers Grow Hot under the Collar over Rising
Federal Fees to Use Black Rock Desert for Festival." *San Francisco Chronicle*, December 30, 2001.

Mauss, Marcel. *The Gift: The Form and Reason for Exchange in Archaic Societies*. Translated by Ian Cunnison. New York: W. W. Norton, 1967 [1925].

McDonough, Tom, ed. *Guy Debord and the Situationist International*. Cambridge, MA: MIT Press, 2002.

Meethan, Kevin. *Tourism in Global Society: Place, Culture, Consumption*.
New York: Palgrave, 2001.

Michalowski, Raymond, and Jill Dubisch. *Run for the Wall: Remembering Viet-
nam on a Motorcycle Pilgrimage*. New Brunswick, NJ: Rutgers University
Press, 2001.

Mitchell, John G. "Public Lands." *National Geographic*, August 2001, 2–29.

Niman, Michael I. *People of the Rainbow: A Nomadic Utopia*. Knoxville: University of Tennessee Press, 1997.

Northrup, Joanne. "Kaleidoscopic Cortege: Art Cars at Burning Man, and
Beyond." In *AfterBurn: Reflections on Burning Man*, edited by Lee Gilmore
and Mark Van Proyen, 131–49. Albuquerque: University of New Mexico
Press, 2005.

Palahniuk, Chuck. *Fight Club*. New York: Henry Holt, 1996.

Pearce, Celia. "Communities of Play: The Social Construction of Identity in Persistent Online Game Worlds." In *Second Person: Role-Playing and Story in
Games and Playable Media*, edited by Noah Wardrip-Fruin and Pat Harri-
gan, 311–18. Cambridge, MA: MIT Press, 2007.

Perry, Paul. *On the Bus: The Complete Guide to the Legendary Trip of Ken Kesey
and the Merry Pranksters and the Birth of the Counterculture*. New York:
Thunder's Mouth Press, 1990.

Pike, Sarah. "Desert Goddesses and Apocalyptic Art: Making Sacred Space at
the Burning Man Festival." In *God in the Details: American Religion in Popular Culture*, edited by Eric Michael Mazur and Kate McCarthy, 155–76.
New York: Routledge, 2001.

———. *Earthly Bodies, Magical Selves: Contemporary Pagans and the Search
for Community*. Berkeley: University of California Press, 2001.

———. "No Novenas for the Dead: Ritual Action and Communal Memory at the
Temple of Tears." In *AfterBurn: Reflections on Burning Man*, edited by Lee
Gilmore and Mark Van Proyen, 195–213. Albuquerque: University of New
Mexico Press, 2005.

Priedite, Alex. "Where High-Tech Meets Low Life and Many a Wood Man Has
Met His Match." *Australian Financial Review*, October 4, 1997, 4.

Rheingold, Howard. *The Virtual Community: Homesteading on the Electronic
Frontier*. New York: HarperPerennial, 1994.

Roberts, Adrian, ed. *Burning Man Live: 13 Years of Piss Clear, Black Rock
City's Alternative Newspaper, 1997–2007*. San Francisco: RE/Search Publications, 2009.

Roof, Wade Clark. *Generation of Seekers: The Spiritual Journeys of the Baby Boom Generation.* San Francisco: HarperSanFrancisco, 1993.

———. *Spiritual Marketplace: Baby Boomers and the Remaking of American Religion.* Princeton: Princeton University Press, 1999.

Santino, Jack, ed. *Halloween and Other Festivals of Death and Life.* Knoxville: University of Tennessee Press, 1994.

Sax, William. *Mountain Goddess: Gender and Politics in a Himalayan Pilgrimage.* New York: Oxford University Press, 1991.

Schechner, Richard. *Between Theater and Anthropology.* Philadelphia: University of Pennsylvania Press, 1985.

———. *Performance Theory.* New York: Routledge, 1988.

———. *The Future of Ritual: Writings on Performance and Culture.* New York: Routledge, 1993.

Schmidt, Leigh Eric. *Restless Souls: The Making of American Spirituality.* San Francisco: HarperSanFrancisco, 2005.

Schudson, Michael. *Discovering the News: A Social History of American Newspapers.* New York: Basic Books, 1978.

———. *The Sociology of News.* New York: W. W. Norton, 2003.

Smith, Jonathan Z. "Religion, Religions, Religious." In *Critical Terms for Religious Studies,* edited by Mark C. Taylor, 269–84. Chicago: University of Chicago Press, 1998.

Smith, Marc A., and Peter Kollock, eds. *Communities in Cyberspace.* New York: Routledge, 1999.

Smith, Valene L., and Maryann Brent, eds. *Hosts and Guests Revisited: Tourism Issues of the Twenty-first Century.* New York: Cognizant Communications Corp., 2001.

Sonner, Scott. "Burning Man Drawing 20,000 to Nevada's Black Rock Desert." *Las Vegas Sun,* September 1, 1999.

St John, Graham. "Alternative Cultural Heterotopia and the Liminoid Body: Beyond Turner at ConFest." *Australian Journal of Anthropology* 12, no. 1 (2001): 47–66.

———, ed. *FreeNRG: Notes from the Edge of the Dance Floor.* Altona, Australia: Common Ground, 2001.

———, ed. *Rave Culture and Religion.* New York: Routledge, 2004.

———, ed. *Victor Turner and Contemporary Cultural Performance.* New York: Berghahn, 2008.

———. *Technomad: Global Raving Countercultures.* London: Equinox, 2009.

Stevens, Richard. "Burning for the Other: Semiotics of a Levinasian Theological Aesthetics in Light of Burning Man." Ph.D. dissertation, Graduate Theological Union, 2003.

Sullivan, James. "Dot-Com Fallout Hits Burning Man: Decline in Attendance Tied to Economic Downturn." *San Francisco Chronicle,* August 27, 2001.

Sylvan, Robin. *Trance Formation: The Spiritual and Religious Dimensions of Global Rave Culture.* New York: Routledge, 2005.

Talen, Bill [Reverend Billy]. *What Should I Do If Reverend Billy Is in My Store?* New York: New Press, 2005.

————. *What Would Jesus Buy? Fabulous Prayers in the Face of the Shopocalypse.* New York: Public Affairs, 2007.

Taylor, Chris. "Burning Man Grows Up." *Business 2.0,* July 3, 2007, 66–70.

Thompson, Don. "Burning Man Festival a Focus for Parties, Religious Yearning." *San Francisco Chronicle,* August 29, 2003.

Turkle, Sherry. *Life on the Screen: Identity in the Age of the Internet.* New York: Simon and Schuster, 1995.

Turner, Fred. *Counterculture to Cyberculture: Stewart Brand, the Whole Earth Network, and the Rise of Digital Utopianism.* Chicago: University of Chicago Press, 2006.

Turner, Victor. *The Ritual Process: Structure and Anti-Structure.* Ithaca, NY: Cornell University Press, 1969.

————. *Dramas, Fields, and Metaphors: Symbolic Action in Human Society.* Ithaca, NY: Cornell University Press, 1974.

————, ed. *Celebration: Studies in Festivity and Ritual.* Washington, DC: Smithsonian Institution Press, 1982.

————. *From Ritual to Theatre: The Human Seriousness of Play.* New York: PAJ Publications, 1982.

————. *The Anthropology of Performance.* New York: PAJ Publications, 1986.

Turner, Victor, and Edith Turner. *Image and Pilgrimage in Christian Culture.* New York: Columbia University Press, 1978.

Upledger, Michael. "The Burning Man Experience." *St. Petersburg (FL) Times,* September 26, 1997.

van Gennep, Arnold. *The Rites of Passage.* Translated by Monika B. Vizedom and Gabrielle L. Caffee. Chicago: University of Chicago Press, 1960 [1909].

Van Proyen, Mark. "The New Dionysianism." In *Sticky Sublime,* edited by Bill Beckley, 165–75. New York: Allworth Press, 2001.

————. "A Tale of Two Surrealities." In *AfterBurn: Reflections on Burning Man,* edited by Lee Gilmore and Mark Van Proyen, 173–93. Albuquerque: University of New Mexico Press, 2005.

Vulliamy, Ed. "Anarchy Rules at Wildest Party on Earth: Ed Vulliamy in Black Rock Desert, Nevada, Joins the Pyro-Fetishists, Cybergeeks and Guys Just Nuts about Guns at the Burning Man Festival." *Observer,* September 6, 1998, 8.

Weber, Max. *The Protestant Ethic and the Spirit of Capitalism.* Translated by Talcott Parsons. New York: Charles Scribner's Sons, 1930 [1904].

————. *The Theory of Social and Economic Organization.* Translated by A. M. Henderson and Talcott Parsons. New York: Oxford University Press, 1947.

Weiners, Brad, and John Plunkett, eds. *Burning Man.* San Francisco: HardWired, 1997.

Werde, Bill. "Burning Man's Dotcom Hangover." *Village Voice,* September 12–18, 2001.

Whiting, Sam. "Modern Primitive Make Burning Man Hottest Ever: Record Crowd Fired up at Annual Arts Festivals." *San Francisco Chronicle,* September 7, 1997.

Wolfe, Tom. *The New Journalism.* New York: Harper and Row, 1973.

Wolkstein, Diane, and Samuel Noah Kramer. *Inanna, Queen of Heaven and Earth: Her Stories and Hymns from Sumer.* New York: Harper and Row, 1983.

Wray, Matt. "Burning Man and the Rituals of Capitalism." *Bad Subjects* 21 (September 1995). Available at http://bad.eserver.org/issues/1995/21/wray.html; accessed January 5, 2009.

Wuthnow, Robert. *After Heaven: Spirituality in America since the 1950s.* Berkeley: University of California Press, 1998.

York, Michael. *Pagan Theology: Paganism as World Religion.* New York: New York University Press, 2003.

DVD Contents

Credits

Parts of chapters 3 and 4 were published as "Of Ordeals and Operas: Reflexive Ritualizing at the Burning Man Festival," in *Victor Turner and Contemporary Cultural Performance*, edited by Graham St John (New York: Berghahn, 2008).

Earlier drafts of chapter 4 were published as "Embers Dust and Ashes: Pilgrimage and Healing at the Burning Man Festival," in *Pilgrimage and Healing*, edited by Jill Dubisch and Michael Winkelman (Tucson: University of Arizona Press, 2005); "Fires of the Heart: Ritual, Pilgrimage, and Transformation at Burning Man," in *AfterBurn: Reflections on Burning Man*, edited by Lee Gilmore and Mark Van Proyen (Albuquerque: University of New Mexico Press, 2005); and "Desert Pilgrimage: Liminality, Transformation, and the Other at the Burning Man Festival," in *On the Road to Being There: Studies in Pilgrimage and Tourism in Late Modernity*, edited by William Swatos (Leiden: Brill Academic Press, 2006).

An earlier version of chapter 5 was published as "Media Mecca: Rituals, Tropes, and Technopagans at the Burning Man Festival," in *Media, Religion, and the Marketplace*, edited by Lynn S. Clark (New Brunswick, NJ: Rutgers University Press, 2007).

Parts of chapter 6 were published as "Change-a-lujah! Destabilizing Normative Religion with Reverend Billy and the Stop Shopping Gospel Choir," *Council of Societies for the Study of Religion Bulletin* 37, no. 1 (2008): 7–10.

Index

Ten Principles (*continued*)
199n2; list of, 38; promotion of, 105;
radical inclusivity, 104, 106, 111,
144; reflections on, 125–26. *See also*
community; decommodification; gifting and gift economy; leave no trace
(LNT) ethos; participation ethos;
radical self-expression; radical
self-reliance
Thar-Taurs of Atlan, The (opera), 86–87
theater: Burning Man as, 16; as transformative influence, 164–65; use of
term, 11, 184n8. *See also* operas;
performances
theme camps: art-focused, 198n66;
dance-oriented, 33–34, 121; description of typical, 33–34; group rituals
in, 96; hierarchy of, 117; Jewish-
oriented, 52–53, 192n20; of opera
performers, 85; oversight of, 34; ritual
"killing" of, 95; village groupings of,
8, 33; specific: Bianca's Smut Shack,
34; Blue Light District (BLD), 183n6;
BRCJCC, 52–53, 192n20; CampArctica, 41; Church of Funk, 33; Death
Guild, 34; HeeBeeGeeBee Healers, 53;
Illumination Village, 198n66;
JiffyLube, 34; Motel 666, 34, 95;
PolyParadise, 34; Safari Camp, 7–8,
96; Spike's Vampire Bar, 33; Spock
Mountain Research Labs, 34; Temple
of Atonement, 34
themes: attitudes toward, 38; design and
promotion of, 35, 76, 77, 189n56;
diversity of, 154; elements of, 35, 38;
first, 28, 35; games reflective of, 74–75;
inspirations for, 195n11; platforms reflective of, 73–77, 80, 81; signs about,
32, 188n44; streets named for, 34,
189n52; use of vs. resistance to, 69,
76. *See also* artworks and installations;
performances; rites and rituals; Temples; themes, specific
themes, specific: American Dream (2008
theme), 38; Body (2000 theme), 35,
86–87; Evolution (2009 theme),
38; Fertility (1997 theme), 35, 83;
Future—Hope and Fear (2006 theme),
35, 38; Inferno (1996 theme), 28, 35,
83; Nebulous Entity (1998 theme), 35;
Psyche (2005 theme), 35; Wheel of
Time (1999 theme), 35, 101. *See also*
Beyond Belief (2003 theme); Floating
World (2002 theme); Green Man
(2007 theme); Seven Ages (2001
theme); Vault of Heaven (2004
theme)

Thompson, Don, 141
toilet facilities, 33
tourism: commodification vs. authenticity
in, 122, 201n49; pilgrimage distinguished from, 120–25; sacred vs.,
105–6, 126. *See also* spectators
trademarks. *See* brand names and trademarks
transformation: author's experience of,
164, 167; catalysts for, 112–14; community and, 106–8; desert environment
and, 20; heterotopia linked to, 22–23;
liminality and communitas in, 13–14;
opening to possibilities of, 21, 53–55,
60–62; participants questioned about,
48, 104, 175, 178, 199n1; performative and reflexive ideology in, 104–5;
playfulness in, 82–83; potential for, in
dialectic between self and community,
106–14, 123–25, 199n6; reflections on
cultural values and, 118–20, 125–26;
release from mundane in, 115; ritual
and, 98–102; spiritual possibilities in,
46–47, 48
tribalism: elements of, 61, 99–100, 128;
media depictions of, 15, 138–39,
150–51. *See also* primitivism
tribe.net, 144, 146, 207–8n74
Tuchman, Gaye, 136
Turkle, Sherry, 145
Turner, Alex, 99
Turner, Edith, 114–16, 120
Turner, Fred, 143
Turner, Rory, 99
Turner, Victor: communications theory
and, 129; critiques of, 82, 184n13,
197n33; influences on, 99–100, 156,
198–99n69; on liminality and communitas, 13, 21, 70, 82–83, 84, 86, 99–
100, 117, 119, 197n33; on pilgrimage,
105, 114–18; on pilgrim and tourist,
120; on playfulness, 82–83; on popular
culture and countercultures, 100–101,
156; on structure and anti-structure,
14, 82, 114, 119; on subjunctive mood,
197n35
Twan (Burner), 84

ukiyo-e (style), 35, 189n58
Unitarian Universalism, 95
universal connections, 56–57
University of Nevada, Reno, 201n36
U.S. Forest Service, 39, 186n24
utopia, 22, 166

VanAlkemade, Rob, 208n2
van Gennep, Arnold, 13, 21, 100

Text:	10/13 Sabon
Display:	Sabon
Compositor:	Westchester Book Group
Indexer:	Margie Towery
DVD Producer:	Elizabeth Gilmore
Printer:	Maple-Vail Book Manufacturing Group